AUSTRALIAN WOMEN'S STORIES

AN OXFORD ANTHOLOGY
SELECTED BY KERRYN GOLDSWORTHY

OXFORD
UNIVERSITY PRESS

OXFORD

UNIVERSITY PRESS

253 Normanby Road, South Melbourne, Victoria, Australia 3205

Oxford University Press is a department of the University of Oxford.
It furthers the University's objective of excellence in research, scholarship,
and education by publishing worldwide in

Oxford New York

Athens Auckland Bangkok Bogotá Buenos Aires Calcutta
Cape Town Chennai Dar es Salaam Delhi Florence Hong Kong Istanbul
Karachi Kuala Lumpur Madrid Melbourne Mexico City Mumbai Nairobi
Paris Port Moresby São Paulo Singapore Taipei Tokyo Toronto Warsaw

with associated companies in
Berlin Ibadan

OXFORD is a registered trade mark of Oxford University Press
in the UK and certain other countries

National Library of Australia
Cataloguing-in-Publication data:

Australian women's stories: an Oxford anthology.

ISBN 0 19 551295 2.

1. Short stories, Australian—Women authors.
I. Goldsworthy, Kerryn, 1953– .

A823.01089287

Edited by Cathryn Game
Text designed by Steve Randles
Typeset by Solo Typesetting
Printed through OUP China

CONTENTS

Preface   v
Introduction   1

Mary Fortune (1833?–1910)
   The Illumined Grave   10
Jessie Couvreur ('Tasma') (1848–97)
   Monsieur Caloche   33
Barbara Baynton (1857–1929)
   The Chosen Vessel   53
Henry Handel Richardson (1870–1946)
   And Women Must Weep   61
Ethel Turner (1870–1958)
   The Carrying of the Baby   68
Ethel Anderson (1883–1958)
   Peronel McCree, and the Sin Called Pride:
   The Arch-sin   73
Katharine Susannah Prichard (1883–1969)
   Flight   94
Marjorie Barnard (1897–1987)
   The Persimmon Tree   109
Christina Stead (1902–83)
   The Old School   113
Margaret Trist (1914–86)
   Twenty Strong   123
Jessica Anderson (1916–)
   Under the House   129
Olga Masters (1919–86)
   The Christmas Parcel   142
Oodgeroo Noonuccal (1920–93)
   Mai (Black Bean)   160
Elizabeth Jolley (1923–)
   My Father's Moon   162

Thea Astley (1925–)
  It's Raining in Mango   182
Marian Eldridge (1936–97)
  The Woman at the Window   200
Barbara Hanrahan (1939–91)
  Butterfly   211
Robin Sheiner (1940–)
  My Sister's Funeral   215
Carmel Bird (1940–)
  The Hair and the Teeth   223
Beverley Farmer (1941–)
  The Harem   229
Helen Garner (1942–)
  What We Say   240
Joan London (1948–)
  The Girls Love Each Other   245
Susan Hampton (1949–)
  Conrad's Bear   255
Kate Grenville (1950–)
  The Test is, if They Drown   262
Alexis Wright (1950–)
  The Serpent's Covenant   273
Gail Jones (1955–)
  Other Places   284
Lucy Sussex (1957–)
  A Tour Guide in Utopia   307
Gillian Mears (1964–)
  Cousins   315
Beth Yahp (1964–)
  The Beautiful Hour   325

Contributors   339
Sources and Acknowledgments   345

PREFACE

I am grateful to Peter Rose of Oxford University Press for his invitation to compile this anthology, and for the fun of talking to him about it. I want to thank Eleanor Hogan for her diligent research and the independent spirit in which she undertook it, and the Faculty of Arts at the University of Melbourne for the grant that made her research possible. I would also like to thank the English Department at the University of Adelaide for making me welcome there. Several friends and colleagues gave me suggestions and information about the contents of this collection: Delys Bird, Susan Lever, Sue Martin, Lyn McCredden, Paul Salzman, and Lucy Sussex have all helped me out.

This book is dedicated to the memory of my mother.

INTRODUCTION

What is an Australian woman?

Is she Mary Wilson Fortune, born in Ireland, taken as a child by her father to Canada, arriving on the Australian goldfields in 1855 as a young woman of twenty-two and becoming one of the voices that still speak to us today of the country's colonial past?

Is she Marjorie Barnard, who was born in Sydney in 1897, lived there for all of her ninety years, made important contributions of various kinds to the national literary culture, and wrote a scholarly and widely read history of her country?

Is she Oodgeroo of the Tribe Noonuccal, Custodian of the land Minjerribah, her totem the carpet snake, born in 1920 on Stradbroke Island and known for twenty-five years in public life as the poet Kath Walker before taking her tribal name?

Or is she Beth Yahp, born in Malaysia in 1964, arriving in Australia twenty years later to enrich its literature with her poetic fictions and to make it her home?

Many of the other writers whose work is included in this collection have, or had, complex relationships with Australia. Henry Handel Richardson left for Europe as a young woman to study music and made only one brief return visit, many years later; but her trilogy *The Fortunes of Richard Mahony* is a large-scale narrative of the nation's formative years and a classic text in Australian literature. Christina Stead, born in Sydney the year after Federation, lived in Australia for thirty-five of her eighty-one years and wrote extensively of her Australian experience in novels and stories, but was refused the Britannica Australia award in 1967 on the grounds that she had lived and worked overseas for decades and was therefore somehow no longer an Australian. Elizabeth Jolley, daughter of an English father and a Viennese mother, grew up in the English Midlands and migrated to Western Australia with her husband in her mid thirties, in 1959; whereas much of her fiction reflects this background, all of her books were written and published in Australia, where she has made her reputation as well as her home.

Many of the stories in this book examine not only the question of what it is to be Australian but also the question of what it is to be a woman. In Lucy Sussex's 'A Tour Guide in Utopia', a charming young time-traveller from 1893 rejoices in amazement, a hundred years later, to see a female Member of Parliament—but then, when she sees that her hair is dyed and her face made up, denounces her as a painted harlot. In Jessie Couvreur's 'Monsieur Caloche', the woman is disguised as a man; in Mary Fortune's 'The Illumined Grave', she has become a ghost; in Oodgeroo's 'Mai', she turns into a tree.

And in Kate Grenville's 'The Test is, if They Drown', the general feeling among the characters is that a woman who does not conform to the accepted standards of womanliness must perforce be a witch. 'I watch Miss Spear as she turns the corner, and wonder what she is. Women don't wear hats like that . . . Women don't wear sandshoes and no socks so their ankles show . . . And women don't chop the heads off dandelions with a stick as she's doing now. If Mrs Longman at school with her smooth chignon and her dainty handkerchiefs is a woman, where does that leave Miss Spear?'

If even 'What is a woman?' can be seen as a difficult question, consider how much more difficult is the question 'What is a woman's story?' The easy answer, and one of the organising principles of this book, is of course: 'A story told by a woman'. But when it comes to stories *about* women, or stories *for* women, it's hard to answer or even just to discuss this question without falling into the trap of identifying certain themes and subjects as 'women's business' and thereby reinforcing the kinds of gender stereotypes that both women and men have been struggling so hard, over the last twenty or thirty years, to escape.

On the other hand, some of the most powerful stories in this book, like Olga Masters' 'The Christmas Parcel', are directly concerned with the shifting, relative values of various human qualities, as well as of various goods and services, and the ways in which those values are gendered. In this story a complex nexus of cash, class, gender, and sexuality is relentlessly, and very movingly, exposed. And as the ending of this story makes clear, certain objects, feelings, and beliefs can be loosely posited as part of what might be called female culture. Domestic life and the private sphere, with their traditionally 'female' activities, occupy the foreground in many of these stories, and, particularly in the contemporary stories, their significance and centrality to life in general are either defiantly asserted or simply taken for granted by the writers.

Cooking and food, for example—again, memorably, in 'The Christmas Parcel'—assume in some of these stories the importance that they have in everybody's real life and, beyond that, a symbolic value. At the end of Gillian Mears' story 'Cousins', loneliness and madness are assuaged by the comforting routines and substances of cookery: 'And I grow happier, thinking of the placing of yolks into a double saucepan; the beating of them into thick yellow ribbons; the rituals and the certainties of the kitchen; the sensual plucking of strawberries from the big beds out the back; the safe feelings.'

Clothing, that other staple item of daily life, also features strongly in the work of female writers. There are, for instance, so many stories by women about a particular dress and its meaning in the life of the character who wears it that tales of 'the dress' could almost be called a subgenre of the short story. In a pre-feminist culture in which physical appearance and traditional ideas of 'femininity' dominated most women's lives, the details of a particular dress, the occasion on which it was worn, and the accretions of meaning that gathered around it could assume enormous significance for women. The Canadian writer Alice Munro once wrote a story called 'Red Dress—1946', and it seems to me that almost every woman in twentieth-century Western culture has had a story to tell, written or unwritten, called 'X Dress—19XX': a story marking some life crisis, and in which details of colour, cut, and stitching assume the status of a secret, female language.

This is mischievously parodied by Ethel Anderson in 'Peronel McCree and the Sin Called Pride': 'It was made with a plain bodice in the hour-glass shape then fashionable. The red plush was folded back, a few inches below the waist in a style called "a fisher-girl sacque". Below this frills fell to the instep, and *lissé* pleats showed beneath them. The neck was cut in a modest square, much frilled. The elbow sleeves were also frilled, and finished with red plush bows.' Perhaps predictably, and certainly subversively, this restitched hand-me-down, subsidised by the egg money, is *not* the dress in which Peronel causes a sensation at the Government House ball.

In other stories, the importance of the Dress is used to make more serious points about poverty, or indeed other manifestations of oppression. Dolly in Henry Handel Richardson's 'And Women Must Weep' is very cleverly named; the dressing-up of a young woman for her first ball reduces her to an object, to be looked at and to be passively, helplessly chosen or rejected. The diminutive 'Dolly' reduces her further: not just a doll but a *little* doll. At the end of the evening, the fact that nobody has wanted to dance with her is pitilessly reflected by the state of her tell-tale ball-gown, 'now crushed to nothing from so much sitting'.

Even more disturbing is the very strange garment that features in Christina Stead's 'The Old School': another humiliating dress, worn this time by a child living in such extreme poverty that she never brings any lunch to school. 'Maidie had only stayed away . . . because she had no dress to wear. Now she had a dress, "It's made out of a sheet." "Flour bags?" "No, it's a sheet." The teacher, curious, went right up to Maidie's desk and studied the dress. It was soft old thick cotton, made in fashion, with a deep yoke, long sleeves into wristbands, several inch wide pleats into a waistband, tucks and a wide hem to let down. It was white and remained white, though certain marks (which made them say flour bags) had faded with washing.'

The list of dressmaking details underlines the unbearable pathos of making such a dress 'in fashion'; these details, more appropriate to the catwalk, stand in stark contrast to the realities of Maidie's life. Stead also explores the way that certain other items of clothing function as signifiers of class and hint at certain connections between class and sexuality: 'Blucher boots were stiff work-boots with heavy soles, cheap and long wearing . . . the very word was socially significant: "he's wearing blucher boots!" The nice girls looked down and away in shame, the dirty girls grinned.'

The plot of Jessie Couvreur's 'Monsieur Caloche' turns on the idea of clothing as a reliable index of gender itself. Lucy Sussex, writing 'A Tour Guide in Utopia' a century later, can use the very gender-specific clothing of the nineteenth century as the source of a joke: ' "Thank you, Sir," she said, releasing me. I nodded in reply, wondering how to say I was a Ms—despite my cropped hair, jeans and Docs.' But in 'Monsieur Caloche', the central character—scarred by smallpox and convinced that the loss of her beauty means that she is somehow no longer a real woman—manages to pass for a man by virtue of her clothes and in spite of the extremely 'feminine' physical appearance about which the narrator drops such heavy and frequent hints throughout the course of the story.

'Monsieur Caloche' is one of the several stories in this book about women who for one reason or another have fallen through the net of male desire. In a patriarchal society in which the function of a woman is to attract a husband and have children with him, the solitary woman is an anomaly, covertly or openly despised; several of these stories, from different historical periods and from different narrative points of view, explore the world of wall-flowers, spinsters, and other such dropouts, and critique rather sternly the social structures and gender norms against which these women must struggle.

Sometimes, although not always, it is a relatively simple question of physical beauty. 'Monsieur' Henriette Caloche is a scarred ex-beauty driven to disguise herself as a man in order to make an independent living, as it's now unlikely that anyone will marry her. Miss Spear in 'The Test is, if They Drown' was 'never anything to write home about' in the first place. Dolly in 'And Women Must Weep', perhaps the most intriguing member of this sad little team, is by contrast a pretty girl but one who simply 'doesn't take'—a fact explained in the end by her own reluctantly radical views: 'For really, truly, right deep down in her, she hadn't wanted "the gentlemen" any more than they'd wanted her: she had only had to pretend to.'

Marjorie Barnard's two solitary women in 'The Persimmon Tree', a story whose treatment of this theme is at once more sophisticated and more elusive, are presented simply as human subjects with feelings and secrets. The story's homoerotic undertones create a kind of closed circuit of meaning from which the question of these women's past or present relations with men has been excluded. Joan London's more explicit treatment of this theme shows women actively rejecting the company of men and turning to each other for companionship and support as well as for sex: ' "There's no boyfriends," I said . . . Then I found myself saying it, as if it had been on my mind all the time: "The girls love each other these days." '

The unnamed narrator in Gail Jones' 'Other Places' is a wallflower of a different kind, left isolated by her two male companions' passion for each other; the solitariness of Gillian Mears' narrator in 'Cousins' is exacerbated by the married happiness of the middle-aged cousin who was first lover, twenty years before, and by her memory of that time. But perhaps the most chilling of these solitary women is Marian Eldridge's Sharon in 'The Woman at the Window', whose desperately isolated situation has been brought about not by her lack of sexual attractiveness but by the helpless disorders and excesses of her sexual history.

One of the most interesting things about these 'lone woman' stories is that even the earliest ones challenge the social values that construct these women as failures. Most of the stories in this book, in fact, offer challenge or resistance to some aspect of male dominance and patriarchal values. Barbara Baynton's 'The Chosen Vessel' is among other things a bitter and savage critique of the corruptions and collusions of two powerful patriarchal institutions, politics and religion—which unwittingly conspire, in this story, to allow a woman to meet her death at the hands of a violent man.

Henriette Caloche also meets her death at the hands of a violent man; the power that she exerts is posthumous, as Sir Matthew Bogg is transformed by her influence and puts his ruthlessly acquired wealth to charitable use. Dolly in 'And Women Must Weep' resists the notion that she is required to 'want the gentlemen', and her resistance, while subconscious, is clearly visible to them. The focus of 'The Persimmon Tree' is exclusively on female subjectivity, and the story subverts masculinity simply by ignoring it; and in 'The Christmas Parcel' the homely household contents of the mysterious parcel reaffirm female solidarity and innocence of corrupted sexual trading, and delicately underline the failure of the father: 'Mr Churcher stared at his hands as if for the first time he realized they were holding nothing.'

Some of the writers here treat the same theme with equal effectiveness but far more light-heartedly. Ethel Anderson's Peronel McCree uses her traditional feminine skills with a needle to puncture patriarchal self-importance by transforming a masculine garment, symbolic of the power of the Church, into something that will serve her own secular, sexual, feminine ends. But perhaps the story most directly subversive of patriarchal power is Barbara Hanrahan's 'Butterfly', a wonderfully funny and sinister response to Freud and hymn of praise to female anatomy, with its child's-eye view of Cousin Henry's penis: '. . . then it got really stiff and stood poking at me like somebody's finger telling you off.'

My criteria for choosing these stories were as mixed as such things usually are. A book of 'women's stories' can easily become a piece of propaganda. I have tried to put together something more complex and interesting than that; although many of these stories offer richly justifiable critiques of patriarchal society and its masculine values, most of them treat their actual male characters with some sympathy and offer, at least implicitly, some ideas about the ways in which men and women might live together more successfully.

I have tried to offer a wide range not only of subject matter but also of different storytelling modes. Some of these stories are very 'plotty', like 'Monsieur Caloche' in its nineteenth-century fashion, or Oodgeroo's 'Mai', with the closely woven narrative chain of cause and effect on which all such myths of origin depend.

Others, like 'The Test is, if They Drown' or Susan Hampton's 'Conrad's Bear', have what might be called psychological plots. Barbara Hanrahan's 'Butterfly', with the deliberate impressionism and inconsequentiality of her *faux-naif* style, has no plot at all.

The idea of a 'women's tradition' in Australian writing interested me, and there are some satisfying connections, across many years, to be made among some of these stories. Lucy Sussex is not just a fiction writer but is also the scholar who recovered and discovered so much of what we now know about the life and work of Mary Fortune. Helen Garner's 'What We Say' contains a reference to 'The Chosen Vessel', and their common subject matter goes to the heart of what it means to be a woman: what Germaine Greer has called the visceral nature of femaleness, the physical fact of living in a woman's body and the consequences that fact can have in a woman's life.

Obviously there are space constraints in a book like this; all anthologists wish they had twice as many pages to play with, and must make hard choices. Long stories are usually sacrificed to this consideration; Gail Jones' 'Other Places' survived the cut because it is one of the most minutely crafted and sophisticated stories I have ever read; because it demonstrates a new kind of hybrid writing; and because—like Katharine Susannah Prichard's 'Flight', Thea Astley's 'It's Raining in Mango', and Alexis Wright's 'The Serpent's Covenant'—it deals in a powerful and uncompromising way with a shameful aspect of Australia's history that must not be allowed to be forgotten.

And, for me most importantly, this story makes—acts out, in its telling—a point crucial for writers with any concern at all for the question of their relationship and their responsibility to society, and of the connections between public and private life: 'I tried to imagine the ways in which the individual kiss and all its individualising implications might be installed and respected in the larger occurrences of a country's history. And simply could not.'

Political and social considerations give writers powerful material to work with. I was astonished, after I had made the final choice of stories, to go through them one by one and realise just how many of them, including those seemingly dealing with 'private life', are stories partly or wholly about poverty. Perhaps the effects of poverty bring out writers' best imaginative responses and the most eloquent ways of expressing them. And perhaps women in particular think a lot about poverty because of the tiny proportion of the world's wealth in their possession. Perhaps women are more likely to think more often about the problems of feeding children and keeping children warm—and about what a woman might be able to trade in order to solve these problems. 'That Fred Rossmore!' says Mrs Churcher in 'The Christmas Parcel', of the lecherous grocer to whom so much money is already owed. ' "He touches diddies if you let him . . . And up here." She touched the morrocain stretched across her chest. Gloria considered this a small price to pay for butter, bacon, tinned peaches and biscuits, but dared not say so.'

Other stories—'What We Say', 'The Persimmon Tree', 'The Serpent's Covenant'—were chosen not only because of the beauty of what they say but also because of the power of what they leave unsaid. Still others—Elizabeth Jolley's 'My Father's Moon', Beverley Farmer's 'The Harem', Carmel Bird's 'The Hair and the Teeth'—contain symbols that go on burning in the reader's mind for a long time after the story ends: the Easter moon, the crystal egg, the locks of golden hair.

And some stories have been included simply because they have earned and re-earned their place over and over, surviving changes in taste and upheavals in questions of literary value over the decades; 'The Chosen Vessel' and 'The Persimmon Tree' simply could not have been left out of this book, and are unlikely ever to disappear from view for very long, if at all, in Australian literary history.

The Illumined Grave

There is some delightful scenery in the Warego district, and between Casyam township and the Burlington Ranges are some of the very finest portions of it. At least, so I thought, for the twentieth time, one glorious autumn day, as I rode through the Manners Run on my return from a visit to Casyam.

The run of Mr Harley Manners was one of the finest in the colony, and spread over no small proportion of the district. It was well watered and richly pastured, and its owner was reputed one of the richest squatters in the colony. Riding slowly over the well-grassed plain, through which the road wound, I was admiring the home station, with its substantial and elegant stone buildings—a glimpse of which could be had from where I was—when the sound of a horse's feet on the road behind me attracted my attention, and I looked round, to find myself joined by Mr Manners himself.

'Good afternoon, Sinclair. Where are you bound for?' he asked.

'Campward,' I replied; 'I was just admiring your homestead, Mr Manners; it must be very pleasant to be master of such a place.'

'Ah! one gets used to be comfortable, you know. You're not very busy just now?'

'No. Why do you ask?'

'Because I've been thinking of riding over to you the last two or three days. I want a little of your help, I think. Is there anything to prevent you stopping at Manneria all night?

'Nothing whatever. I am quite at your service.'

'That's right—you detectives have the best billets in the colony, I do believe. Ah, well! never mind contradicting me just now, for I have a queer story to tell you, and our ride homeward will afford an excellent opportunity for my doing so. By the way, Mr Bruce of Broadbraes is stopping with me just now.'

'Indeed! Has he ever heard any word of his lost daughter yet?'

'Not the least tidings—not a word.'

'It is very strange indeed; but now for your communication;' and turning our horses' heads toward Manneria, as Mr Manners called his station, I waited to hear what strange story he had to tell in my line.

'You know the Gully Hut, as they call it?' he began—'the one that lies at the foot of the Bald Hill, at the back of the run?'

'Yes—that was the one we called at, the day we went kanga-rooing with Captain Chymes.'

'Exactly. Well, the same hutkeeper that you saw on that occasion is there still; but there is another shepherd stationed there now—one who has only been in my employment about two months. This man tells, and persists in the truth of, one of the most singular stories I have ever heard. I hope you won't laugh while I tell it, for I give you fair warning that it has made a great impression upon myself.'

'I have seen and heard too many unaccountable things myself, Mr Manners,' I replied, 'to scoff at any man's opinion; pray continue your relation.'

'Shortly after this new shepherd—whose name is Strong—came, he was unfortunate enough to lose nearly half his flock in some of the gorges running into the Darlingford Ranges. He was naturally anxious, and having folded what remained of the sheep near the hut, he took his supper and started back toward the vicinity of the ranges, determined to spend the moonlight hours in a strict search for the missing flock. Mind you, I tell the story as Strong himself has told it many times to me and to others, and he never makes the least variation in the tale.'

'Go on,' I said, being deeply interested already.

'It was a very dark night when Strong started from the hut, and he knew that it would be some hours before the moon arose, but as he knew the direction well, and was a good bushman, he did not hesitate to go. He called his dog; but it appears that the animal, considering his day's work done, preferred the chimney to a dark tramp over the plains, and so he did not follow him. Well, Strong reached the foot of one of the ranges, and wrapping himself in a blanket he had brought for the purpose, he chose a sheltered spot under a granite boulder, and laid himself down to sleep until the moon arose. The man thinks that an hour or two must have elapsed when he opened his eyes after a sound sleep. What awakened him he could not tell, but he declares that an icy wind seemed to flow over his face, and he started to a sitting posture, with every hair standing erect upon his head with terror.'

'And what did he see?' I asked, as Mr Manners paused to draw breath, and observe what effect his relation had upon me.

'I am going to tell you,' he replied. 'As Strong sat up, he saw at the foot of a high granite boulder, directly opposite to him, a phenomenon so strange that it riveted his eyes and every feeling. It was dark as pitch, and I have mentioned that Strong had chosen his camping place among the scattered boulders at the foot of the Bald Hill. Of course, the man knew he was among the rocks, but the darkness was so intense when he opened his eyes after awaking from his sleep, that had it not been for a supernatural light that burned opposite, he would have seen nothing.'

'A supernatural light!' I interjected.

'Yes—a pale blue light that hovered over a spot of ground at the foot of a boulder—a light that trembled and died, and came and went; sometimes illuminating faintly the face of the over-hanging rock, and sometimes going low over the spot from which it always appeared to emanate, and sometimes again rising up in flickering tongues of lambent flame, and shaping itself into strange and unearthly forms.'

Mr Manners spoke with such a low and tremulous voice, that I looked into his face, and was astonished to see it pale and rigid.

'You seem strangely affected with this story,' I said—'one would fancy you believed it.'

'Believe it! I have seen it myself, and I seem to see it yet, and to feel the horrid chill that the sight bred in my very marrow!'

'Saw it yourself! I thought you were but repeating your shepherd's story.'

'Yes, yes—but let me finish, and then I will explain. Strong declares he has seen this singular sight many times, and always on the same spot, but he saw, or says he saw, what did not become visible to me, a shadowy female form distinctly visible between the floating light and the boulder—a form in a white robe covered with blood, and heavy black hair, dishevelled, and matted with gore.'

'And how was it that you came to witness this strange scene yourself, Mr Manners?'

'Well, the tale got among the station hands, and made such a commotion, that my curiosity was excited. Besides, I quite believed that the man was either the victim of his own superstition, or imposing on the credulity of his mates; so I got him to show me the spot, and I watched one dark night, and saw what I have described to you, minus the figure of a female; that I did not see.'

'Was Strong aware that you were about to keep watch yourself?' I asked.

'He was not. Oh, the light could not be made by any human contrivance! If you see it, as I believe you will, you will acknowledge that at once.'

'You believe it to be a real ghostly affair then?'

'Well, I do not quite, or I should not have thought of your assistance. But I have another circumstance to mention, and to this Strong also called my attention. Not one of the sheep will pass over that spot in broad daylight. Through the many scattered boulders that lie on the grass around, are worn a hundred tracks by their numerous feet, but there is not a blade of grass bent between the rocks where that light lives.'

'Oh!' I said.

'Well, do you see anything?' he asked, looking into my thoughtful face anxiously. 'You are a man of education, I know, Sinclair, and have read much. You will, I have no doubt, have encountered scientific explanations of those luminous gaseous exhalations that have been seen floating over the graves in church-yards by night. Does any such possibility suggest itself in the present instance?'

'We know such things are verified facts,' I replied; 'but the female form?'

'I did not see it. Let us make every allowance for the superstitious exaggeration of an ignorant man.'

'I should like to see this luminous appearance,' I observed, after a thoughtful pause.

'Well, let us go to-night.' exclaimed Mr Manners, eagerly. 'I am most anxious to see the matter cleared up, and it is dark moon now; I shall be most happy to accompany you. A man like you won't mind a few hours camping out, and we can ride over.'

'No, I don't mind camping out, but, with your approval, I should prefer seeing the shepherd Strong first.'

'Very well—but why? Do you think he can have anything to do with it? but of course not—it is not possible. However, here is Manneria, and I hope you are ready for dinner.'

The circumstances which Mr Manners had just related to me made a powerful impression upon my mind; and no wonder that it was so, for they were very singular, and altogether out of the common run of things. I could not altogether divest myself of the idea, however, that Strong had some untold connection with the matter; and I pondered upon my view of it all the time I was preparing myself for dinner.

At the table I met the Mr Bruce whom my host had mentioned—a quiet, reserved man, of Scotch birth, whose station adjoined the widely spreading one of Mr Manners, and whose face still bore traces of the bitter and singular bereavement he had suffered twelve months before. Mr Bruce had been the father of an only daughter, who, as the sole heir of a wealthy squatter, had many suitors. She favoured none of them, however. She was intellectual, and devoted to reading; disliked general society, and indulged, during their occasional residence at Broadbraes, in lonely rides on horseback. One day, she mounted her favourite mare and went out as usual, unquestioned, and she never returned, nor were any traces or tidings ever discovered of either the young lady or the horse she rode. It is needless to say that every effort was made that money could further, but in vain—her fate was enveloped in mystery; and that was the short sad story of a father's bereavement.

There were no ladies at Manneria, and we were but a dull trio that evening. I was glad when bedtime came, so that I might sleep away the interval between that time and my visit to the shepherd whom I was to anxious to see.

Well, morning came, and immediately after breakfast I prepared for a start to the Gully Hut, with the locality of which I was already well acquainted. Mr Manners wished to accompany me, but Mr Bruce looked so lonely, that I had little difficulty in persuading him to remain at home and try to entertain him.

'But mind, Sinclair,' he said, at parting, 'you are to be back to dinner, and not to attempt visiting the spirit-light without me.'

I was not disappointed to find the hutkeeper only at my destination, as, of course, I was aware that the shepherd would in all likelihood be out with his flock, but the man told me in what direction I should find Strong, and two miles' pleasant ride brought me within sight of the large flock, spread over one of the finest plains in the district, quietly and peacefully grazing, while the shepherd lay under the shade of a tree idly gazing up at the unflecked sky above him. He was, perhaps, half-dozing, but at any rate, he did not hear my approach, and started up when I addressed him.

'Yours is a lonely life, my man, and you have plenty of time for meditation.'

'Yes, rather too much,' he answered, looking at me keenly as I fastened my horse to a sapling, and seated myself beside him. I returned the look for a minute or two, and saw a man under thirty years of age, of a fair complexion, and with a mild and rather timorous expression of countenance.

'You wonder what I want,' I said, in reply to his look; 'well, I've ridden over from Manneria to hear you tell this strange story about the ghostly light. Mr Manners has been telling me something of it, and I am anxious to hear more.'

'He saw it himself,' replied the man, in a solemn tone.

'Yes, but he did not see the apparition.'

'No, *he* won't see that,' he replied, shaking his head.

'Why?'

'There are some people that spirits will appear to, and some they won't.'

'Oh, you quite believe in ghosts, then? But tell me all you know about it, for I am very anxious, and much interested.'

'I can tell you no more than Mr Manners has told you, but I will tell you over again if you like,' and he began in an impressive manner to relate the same strange narrative which I had already heard. I say, in an impressive manner, for the man evidently believed fully in the spiritual appearance which he declared he had seen now upon several occasions, and trembled with unfeigned horror as he narrated the story.

'And the cattle still avoid the spot?' I asked, after a silence of some moments' duration.

'Yes, you can see that for yourself in broad daylight.'

'Now, tell me your candid opinion, Strong,' I said—'what do you think is the occasion of these singular appearances? Do you really think they are supernatural, or are some of the station hands amusing themselves by hoaxing you?'

'Hoaxing me! Do you think I am blind? How could anyone make up such sights? No, no, it's nothing of this world!'

'What is it, then, in your opinion, Strong?'

'I believe a murder has been committed on that spot, and that the spirit of the departed is crying out for vengeance; that's what I believe, and nothing will convince me to the contrary.'

Strong spoke in a state of great excitement. His face flushed and his dull eyes lighted up, and I was still more convinced that there was no imposition on his part at least.

'Have you ever heard of flames of light appearing over graves in churchyards?' I asked him, 'in dark nights, just as you describe this?'

'No; do they?'

'Yes, so men of science declare; and that the light is occasioned by the escape of noxious gases generated by the decomposition of the dead bodies.'

'Then, by Jove, it's buried there!' he exclaimed, excitedly.

'What's buried there?'

'The corpse of the murdered person.'

'Did that never strike you before?' I asked.

'Never. I thought the spirit appeared to me always because—because—'

'Because what?' I inquired, as he stammered and hesitated.

'Because spirits show themselves always to some people, as I told you before.'

'I wish the police would take it in hand,' he said, after a pause, rising at the same time, and wiping the perspiration off his face with an old rag that had once been a handkerchief. 'I wish they'd dig it up and see.'

'Why don't you tackle it yourself, man?' I inquired.

'Oh! I daren't,' was the shuddering answer; 'I daren't.'

'Well, be satisfied,' I responded, 'I am in the police; and, believe me, I'll see it through. However, don't interfere with the place any way, for I want to have a look at that luminous phenomenon myself.'

The shepherd looked at me thoughtfully as I unfastened my horse and prepared to mount; and then he turned suddenly away and whistled shrilly to his dog.

'There is some singular consciousness about that Strong,' I remarked to Mr Manners, on my return; 'but it can only be the overwrought fears of a superstitious character. If there was any guilt about him he would not be so anxious for the interference of the police, or so willing to draw attention to his spiritual visitation.'

'He is a simple, dreamy sort of man,' observed the squatter, 'and always appears in deep meditation; but this visitation has doubtless made a deep impression on his mind, and I do not wonder, for it has upon mine, which, I hope, is not unduly loaded with superstition. By the bye, Mr Bruce has been very anxious for your return. When he heard that you were a detective he seemed to wish to speak of his daughter.'

Following my host into the drawing-room, I joined the sad-looking and bereaved father, who immediately drew me apart, and entered upon the subject that engrossed all his thoughts.

'I only knew that you were a detective officer about an hour ago, my dear sir,' he began, 'and I think myself most fortunate in having lighted upon you in this matter. I have heard your name, and know that you bear a high character in your profession.'

I could only bow to this compliment, and permit Mr Bruce to proceed.

'Of course you have heard of my loss,' he continued, in a husky voice. 'I have not got over it yet. If it had been a stroke from the hand of the Great Disposer of events, I could have borne it better; but thus, it—it crushes me.'

'My dear sir, hitherto every search for crime has proved ineffectual; why, then, give way to utter hopelessness? Why not try to believe that it is but an elopement, which may some day be explained and forgiven?'

He shook his head mournfully as he answered—'No, no, it is murder. I feel it *here*.'

And he placed his hand on his breast.

'You can have no foundation for such a dreadful conclusion, dear sir, except the mysteriousness of your daughter's disappearance; and the conclusion you have come to is the very worst that fate could have overwhelmed you with. Surely you know nothing to warrant it, with which the police are not already acquainted?'

'Nothing, save that there is one man living whose very name rankles in my blood, against whom my hand would involuntarily arm itself for vengeance—a man whose eye falls beneath mine, and whose forehead grows damp with fear as he stoops it before me.'

'And the name of that man?—may I know it?'

'His name is Richard Commings.'

'What! Commings of Booyong? Why, Mr Bruce, he was not in the district at the time of your loss. He only returned from Sydney about a fortnight ago.'

'I know it; yet I am convinced that he has had his hands in the blood of my child.'

The poor man spoke so wildly, and with such determination, that I feared his reason was deserting him, and tried to calm and soothe him, while I secretly made a sign for Mr Manners to approach.

'Did Commings ever pay Miss Bruce any attention?' I asked.

'No, not that I am aware of, but he is a bad man, and his sins are branded in his face. Nay, I see you think me raving, but to the death I will pursue him; yea, to the very gates of hell, till I bring him to justice!'

It required the united efforts of Mr Manners and myself to soothe the excited gentleman, and nothing but the most solemn promises on my part that I would set all my energies to work against Commings, caused him to compose himself. But before the dinner was announced, he was restored to his usual melancholy quiet, satisfied with my promise of immediate action.

Deeply as Mr Manners was affected by the sudden excitement and sad melancholy of his friend, it made no change in his determination to accompany me to witness with my own eyes the spectral light of which I had heard. So, leaving Mr Bruce in his own apartment, preparing for rest, we started on horseback for the spot.

The moon was still high, but we had made every preparation for disposing ourselves as comfortably as circumstances would permit, before it finally disappeared and left the earth to darkness, and the time when 'spirits walk the earth.' On our saddles were strapped well lined rugs, and a flask of renovating 'fire water' was not forgotten.

I felt a strange eagerness for the termination of our adventure, as we cantered, almost silently, over the moonlit grass. I was always slightly inclined to be superstitious, in spite of hard friction in the commonplace world; and, in spite of common sense and reason, and all the remainder of the objective faculties, I had some faint hope of myself seeing the spectral form, hitherto only visible to the shepherd Strong.

In a still clear light we reached the interesting locality, and having tied our horses in the shelter of an overhanging rock at a short distance, we turned toward the spot indicated by Mr Manners.

'Here it is, close to that boulder, and there is the place opposite, from whence I witnessed the appearance.'

I firstly took a careful survey of the spot itself. The locality was a gentle slope at the foot of a hill, dotted with young trees and sprinkled with numerous granite boulders. Some of these rocks were high and steep, and half covered with creeping verdure; others were water-worn and grey, lying singly here and there, as if tossed from the hands of some playful Titan.

In some places the rocks lay closely together, and were guarded by tall peppermint trees that hung over them dark and silent. Sheep tracks gleamed white in the moonlight among the boulders, save only in that one nook where the grass slept greenly and untrodden. Here three or four rocks clustered within a few yards of each other, and the low moon threw their long dark shadows athwart the dim grass; but just where Mr Manners directed my attention, the full light of the orb lay, as it stole lowly between opening boulders, and across the broad level plain.

I stooped down and examined the spot. No grass grew upon it, for it lay under the branches of a tree, where the decaying of fallen vegetable matter mingled with the crumbled granite sand of the adjacent boulder. It had not been disturbed, at least lately, for the pretty carved-like seeds of the tree above it lay half an inch thick on the spot, and rustled as I passed my hand over them.

'Well, there is nothing to be seen, as yet, at any rate,' I said; 'and I vote that we take up our quarters and wait quietly.'

We did so. Folding our rugs around us, and fortifying ourselves with a sip from the ready flask, we lay down in the shelter of the rock indicated by Mr Manners, where it was already nearly as dark as midnight, the moon having now sunk below the boulder that formed our shelter.

Not a word was spoken; we both lay in a half erect posture, our heads partially supported by the granite and partially by the ample rugs. I cannot answer for my companion, but I will avouch for myself that, in spite of the soporific tendency of the spirit I had imbibed, I never took my eyes from the marvellous spot until every vestige of moonlight had deserted it. Nor even then; though I had no visible object upon which to exercise my vision, I still stared in the same direction.

Was the moon really down? Did not a ray still linger on that interesting spot—a ray that moved as the foliaged branch of some intervening tree swayed gently in the night air? No, in the direction of the lost orb all was dark as the grave.

The grave! Was the grave dark? Was *that* spot a grave, and did a lurid flame float and wave over it close to the ground, and flicker and become faint and die out? See! it glows in distinctness, and sweeps like flame bending before a breeze down to the exhaling earth, only to become steady again, and cast a death-like reflection up to the face of the rock beside it, where it played like the moonlight upon waters.

'Good heavens preserve us! Sinclair,' whispered Manners, grasping my arm with a grip like that of a vice, 'is not that a terrible sight? God be merciful to us, it is not human!'

'Hush!' I answered, softly. 'If it is what we suspect, science explains the mystery simply. I shall not tremble till we see the apparition; should it appear, then—ha! what's that!'

The exclamation was wrung from me by the touch of cold fingers clasping mine, while the death-light grew momentarily bright, and then died out entirely, as a lonely, weird-sounding wind swept down the gully and sighed among the trees around us.

'I say, come out of this, Sinclair,' whispered Manners hoarsely, almost dragging me to my feet as he did so; 'flesh and blood could not stand the horror that is growing on me, and keep his senses. For mercy sake, let us go home!'

Truth to say I was nothing loath; the chill of those unearthly fingers still *burned* my hand, and something else remained there, of which I said not one word until we had mounted our horses, and were riding toward Manneria as rapidly as the darkness would permit.

'What in the name of goodness made you cry out that way, Sinclair?' questioned Manners, at length. 'At the sound of your frightened voice, all the scrap of courage I was nourishing died out.'

'It was very singular—it was *awful*, that's what it was.'

'Yes, it was indeed. Ah! Sinclair, there must be something supernatural in it, for a horror seems impregnating the very atmosphere around the place.'

'It is not that; it was a touch that drew the exclamation from me.'

'A touch!'

'Yes, the touch of cold fingers on mine.'

'Oh! you must be dreaming, or have been, at any rate. Bless us all, that is even worse than Strong's version; but we saw nothing.'

'I could not have been dreaming in the middle of an observation I was making to you. However, there can be no question of the fact; cold fingers touched mine, and left within my hand a something that I still grasp.'

'You are not jesting?'

'I am not indeed,' I replied.

Nor did I at all feel in the mood for jesting; the circumstance that had just occurred was too entirely surrounded by mystery and horror to permit of such a feeling.

'What, then, is it that you have got in your hand, Sinclair?'

'It feels like a bit of paper; but it's no use guessing, we shall soon reach the light.'

Not a word was exchanged between Mr Manners and myself during the remainder of our dark ride, and in silence we alighted and entered the house.

Notwithstanding the lateness of the hour, curiosity forbade our retiring without examining the spiritual communication which I had received; and entering the dining-room, where a fire still smouldered, Mr Manners struck a match and lighted a lamp that remained on the table.

'Now for your missive from the world of spirits,' said he.

And I opened the hand in which I still held the paper tightly enclosed, and showed a piece of discoloured but strong paper, upon which were traced, in a firm hand, a few lines.

The paper was apparently a leaf from a notebook, and the writing would have been illegible had it not been evidently written by some sort of stylus on a soft substance, so that the impression of the words was sharply indented on the paper.

But how shall I attempt to describe the astonishment which overpowered us when we had perused those words! No expressions of mine could convey it to you; and, remembering the poor, half distracted parent that slept under the roof so near us, you will doubtless share our feelings when you have read them also. They were as follows:—

'Seized by Richard Commings, Booyong; fastened to a tree and left. Search among Bald Hill granites.—ANNA BRUCE.'

We were stunned and somewhat temporarily deprived of speech. The paper was read and laid upon the table, and Manners and I looked each other in the face like men suddenly faced by some great difficulty. At length speech came, and it was Manners who spoke.

'Is this some great imposture?'

'Could it be possible that Bruce has done it himself?' I asked, recollecting his hatred of this Commings.

'Done what?'

'Placed this paper in my hand to-night.'

'Not he! How could you believe a father to be so heartless! Why, you are simply accusing or suspecting a man of forging his dead daughter's name for the purpose of getting a man committed for murder. Hideous!'

'Who did it then? Account for it in some way. Was it truly a visitant from the other world that placed this paper between my fingers? Bah! We must find some more reasonable solution of the mystery to satisfy a policeman.'

Manners sighed involuntarily; but then he lighted a candle and turned to leave the room.

'It is altogether too much for me, Sinclair,' he said; 'I feel nervous and unhinged. Let us take daylight on it. Upon my word my heart is sore for that poor Bruce.'

As so was mine. Detective though I was, I felt deeply for the bereaved father as I lay, thoughtfully, in my bed; but I felt other things too. I felt that there was crime and mystery to be unravelled, and that mine would be the task to do it.

In the first place, what a strange coincidence it was that upon the very night of Mr Bruce's unusual outburst, this missive from the dead should find its way into my hands. I had no doubt now that the unfortunate girl had been murdered, for the spot also mentioned in her note was the very one whereon appeared the mysterious light, and I felt certain that beneath it lay the body of the once fair Anna Bruce.

Certainly, it was possible that the paper, or rather the words upon it, might be a forgery. I was entirely ignorant of Miss Bruce's writing, but her disappearance had been too complete and traceless not to arouse the gravest suspicion—and here was confirmation of the worst.

Much as I dreaded the effect of the proceeding, I felt that it would be necessary to show the writing and the signature to Mr Bruce; he alone could judge of and verify its correctness—and besides, he had a right to know, and one which I was not disposed to deny him. Then, again, there was that strange superstitious shepherd, with his anxious watchful manner; he puzzled and strongly interested me, and it was nearly morning before I fell into a sound sleep.

Manners and I had a consultation in the morning. We calmly and coolly discussed the circumstances, and decided upon at once showing Mr Bruce the signature of his lost daughter. That done, with whatever effect, we were to proceed to the scene of our mysterious adventure, and thoroughly explore the supposed grave. It was deputed to me to break the distressing intelligence to the father; and, although I did not like the job, it was more my duty than Mr Manners's, independent of his friendly feelings towards him.

Breakfast was over; and, with an anxious face, my host saw me approach Mr Bruce and seat myself beside him. There was doubtless some unusual expression in my own countenance, for he looked at me keenly, and showed every symptom of one expecting to hear some painful intelligence.

'Mr Bruce, do you recollect our conversation of yesterday, and the determined suspicions you expressed?' I began.

'Yes. What is it?' he asked, in a hoarse whisper. 'Tell it me at once, for God's sake; no circumlocution! I know you have discovered something.'

'Try and keep yourself as calm as possible, my dear fellow,' pleaded Manners. 'Do not excite yourself more than you can possibly help. God knows, you have suffered enough already.'

'I can suffer no more, for I feel the worst has happened long, long ago; tell me then what it is.'

I placed the note in his hand and watched his face as, word by word, he deciphered it. I saw the pallor deepen into a deathly hue, and then flush into a blaze of fury.

'Did I not tell you?' he cried. 'May the vengeance of Heaven overtake him!'

'It is the writing of Miss Bruce, then? You are sure of it?'

'There is no doubt of it—none whatever.'

'Then the business is now in my hands,' I said, rising to go; 'and believe me, dear sir, that if human ingenuity and perseverance can accomplish it, you shall have the satisfaction of seeing your daughter avenged.'

'Heaven prosper you!' he exclaimed, grasping my hand. 'What is it that you go to do?'

'I must have the wretch arrested at once. Meanwhile, Mr Bruce, you must entrust that paper to my keeping for the present.'

He looked at the characters wistfully for a second, and then he handed it to me, turning away at the same time to hide the tears that I saw bursting from his eyes. My heart was heavy enough as I mounted my horse and waited for Mr Manners to join me, but it needed no fresh incentive to urge my exertions towards the conviction of the suspected murderer; the memory of that tearful old man and his terrible bereavement would drive me on his track faster than any consciousness of duty or reward.

'I think it is fortunate that he did not suspect our object,' observed Mr Manners, during our ride. 'He would have insisted on accompanying us; and if it is really as we suspect, the sight would have been maddening.'

'It would indeed. But here we are. That's the place, is it not? And there is Strong, I do believe. He seems to haunt this locality. How are we to manage for some tool?'

'I had better ride round to the Gully Hut; they will doubtless have a shovel or spade there. I'll ask Strong.'

The shepherd was approaching as he spoke, and evidently watching our movements anxiously. He soon reached us, and Mr Manners spoke.

'Have you or Jack got any sort of a spade up at the hut, Strong?'

'Spade, sir, what are you going to do with it?'

'We are going to look for the cause of your ghostly light,' I replied, as he turned an anxious look toward me.

'Ah, I thought so!' he said, with apparent satisfaction. 'I thought as how it would be. Here's one; I brought it on purpose.'

And from behind the very granite rock where the mystery was, he produced a spade, and laid it before Mr Manners.

We dismounted, and fastened our horses to the neighbouring saplings; and then, spade in hand, I approached the place, and began to shovel out the loose, porous, sandy soil. Mr Manners stood near me, his handsome face full of solemn expectation; and Strong leaned against the rock, every feature of his rough countenance expressing terror and awe.

Shovelful after shovelful was tossed out, until quite a little heap lay upon the near sward, and a shallow hole about eighteen inches deep was formed. Not a word passed from one to another; we were too deeply interested to speak, and were each moment more so as we neared the accomplishment or dispersion of our fears.

One more spadeful, and a piece of black folded cloth was visible at the bottom of the hole. I paused, and looked up at Manners, whose face was really painfully agitated.

'Go on!' he whispered, and with an effort, I did so.

Strong did not utter a syllable, but I could hear his hard tremulous breathing as he now bent over me, and almost fancy the throbs of his heart to be painful, so loud and distinct were they. At length, about five feet in length of the same black material was disclosed—in fact, a grave in size, carefully covered with black cloth.

What was under it? I guessed, but dreaded to lift it; and for a full breath of air, which I dared not draw while bending over *that* object, I stepped out on to the grass, back a good bit, and then I leaned on my spade and looked at it. Mr Manners breathed hard, and looked frightedly into the hole; and the shepherd leaned back again on the rock—he looked as if he would faint.

'What is it?' I asked, in a low voice.

'It is the skirt of a cloth habit,' answered Mr Manners, faintly. 'She has been dragged by the shoulders into the grave, and her long black skirt folded up over her body. Poor Anna!'

Laying down the spade, I stepped forward, and catching the material with both hands at the end where the edges were visible, I lifted it up slowly. Only a little caught at the sides, and held by the weight of small portions of the dry sandy soil that still lay upon it, it easily gave way, and permitted me to fold it down over the feet and expose the terrible secret.

Yes, over the feet: and there lay the remains of lovely Anna Bruce, blood bedabbled and decaying; but in a wondrous state of preservation after so long an interment.

Alas! it was truly the face of a murdered one we gazed upon, for under the long golden tresses that swept over the sinking bosom, on the fading brow where their wealth rested, lay a deep wide gash, that severed the white bone, and penetrated to the very brain! I had never seen the girl in life, but my heart grew cold with horror, while at the same time it burned with rage for retribution; and I hastily covered up the face of the dead once more with her own skirt, and began to shovel in the soil again.

'Come, let's to work!' I cried, as it was completed. 'This is no time for idle speculation. Mr Manners, go home to the poor old father; and you, Strong, keep watch here till I send a policeman to relieve you.'

And I mounted my horse, and rode quickly in the opposite direction to that in which we had come.

Such a lovely day to look upon the young dead! Such green, lovely verdure!—such bright soft clouds!—such a wealth of life everywhere! God forbid that the bloody hand should go free after the innocent blood it had spilt! Onward, good Vino—onward to the abode of the murderer!

Booyong was distant from Manneria some nine miles; and halfway between them lay our police camp. From thence I sent a man to take the necessary steps with respect to the corpse, and procured as a companion in my expedition a trooper upon whom I could depend.

It was still early in the day when we reached the station of Mr Richard Commings, and I did not think it necessary to hide our approach in the least, as, so entirely unsuspected as he had been, he was doubtless lapped in fancied security; and yet, how must he feel?

As I turned back in my saddle, I could plainly behold the summit of the Bald Hill. Surely it must carry unceasing remembrance of his crime into his very chamber!

As if the murderer ever forgets—as if he could enjoy *one* moment of security!

Richard Commings was lounging idly in his sitting room, with the weekly paper before him, as we quietly entered; but at the first look into my eyes he seemed to wither away from manhood—to fade like the trembling leaf, that only waits a breeze to fall dead and helpless on the frozen ground.

'You know what it is,' I said, sternly, as I paused before him. 'It is on your forehead as plainly as if you did it yesterday.'

The bewildered being lifted his hand quickly to his brow, as if expecting to really feel there the moisture of blood, and then his head fell forward on the table with a groan of agony.

'I arrest you, Richard Commings, for the murder of Anna Bruce.'

He did not speak or move, and I lifted his head a little to see if he had fainted. Blood on his forehead? Yes, it was there, for his face rested in a pool of it that bubbled from his lips, and spread broadly and rapidly on the oilcloth cover of the table. Not before man's weak tribunal has Richard Commings answered for his crime.

The inquests were over. Poor Anna Bruce has been laid to rest by her broken-hearted father, among the graves of her kindred; and Richard Commings has been hidden from the light he had desecrated. I had ridden to Manneria, and intended spending the night there; and Mr Manners and I were sitting by the fire, sadly talking over the recent melancholy events, when a servant brought in word that a man wished to speak to Mr Manners and me.

'Who is he?' I asked.

'It's Strong, the shepherd,' replied the man.

'Strong!' I exclaimed, remembering his peculiar behaviour respecting this murder. 'Show him up, by all means. You have no objection, Mr Manners?'

'None whatever.'

And in a few minutes Strong entered the apartment, and was accommodated with a seat. He looked pale and nervous, but determined; and as he wiped the damp from his forehead, I noticed that he was thinner than when I had last seen him, which was at the inquest.

'I have something to tell you, gentlemen,' he said, nervously; 'and God knows it will be a relief. As the unfortunate man is gone to his account, I didn't mean to speak at all; but it's killing me, and I don't feel well at all.'

'You don't look well,' I said; 'but I always suspected you knew more of this affair than you chose to tell. That affair of the writing put into my hands, eh?'

'Yes, sir. It was I put it there.'

'I'm glad to hear it, for it was the only part of the thing that reason would not touch. But why did you do it that way?'

'Well, I'll tell you all the story, and then you'll know. Twelve months ago or more I was in the employment of Commings of Booyong.'

'The devil you were!' I could not help interjecting. 'How is it that no one knew you?'

'I was there but a few weeks,' he replied. 'One day, when the master had been away for some time, I was sent with a led horse to meet him at Casyam. That must have been the very day Miss Bruce was murdered. Well, I met Commings, and we started for Booyong. About half-a-mile from the place where we found the body, something stopped him. I have thought over it since; and likely he saw the young lady at a distance, though I didn't. At any rate, he told me to wait at a corner of the road until he came back, as he wanted to pick up a specimen he had left in a certain place. Well, he rode off, and I dare say, was an hour gone. I was beginning to be pretty tired of waiting when he came back, and told me to ride back to Casyam, as he had changed his mind, and was going back to Sydney. "I'll stay all night at Manners's," he said, "or at least I'll dine there. And as I mean to take you with me to Sydney, we'll start with the coach to-morrow. Put up at Frenchy's." That's what he said, as nearly as I can remember.'

It is unnecessary to say that we were deeply interested listeners to this unexpected story. And as Strong really looked unwell, and was trembling like a leaf, Manners poured him out a tumbler half full of wine, and handed it to him, after swallowing which he continued—

'Well, Commings joined me in the evening, and we started by coach early next day. I went to Sydney with him, but he soon gave me the sack, and I took a job at shepherding on a station near Kiama. Of course I knew nothing of what had been done here, but there was a something always drawing me here. I had no peace night or day till I came.

'Well, come I did, and it was so ordered. The very day I put foot in Casyam Mr Manners there engaged me, and I was sent to the very spot almost—to the Gully Hut. I tell you it was ordered,' he continued, after a pause. 'What else made the first story I heard be the strange one of the missing young lady? And what else made me lose the sheep that night, and be sent to sleep where I'd open my eyes on the grave light? Why did she herself beckon me from the middle of the blaze, although she was lying cold and bloody under it?'

The poor man had evidently worked himself up into a superstitious belief that he was ordained to be the instrument of the murderer's punishment in some way, and I feared for his senses as the light of supernatural belief burned in his eyes.

'And so,' he went on hurriedly, 'I found my flock; and as they were scattering through the rocks—all keeping from *that* one though—a piece of paper blew up against my feet with the breeze; that was the piece I put in your hand that night when I watched you at the grave. I knew you'd go.'

'Doubtless the poor girl managed to write those lines while Commings went to send you back to Casyam, Strong. Poor Anna! poor girl!'

'Ah, if I had only known then!' exclaimed the shepherd. 'If I could only have guessed, I might have saved her! But she knew my will, and trusted me to hang the murderer. I did my best, gentlemen—I did my best; but the coward died, you see. God help us all!'

And Strong lifted his hat, and departed.

'That poor fellow will not last long,' I said, as he closed the door behind him; 'or, if he does, it will be, I fear, as an inmate of some asylum.'

'I fear so,' was Mr Manners's reply, as we separated for the night.

So, immediately after such a conversation, it was no wonder that in my sleep I was again digging up the grave of murdered Anna Bruce, and that as I dug, blue, unearthly flames followed the spade as I worked, and lighted up with a hideous pallor the dead face of the buried maiden.

JESSIE COUVREUR ('TASMA')

Monsieur Caloche

Chapter I

A more un-English, uncolonial appearance had never brightened the prosaic interior of Bogg & Company's big warehouse in Flinders Lane. Monsieur Caloche, waiting in the outer office, under fire of a row of curious eyes, was a wondrous study of 'Frenchiness' to the clerks. His vivacious dark eyes, shining out of his sallow face, scarred and seamed by the marks of smallpox, met their inquisitive gaze with an expression that seemed to plead for leniency. The diabolical disease that had scratched the freshness from his face had apparently twisted some of the youthfulness out of it as well; otherwise it was only a young soul that could have been made so diffident by the consciousness that its habitation was disfigured. Some pains had been taken to obviate the effects of the disfigurement and to bring into prominence the smooth flesh that had been spared. It was not chance that had left exposed a round white throat, guiltless of the masculine Adam's apple, or that had brushed the fine soft hair, ruddily dark in hue like the eyes, away from a vein-streaked temple. A youth of unmanly susceptibilities, perhaps—but inviting sympathy rather than scorn—sitting patiently through the dreary silent three-quarters of an hour, with his back to the wall which separated him from the great head of the firm of Bogg & Co.

The softer-hearted of the clerks commiserated with him. They would have liked to show their goodwill, after their own fashion, by inviting him to have a 'drink', but—the possibility of shouting for a young Frenchman, waiting for an interview with their chief! . . . Anyone knowing Bogg, of Bogg & Co., must have divined the outrageous absurdity of the notion. It was safer to suppose that the foreigner would have refused the politeness. He did not look as though whisky and water were as familiar to him as a tumbler of *eau sucrée*. The clerks had heard that it was customary in France to drink absinthe. Possibly the slender youth in his loose-fitting French paletot reaching to his knees, and sitting easily upon shoulders that would have graced a shawl, had drunk deeply of this fatal spirit. It invested him with something mysterious in the estimation of the juniors, peering for traces of dissipation in his foreign face. But they could find nothing to betray it in the soft eyes, undimmed by the enemy's hand, or the smooth lips set closely over the even row of small French teeth. Monsieur Caloche lacked the happy French confidence which has so often turned a joke at the foot of the guillotine. His lips twitched every time the door of the private office creaked. It was a ground-glass door to the left of him, and as he sat, with his turned-up hat in his hand, patiently waiting, the clerks could see a sort of suppression overspreading his disfigured cheeks whenever the noise was repeated. It appeared that he was diffident about the interview. His credentials were already in the hands of the head of the firm, but no summons had come. His letter of recommendation, sent in fully half an hour back, stated that he was capable of undertaking foreign correspondence; that he was favourably known to the house of business in Paris whose principal had given him his letter of presentation; that he had some slight knowledge of the English language; that he had already given promise of distinguishing himself as an *homme de lettres*. This final clause of the letter was responsible for the length of time Monsieur Caloche was kept waiting. *Homme de lettres!* It was a stigma that Bogg, of Bogg & Co., could not overlook. As a practical man, a self-made man, a man who had opened up new blocks of country and imported pure stock into Victoria—what could be expected of him in the way of holding out a helping hand to a scribbler—a pauper who had spent his days in making rhymes in his foreign jargon? Bogg would have put your needy professionals into irons. He forgave no authors, artists, or actors who were not successful. *Homme de lettres!* Coupled with his poverty it was more unpardonable a title than jail-bird. There was nothing to prove that the latter title would not have fitted Monsieur Caloche as well. He was probably a ruffianly Communist. The French Government could not get hold of all the rebels, and here was one in the outer office of Bogg & Co. coolly waiting for a situation.

Not so coolly, perhaps, as Bogg, in his aggrieved state of mind, was ready to conclude. For the day was a hot-wind day, and Bogg himself, in white waistcoat and dust-coat, sitting in the cool depths of his revolving chair in front of the desk in his private office, was hardly aware of the driving dust and smarting grit emptied by shovelfuls upon the unhappy people without. He perspired, it is true, in deference to the state of his big thermometer, which even here stood above 85° in the corner, but having come straight from Brighton in his private brougham, he could wipe his moist bald head without besmearing his silk handkerchief with street grime. And it was something to be sitting here, in a lofty office, smelling of yellow soap and beeswax, when outside a north wind was tormenting the world with its puffs of hot air and twirling relays of baked rubbish and dirt. It was something to be surrounded by polished mahogany, cool to the touch, and cold iron safes, and maps that conveyed in their rippling lines of snowy undulations far-away suggestions of chill heights and mountain breezes. It was something to have iced water in the decanter at hand, and a little fountain opposite, gurgling a running reminder of babbling brooks dribbling through fern-tree valleys and wattle-studded flats. Contrasting the shaded coolness of the private office with the heat and turmoil without, there was no cause to complain.

Yet Bogg clearly had a grievance, written in the sour lines of his mouth, never too amiably expanded at the best of times, and his small, contracted eyes, full of shrewd suspicion-darting light. He read the letter sent in by Monsieur Caloche with the plentiful assistance of the tip of his broad forefinger, after a way peculiar to his early days, before he had acquired riches, or knighthood, or rotundity.

For Bogg, now Sir Matthew Bogg, of Bogg and Company, was a self-made man, in the sense that money makes the man, and that he had made the money before it could by any possibility make him. Made it by dropping it into his till in those good old times when all Victorian storekeepers were so many Midases, who saw their spirits and flour turn into gold under their handling; made it by pocketing something like three thousand per cent upon every penny invested in divers blocks of scrubby soil hereafter to be covered by those grand and gloomy bluestone buildings which make of Melbourne a city of mourning; made it by reaching out after it, and holding fast to it, whenever it was within spirit-call or finger-clutch, from his early grog-shanty days, when he detected it in the dry lips of every grimy digger on the flat, to his later station-holding days, when he sniffed it in the drought which brought his neighbours low. Add to which he was lucky—by virtue of a certain inherent faculty he possessed in common with the Vanderbilts, the Stewarts, the Rothschilds of mankind—and far-seeing. He could forestall the news in the *Mark Lane Express*. He was almost clairvoyant in the matter of rises in wool. His luck, his foresight, were only on a par with his industry, and the end of all his slaving and sagacity was to give him at sixty years of age a liver, a paunch, an income bordering on a hundred thousand pounds, and the title of Sir Matthew Bogg.

It was known that Sir Matthew had worked his way to the colonies, acting indiscriminately as pig-sticker and deck-swabber on board the *Sarah Jane*. In his liverless, paunchless, and titleless days he had tossed for coppers with the flat-footed sailors on the forecastle. Now he was bank director, railway director, and a number of other things that formed a graceful flourish after Sir Matthew, but that would have sounded less euphonious in the wake of plain 'Bogg'. Yet 'plain Bogg' Nature had turned him out, and 'plain Bogg' he would always remain while in the earthly possession of his round, overheated face and long, irregular teeth. His hair had abandoned its lawful territory on the top of his head, and planted itself in a vagrant fashion, in small tufts in his ears and nostrils. His eyebrows had run riot over his eyes, but his eyes asserted themselves through all. They were eyes that, without being stronger or larger or bolder than any average pair of eyes to be met with in walking down the street, had such a knack of 'taking your measure' that no one could look at them without discomfiture. In the darkened atmosphere of the Flinders Lane office, Sir Matthew knew how to turn these colourless unwinking orbs to account. To the maliciously inclined among the clerks in the outer office there was nothing more amusing than the crest-fallen appearance of the applicants, as they came out by the ground-glass door, compared with the jauntiness of their entrance. Young men who wanted colonial experience, overseers who applied for managerships on his stations, youths fresh from school who had a turn for the bush, had all had specimens of Sir Matthew's mode of dealing with his underlings. But his favourite plan, his special hobby, was to 'drop on to them unawares'.

There is nothing in the world that gives such a zest to life as the possession of a hobby, and the power of indulging it. We may be pretty certain that the active old lady's white horse at Banbury Cross was nothing more than a hobby-horse, as soon as we find out in the sequel that she 'had rings on her fingers and bells on her toes', and that 'she shall have music wherever she goes'. It is the only horse an old lady could be perpetually engaged in riding with-out coming to grief—the only horse that ever makes us travel through life to the sound of music wherever we go.

From the days when Bogg had the merest shred of humanity to bully, in the shape of a waif from the Chinese camp, the minutes slipped by with a symphony they had never possessed before. As fullness of time brought him an increase of riches and power, he yearned to extend the terror of his sway. It was long before he tasted the full sweetness of making strong men tremble in their boots. Now, at nearly sixty years of age, he knew all the delights of seeing victims, sturdier and poorer than himself, drop their eyelids before his gaze. He was aware that the men in the yard cleared out of his path as he walked through it; that his managers up-country addressed him in tones of husky conciliation; that every eye met his with an air of deprecation, as much as to apologise for the fact of existing in his presence; and in his innermost heart he believed that in the way of mental sensation there could be nothing left to desire. But how convey the impression of rainbow-tints to eyes

that have never opened upon aught save universal blackness? Sir
Matthew had never seen an eye brighten, a small foot dance, at his
approach. A glance of impotent defiance was the only equivalent
he knew for a gleam of humid affection. He was accustomed to
encounter a shifting gaze. The lowest form of self-interest was the
tie which bound his people to him. He paid them as butts, in
addition to paying them as servants. Where would have been his
daily appetiser in the middle of the day if there had been no yard,
full of regulations impossible to obey; no warehouse to echo his
harsh words of fault-finding; no servile men, and slouching fast-
expanding boys, to scuttle behind the big cases, or come forth as if
they were being dragged by hooks, to stand with sheepish expression before him? And when he had talked himself hoarse in town,
where would have been the zest of wandering over his stations, of
surveying his fat bullocks and woolly merinos, if there had been no
accommodating managers to listen reverentially to his loudly
given orders, and take with dejected, apologetic air his continued
rating? The savour of life would have departed—not with the
bodily comfort and the consequence that riches bring, but with
the power they confer of asserting yourself before your fellow-
men after any fashion you please. Bogg's fashion was to bully them,
and he bullied them accordingly.

But, you see, Monsieur Caloche is still waiting; in the
position, as the junior clerks are well aware, of the confiding calf
awaiting butchery in a frolicsome mood outside the butcher's
shop. Not that I would imply that Monsieur Caloche frolicked,
even metaphorically speaking. He sat patiently on with a sort of sad
abstracted air; unconsciously pleating and unpleating the brim of
his soft Paris hat, with long lissome fingers that might have
broidered the finest silk on other than male hands. The flush of
colour, the slight trembling of lips, whenever there was a noise
from within, were the only signs that betrayed how acutely he was
listening for a summons. Despite the indentations that had marred
for ever the smoothness of the face, and pitted the forehead and
cheeks as if white gravel had been shot into them, the colour that
came and went so suddenly was pink as rose-coloured lake.

It stained even the smooth white neck and chin, upon which the faintest traces of down were not yet visible to the scrutinising eyes of the juniors.

Outside, the north wind ran riot along the pavement, upsetting all orderly arrangements for the day with dreadful noise and fussiness, battering trimly dressed people into red-eyed wretches heaped up with dust; wrenching umbrellas from their handles, and blinding their possessors trying to run after them; filling open mouths with grit, making havoc with people's hats and tempers, and proving itself as great a blusterer in its character of a peppery emigrant as in its original *rôle* of the chilly Boreas of antiquity.

Monsieur Caloche had carefully wiped away from his white wristband the dust that it had driven into his sleeve, and now the dust on his boots—palpably large for the mere slips of feet they enclosed—seemed to give him uneasiness; but it would seem that he lacked the hardihood to stoop and flick it away. When, finally, he extended surreptitiously a timid hand, it might have been observed of his uncovered wrist that it was singularly frail and slender. This delicacy of formation was noticeable in every exterior point. His small white ear, setting close to his head, might have been wrapped up over and over again in one of the fleshy lobes that stretched away from Sir Matthew's skull. Decidedly, the two men were of a different order of species. One was a heavy mastiff of lupine tendencies—the other a delicate Italian greyhound, silky, timorous, quivering with sensibility.

And there had been time for the greyhound to shiver long with expectancy before the mastiff prepared to swallow him up.

It was a quarter to twelve by the gloomy-faced clock in the outer office, a quarter to twelve by all the clerks' watches, adjusted every morning to the patriarch clock with unquestioning faith, when Monsieur Caloche had diffidently seated himself on the chair in the vicinity of the ground-glass door. It was half-past twelve by the gloomy-faced clock, half-past twelve by all the little watches that toadied to it, when Sir Matthew's bell rang. It was a bell that must have inherited the spirit of a fire-bell or a doctor's night-bell. It had never been shaken by Sir Matthew's fingers without causing a fluttering in the outer office. No one knew what hair-suspended sword might be about to fall on his head before the messenger returned. Monsieur Caloche heard it ring, sharply and clamorously, and raised his head. The white-faced messenger, returning from his answer to the summons, and speaking with the suspension of breath that usually afflicted him after an interview with Sir Matthew, announced that 'Mister Caloosh' was wanted, and diving into the gloomy recess in the outer office, relapsed into his normal occupation of breathing on his penknife and rubbing it on his sleeve.

Monsieur Caloche meanwhile stood erect, more like the startled greyhound than ever. To the watchful eyes of the clerks, staring their full at his retreating figure, he seemed to glide rather than step through the doorway. The ground-glass door, attached by a spring from the inside, shut swiftly upon him, as if it were catching him in a trap, and so hid him in full from their curious scrutiny. For the rest, they could only surmise. The lamb had given itself up to the butcher's knife. The diminutive greyhound was in the mastiff's grip.

Would the knife descend on the instant? Would the mastiff fall at once upon the trembling foreigner, advancing with sleek uncovered head, and hat held in front by two quivering hands? Sir Matthew's usual glare of reception was more ardent than of custom as Monsieur Caloche approached. If every 'foreign adventurer' supposed he might come and loaf upon Bogg, of Bogg & Company, because he was backed up by a letter from a respectable firm, Sir Matthew would soon let him find out he was mistaken! His glare intensified as the adventurous stripling glided with softest footfall to the very table where he was sitting, and stood exactly opposite to him. None so adventurous, however, but that his lips were white and his bloodless face a pitiful set-off to the cruelly prominent marks that disfigured it. There was a terror in Monsieur Caloche's expression apart from the awe inspired by Sir Matthew's glare which might have disarmed a butcher or even a mastiff. His large, soft eyes seemed to ache with repressed tears. They pleaded for him in a language more convincing than words,

'I am friendless—I am a stranger—I am—' but no matter! They cried out for sympathy and protection, mutely and unconsciously.

But to Sir Matthew's perceptions visible terror had only one interpretation. It remained for him to 'find out' Monsieur Caloche. He would 'drop on to him unawares' one of these days. He patted his hobby on the back, seeing a gratification for it in prospective, and entering shortly upon his customary stock of searching questions, incited his victim to reply cheerfully and promptly by looking him up and down with a frown of suspicion.

'What brought you 'ere?'

'Please?' said Monsieur Caloche, anxiously.

He had studied a vocabulary opening with 'Good-day sir. What can I have the pleasure of doing for you this morning?' The rejoinder to which did not seem to fit in with Sir Matthew's special form of inquiry.

'What brought you 'ere, I say?' reiterated Sir Matthew, in a roar, as if deafness were the only impediment on the part of foreigners in general to a clear comprehension of our language.

'De sheep, Monsieur! *La Reine Dorée*,' replied Monsieur Caloche, in low-toned, guttural, musical French.

'That ain't it,' said Sir Matthew, scornfully. 'What did you come 'ere for? What are you fit for? What can you do?'

Monsieur Caloche raised his plaintive eyes. His sad desolation was welling out of their inmost depths. He had surmounted the first emotion that had driven the blood to his heart at the outset, and the returning colour, softening the seams and scars in his cheeks, gave him a boyish bloom. It deepened as he answered with humility, 'I will do what Monsieur will! I will do my possible!'

'I'll soon see how you shape,' said Sir Matthew, irritated with himself for the apparent difficulty of thoroughly bullying the defenceless stranger. 'I don't want any of your parley-vooing in my office—do you hear! I'll find you work—jolly quick, I can tell you! Can you mind sheep? Can you drive bullocks, eh? Can you put up a post and rail? You ain't worth your salt if you can't use your 'ands!'

He cast such a glance of withering contempt on the tapering white fingers with olive-shaped nails in front of him that Monsieur Caloche instinctively sheltered them in his hat. 'Go and get your traps together! I'll find you a billet, never fear!'

'*Mais, Monsieur*—'

'Go and get your traps together, I say! You can come 'ere again in an hour. I'll find you a job up-country!' His peremptory gesture made any protest on the part of Monsieur Caloche utterly unavailing. There was nothing for him to do but to bow and to back in a bewildered way from the room. If the more sharp-eared of the clerks had not been in opportune contiguity to the ground-glass door during Sir Matthew's closing sentences, Monsieur Caloche would have gone away with the predominant impression that 'Sir Bang' was an *enragé*, who disapproved of salt with mutton and beef, and was clamorous in his demands for 'traps', which Monsieur Caloche, with a gleam of enlightenment in the midst of his heart-sickness and perplexity, was proud to remember meant 'an instrument for ensnaring animals'. It was with a doubt he was too polite to express that he accepted the explanation tendered him by the clerks, and learned that if he 'would strike while the iron is hot' he must come back in an hour's time with his portmanteau packed up. He was a lucky fellow, the juniors told him, to jump into a billet without any bother; they wished to the Lord they were in *his* shoes, and could be drafted off to the Bush at a moment's notice.

Perhaps it seemed to Monsieur Caloche that these congratulations were based on the Satanic philosophy of 'making evil his good'. But they brought with them a flavour of the human sympathy for which he was hungering. He bowed to the clerks all round before leaving, after the manner of a court-page in an opera. The hardiest of the juniors ran to the door after he was gone. Monsieur Caloche was trying to make head against the wind. The warm blast was bespattering his injured face. It seemed to revel in the pastime of filling it with grit. One small hand was spread in front of the eyes—the other was resolutely holding together the front of his long, light paletot, which the rude wind had sportively thrown open. The junior was cheated of his fun. Somehow the sight did not strike him as being quite as funny as it ought to have been.

Chapter II

The station hands, in their own language, 'gave Frenchy best'. No difference of nationality could account for some of his eccentricities. As an instance, with the setting in of the darkness he regularly disappeared. It was supposed that he camped up a tree with the birds. The wit of the wood-shed surmised that 'Froggy' slept with his relatives, and it would be found that he had 'croaked' with them one of these odd times. Again, there were shearers ready to swear that he had 'blubbered' on finding some sportive ticks on his neck. He was given odd jobs of wool-sorting to do, and was found to have a mania for washing the grease off his hands whenever there was an instant's respite. Another peculiarity was his aversion to blood. By some strange coincidence, he could never be found whenever there was any slaughtering on hand. The most plausible reason was always advanced for necessitating his presence in some far-distant part of the run. Equally he could never be induced to learn how to box—a favourite Sunday morning and summer evening pastime among the men. It seemed almost to hurt him when damage was done to one of the assembled noses. He would have been put down as a 'cur' if it had not been for his pluck in the saddle, and for his gentle winning ways. His pluck, indeed, seemed all concentrated on his horsemanship. Employed as a boundary-rider, there was nothing he would not mount, and the station hands remarked, as a thing 'that beat them once and for all', that the 'surliest devils' on the place hardly every played up with him. He employed no arts. His bridle-hand was by no means strong. Yet it remained a matter of fact that the least amenable of horses generally carried him as if they liked to bear his weight. No one being sufficiently learned to advance the hypothesis of magnetism, it was concluded that he carried a charm.

This power of touch extended to human beings. It was almost worth while spraining a joint or chopping at a finger to be bandaged by Monsieur Caloche's deft fingers. His horror of blood never stood in his way when there was a wound to be doctored. His supple hands, browned and strengthened by his outdoor work, had a tenderness and a delicacy in their way of going to work that made the sufferer feel soothed and half-healed by their contact. It was the same with his manipulation of things. There was a refinement in his disposition of the rough surroundings that made them look different after he had been among them.

And not understood, jeered at, petted, pitied alternately—with no confidant of more sympathetic comprehension than the horse he bestrode—was Monsieur Caloche absolutely miserable? Granting that it were so, there was no one to find it out. His brown eyes had such an habitually wistful expression, he might have been born with it. Very trifles brought a fleeting light into them—a reminiscence, perhaps that while it crowned him with 'sorrow's crown of sorrow', was yet a reflection of some past joy. He took refuge in his ignorance of the language directly he was questioned as to his bygone life. An embarrassed little shrug, half apologetic, but powerfully conclusive, was the only answer the most curious examiner could elicit.

It was perceived that he had a strong objection to looking in the glass, and invariably lowered his eyes on passing the cracked and uncompromising fragment of mirror supported on two nails against the planking that walled the rough, attached kitchen. So decided was this aversion that it was only when Bill, the blacksmith, asked him chaffingly for a lock of his hair that he perceived with confusion how wantonly his silken curls were rioting round his neck and temples. He cut them off on the spot, displaying the transparent skin beneath. Contrasted with the clear tan that had overspread his scarred cheeks and forehead, it was white as freshly drawn milk.

He was set down on the whole as given to moping; but, taking him all round, the general sentiment was favourable to him. Possibly it was with some pitiful prompting of the sort that the working manager sent him out of the way one still morning, when Sir Matthew's buggy, creaking under the unwelcome preponderance of Sir Matthew himself, was discerned on its slow approach to the homestead. A most peaceful morning for the initiation of Sir Matthew's blustering presence! The sparse gum-leaves hung as motionless on their branches as if they were waiting to be photographed. Their shadows on the yellowing grass seemed painted into the soil. The sky was as tranquil as the plain below. The smoke from the homestead reared itself aloft in the long, thinly drawn column of grey. A morning of heat and repose, when even the sunlight does not frolic and all nature toasts itself, quietly content. The dogs lay blinking at full length, their tails beating the earth with lazy, measured thumps. The sheep seemed rooted to the patches of shade, apathetic as though no one wore flannel vests or ate mutton-chops. Only the mingled voices of wild birds and multitudinous insects were upraised in a blended monotony of subdued sounds. Not a morning to be devoted to toil! Rather, perchance, to a glimmering perception of a golden age, when sensation meant bliss more than pain, and to be was to enjoy.

But to the head of the firm of Bogg & Company, taking note of scattered thistles and straggling wire fencing, warmth and sunshine signified only dry weather. Dry weather clearly implied a fault somewhere, for which somebody must be called to account. Sir Matthew had the memory of a strategist. Underlying all considerations of shorthorns and merinos was the recollection of a timid foreign lad to be suspected for his shy, bewildered air—to be suspected again for his slim white hands—to be doubly suspected and utterly condemned for his graceful bearing, his appealing eyes, that even now Sir Matthew could see with their soft lashes drooping over them as he fronted them in his darkened office in Flinders Lane. A scapegoat for dry weather, for obtrusive thistles, for straggling fencing! A waif of foreign scum to be found out! Bogg had promised himself that he would 'drop on to him unawares'. Physically, Bogg was carried over the ground by a fast trotter; spiritually, he was borne along on his hobby, ambling towards its promised gratification with airy speed.

The working manager, being probably of Bacon's way of thinking, that 'dissimulation is but a faint kind of policy', did not, in his own words, entirely 'knuckle down' to Sir Matthew. His name was Blunt—he was proud to say it—and he would show you he could make his name good if you 'crossed' him. Yet Blunt could bear a good deal of 'crossing' when it came to the point. Within certain limits, he concluded that the side on which his bread was buttered was worth keeping uppermost, at the cost of some hard words from his employer.

And he kept it carefully uppermost on this especial morning, when the quietude of the balmy atmosphere was broken by Sir Matthew's growls. The head of the firm, capturing his manager at the door of the homestead, had required him to mount into the double-seated buggy with him. Blunt reckoned that these tours of inspection in the companionship of Bogg were more conducive to taking off flesh than a week's hard training. He listened with docility, nevertheless, to plaints and ratings—was it not a fact that his yearly salaries had already made a nest-egg of large proportions?—and might have listened to the end, if an evil chance had not filled him with a sudden foreboding. For, picking his way over the plain, after the manner of Spenser's knight, Monsieur Caloche, on a fleet, newly broken-in two-year-old, was riding towards them. Blunt could feel that Sir Matthew's eyes were sending out sparks of wrath. For the first time in his life he hazarded an uncalled-for opinion.

'He's a good working chap, that, sir!'—indicating by a jerk of the head that the lad now galloping across the turf was the subject of his remark.

'Ah!' said Sir Matthew.

It was all he said, but it was more than enough.

Blunt fidgeted uneasily. What power possessed the boy to make him show off his riding at this juncture? If he could have stopped him, or turned him back, or waved him off!—but his will was impotent.

Monsieur Caloche, well back in the saddle, his brown eyes shining, his disfigured face flushed and glowing, with wide felt-hat drawn closely over his smooth small head, with slender knees close pressed to the horse's flanks, came riding on, jumping small logs, bending with flexible joints under straggling branches, never pausing, in his reckless course, until on a sudden he found himself almost in front of the buggy, and, reining up, was confronted in full by the savage gleam of Sir Matthew's eyes. It was with the old scared expression that he pulled off his wideawake and bared his head, black and silky as a young retriever's. Sir Matthew knew how to respond to the boy's greeting. He stood up in the buggy and shook his fist at him; his voice, hoarse from the work he had given it that morning, coming out with rasping intensity.

'What the devil do you mean by riding my 'orses' tails off, eh?'

Monsieur Caloche, in his confusion, straining to catch the full meaning of the question, looked fearfully round at the hind-quarters of the two-year-old, as if some hitherto unknown phenomenon peculiar to Australian horses might in fact have suddenly left them tailless.

But the tail was doing such good service against the flies at the moment of his observations, that, reassured, he turned his wistful gaze upon Sir Matthew.

'Monsieur,' he began apologetically, 'permit that I explain it to you. I did ga-lopp.'

'You can ga-lopp to hell!' said Sir Matthew with furious mimicry. 'I'll teach you to ruin my 'orses' legs!'

Blunt saw him lift his whip and strike Monsieur Caloche on the chest. The boy turned so unnaturally white that the manager looked to see him reel in his saddle. But he only swayed forward and slipped to the ground on his feet. Sir Matthew, sitting down again in the buggy with an uncomfortable sensation of some undue excess it might have been as well to recall, saw his white face for the flash of an instant's space, saw its desperation, its shame, its trembling lips; then he was aware that the two-year-old stood riderless in front of him, and away in the distance the figure of a lad was speeding through the timber, one hand held against his chest, his hat gone and he unheeding, palpably sobbing and crying in his loneliness and defencelessness as he stumbled blindly on.

Runaway boys, I fear, call forth very little solicitude in any heart but a mother's. A cat may be nine-lived, but a boy's life is centuple. He seems only to think it worth keeping after the best part of it is gone. Boys run away from schools, from offices, from stations, without exciting more than an ominous prognostication that they will go to the bad. According to Sir Matthew's inference, Monsieur Caloche had 'gone to the bad' long ago—*ergo* it was well to be rid of him. This being so, what utterly inconsistent crank had laid hold of the head of the great firm of Bogg & Company, and tortured him through a lengthy afternoon and everlasting night, with the vision of two despairing eyes and a scarred white face? Even his hobby cried out against him complainingly. It was not for this that it had borne him prancing along. Not to comfort him night and day with eyes so distressful that he could see nothing else. Would it be always so? Would they shine mournfully out of the dim recesses of his gloomy office in Flinders Lane, as they shone here in the wild bush on all sides of him?—so relentlessly sad that it would have been a relief to see them change into the vindictive eyes of the Furies who gave chase to Orestes. There was clearly only one remedy against such a fate, and that was to change the nature of the expression which haunted him by calling up another in its place. But how and when!

Sir Matthew prowled around the homestead the second morning after Monsieur Caloche's flight, in a manner unaccountable to himself. That he should return 'possessed' to his elaborate warehouse, where he would be alone all day—and his house of magnificent desolation, where he would be alone all night, was fast becoming a matter of impossibility. What sums out of all proportion would he not have forfeited to have seen the white-faced foreign lad, and to be able to pay him out for the discomfort he was causing him—instead of being bothered by the sight of his 'cursed belongings' at every turn! He could not go into the stable without seeing some of his gimcracks; when he went blustering into the kitchen it was to stumble over a pair of miniature boots, and a short curl of hair, in silken rings, fell off the ledge at his very feet. There was only one thing to be done! Consulting with Blunt, clumsily enough, for nothing short of desperation would have induced Sir Matthew to approach the topic of Monsieur Caloche, he learned that nothing had been seen or heard of the lad since the moment of his running away.

'And 'twasn't in the direction of the township, neither,' added Blunt, gravely. 'I doubt the sun'll have made him stupid, and he'll have camped down some place on the run.'

Blunt's insinuation anent the sun was sheer artifice, for Blunt, in his private heart, did not endorse his own suggestion in the least degree. It was his belief that the lad had struck a shepherd's hut, and was keeping (with a show of common-sense he had not credited him with) out of the way of his savage employer. But it was worth while making use of the artifice to see Sir Matthew's ill-concealed uneasiness. Hardly the same Sir Matthew, in any sense, as the bullying growler who had driven by his side not two days ago. For *this* morning the double-seated buggy was the scene of neither plaints nor abuse. Quietly over the bush track—where last Monsieur Caloche, with hand on his breast, had run sobbing along—the two men drove, their wheels passing over a wideawake hat, lying neglected and dusty in the road. For more than an hour and a half they followed the track, the dusty soil that had been witness to the boy's flight still indicating at intervals traces of a small footprint. The oppressive calm of the atmosphere seemed to have left even the ridges of dust undisturbed. Blunt reflected that it must have been 'rough on a fellow' to run all that way in the burning sun. It perplexed him, moreover, to remember that the shepherd's hut would be now far in their rear. Perhaps it was with a newly born sense of uneasiness on his own account that he flicked his whip and made the trotter 'go', for no comment could be expected from Sir Matthew, sitting in complete silence by his side.

To Blunt's discerning eyes the last of the footprints seemed to occur right in the middle of the track. On either side was the plain. Ostensibly, Sir Matthew had come that way to look at the sheep.

There was, accordingly, every reason for turning to the right and driving towards a belt of timber some hundred yards away, and there were apparently more forcible reasons still for making for a particular tree—a straggling tree, with some pretensions to a meagre shade, the sight of which called forth an ejaculation, not entirely coherent, from Blunt.

Sir Matthew saw the cause of Blunt's ejaculation—a recumbent figure that had probably reached 'the quiet haven of us all'— it lay so still. But whether quiet or no, it would seem that to disturb its peace was a matter of life or death to Sir Matthew Bogg. Yet surely here was satiety of the fullest for his hobby! Had he not 'dropped on to the "foreign adventurer" unawares'? So unawares, in fact, that Monsieur Caloche never heeded his presence, or the presence of his working manager, but lay with a glaze on his half-closed eyes in stiff unconcern at their feet.

The clerks and juniors in the outer office of the great firm of Bogg & Co. would have been at some loss to recognise their chief in the livid man who knelt by the dead lad's side. He wanted to feel his heart, it appeared, but his trembling fingers failed him. Blunt comprehended the gesture. Whatever tenderness Monsieur Caloche had expended in his short lifetime was repaid by the gentleness with which the working manager passed his hand under the boy's rigid neck. It was with a shake of the head that seemed to Sir Matthew like the fiat of his doom that Blunt unbuttoned Monsieur Caloche's vest and discovered the fair, white throat beneath. Unbuttoning still—with tremulous fingers, and a strange apprehension creeping chillily over him—the manager saw the open vest fall loosely asunder, and then—

Yes; then it was proven that Sir Matthew's hobby had gone its extremest length. Though it could hardly have been rapture at its great triumph that filled his eyes with such a strange expression of horror as he stood looking fearfully down on the corpse at his feet. For he had, in point of fact, 'dropped on to it unawares'; but it was no longer Monsieur Caloche he had 'dropped on to', but a girl with a breast of marble, bared in its cold whiteness to the open daylight, and to his ardent gaze. Bared, without any protest from the half-closed eyes, unconcerned behind the filmy veil which glazed them. A virgin breast, spotless in hue, save for a narrow purple streak, marking it in a dark line from the collarbone downwards. Sir Matthew knew, and the working manager knew, and the child they called Monsieur Caloche had known, by whose hand the mark had been imprinted. It seemed to Sir Matthew that a similar mark, red hot like a brand, must now burn on his own forehead for ever. For what if the hungry Australian sun, and emotion, and exhaustion had been the actual cause of the girl's death? He acknowledged, in the bitterness of his heart, that the 'cause of the cause' was his own bloodstained hand.

It must have been poor satisfaction to his hobby, after this, to note that Blunt had found a tiny pocket-book on the person of the corpse, filled with minute foreign handwriting. Of which nothing could be made? For, with one exception, it was filled with French quotations, all of the same tenor—all pointing to that one conclusion—and clearly proving (if it has not been proved already) that a woman who loses her beauty loses her all. The English quotation will be known to some readers of Shakespeare. 'So beauty blemished once for ever's lost!' Affixed to it was the faintly traced signature of Henriette Caloche.

So here was a sort of insight into the mystery. The 'foreign adventurer' might be exonerated after all. No baser designs need be laid at the door of dead 'Monsieur Caloche' than the design of hiding the loss which had deprived her of all glory in her sex. If, indeed, the loss were a *real* one! For beauty is more than skin-deep, although Monsieur Caloche had not known it. It is of the bone, and the fibre, and the nerves that thrill through the brain. It is of the form and the texture too, as anyone would have allowed who scrutinised the body prone in the dust. Even the cruel scars seemed merciful now, and relaxed their hold on the chiselled features, as though 'eloquent, just, and mightie Death' would suffer no hand but his own to dally with his possession.

It is only in Christmas stories, I am afraid, where, in deference to so rollicking a season, everything is bound to come right in the end, that people's natures are revolutionised in a night, and from narrow-minded villains they become open-hearted seraphs of charity. Still, it is on record of the first Henry that from the time of the sinking of the *White Ship* 'he never smiled again'. I cannot say that Sir Matthew was never known to smile, in his old sour way, or that he never growled or scolded, in his old bullying fashion, after the discovery of Monsieur Caloche's body. But he was nonetheless a changed man. The outside world might rightly conjecture that henceforth a slender, mournful-eyed shadow would walk by his side through life. But what can the outside world know of the refinement of mental anguish that may be endured by a mind awakened too late? In Sir Matthew's case—relatively as well as positively. For constant contemplation of a woman's pleading eyes and a dead statuesque form might give rise to imaginings that it would be maddening to dwell upon. What a wealth of caresses those still little hands had had it in their power to bestow! What a power of lighting up the solemnest office, and—be sure—the greatest, dreariest house, was latent in those dejected eyes!

Brooding is proverbially bad for the liver. Sir Matthew died of the liver complaint, and his will was cited as an instance of the eccentricity of a wealthy Australian, who never having been in France, left the bulk of his money to the purpose of constructing and maintaining a magnificent wing to a smallpox hospital in the south of France. It was stipulated that it should be called the 'Henriette' wing, and is, I believe, greatly admired by visitors from all parts of the world.

The Chosen Vessel

She laid the stick and her baby on the grass while she untied the rope that tethered the calf. The length of the rope separated them. The cow was near the calf, and both were lying down. Feed along the creek was plentiful, and every day she found a fresh place to tether it, since tether it she must, for if she did not, it would stray with the cow out on the plain. She had plenty of time to go after it, but then there was her baby; and if the cow turned on her out on the plain, and she with her baby,—she had been a town girl and was afraid of the cow, but she did not want the cow to know it. She used to run at first when it bellowed its protest against the penning up of its calf. This satisfied the cow, also the calf, but the woman's husband was angry, and called her—the noun was cur. It was he who forced her to run and meet the advancing cow, brandishing a stick, and uttering the threatening words till the enemy turned and ran. 'That's the way!' the man said, laughing at her white face. In many things he was worse than the cow, and she wondered if the same rule would apply to the man, but she was not one to provoke skirmishes even with the cow.

It was early for the calf to go to 'bed'—nearly an hour earlier than usual; but she had felt so restless all day. Partly because it was Monday, and the end of the week that would bring her and the baby the companionship of his father, was so far off. He was a shearer, and had gone to his shed before daylight that morning. Fifteen miles as the crow flies separated them.

There was a track in front of the house, for it had once been a wine shanty, and a few travellers passed along at intervals. She was not afraid of horsemen; but swagmen, going to, or worse coming from, the dismal, drunken little township, a day's journey beyond, terrified her. One had called at the house today, and asked for tucker.

That was why she had penned up the calf so early. She feared more from the look of his eyes, and the gleam of his teeth, as he watched her newly awakened baby beat its impatient fists upon her covered breasts, than from the knife that was sheathed in the belt at his waist.

She had given him bread and meat. Her husband she told him was sick. She always said that when she was alone and a swagman came; and she had gone in from the kitchen to the bedroom, and asked questions and replied to them in the best man's voice she could assume. Then he had asked to go into the kitchen to boil his billy, but instead she gave him tea, and he drank it on the wood heap. He had walked round and round the house, and there were cracks in some places, and after the last time he had asked for tobacco. She had none to give him, and he had grinned, because there was a broken clay pipe near the wood heap where he stood, and if there were a man inside, there ought to have been tobacco. Then he asked for money, but women in the bush never have money.

At last he had gone, and she, watching through the cracks, saw him when about a quarter of a mile away, turn and look back at the house. He had stood so for some moments with a pretence of fixing his swag, and then, apparently satisfied, moved to the left towards the creek. The creek made a bow round the house, and when he came to the bend she lost sight of him. Hours after, watching intently for signs of smoke, she saw the man's dog chasing some sheep that had gone to the creek for water, and saw it slink back suddenly, as if it had been called by some one.

More than once she thought of taking her baby and going to her husband. But in the past, when she had dared to speak of the dangers to which her loneliness exposed her, he had taunted and sneered at her. 'Needn't flatter yerself,' he had told her, 'nobody 'ud want ter run away with yew.'

Long before nightfall she placed food on the kitchen table, and beside it laid the big brooch that had been her mother's. It was the only thing of value that she had. And she left the kitchen door wide open.

The doors inside she securely fastened. Beside the bolt in the back one she drove in the steel and scissors; against it she piled the table and the stools. Underneath the lock of the front door she forced the handle of the spade, and the blade between the cracks in the flooring boards. Then the prop-stick, cut into lengths, held the top, as the spade held the middle. The windows were little more than portholes; she had nothing to fear through them.

She ate a few mouthfuls of food and drank a cup of milk. But she lighted no fire, and when night came, no candle, but crept with her baby to bed.

What woke her? The wonder was that she had slept—she had not meant to. But she was young, very young. Perhaps the shrinking of the galvanised roof—hardly though, since that was so usual. Yet something had set her heart beating wildly; but she lay quite still, only she put her arm over her baby. Then she had both round it, and she prayed, 'Little baby, little baby, don't wake.'

The moon's rays shone on the front of the house, and she saw one of the open cracks, quite close to where she lay, darken with a shadow. Then a protesting growl reached her; and she could fancy she heard the man turn hastily. She plainly heard the thud of something striking the dog's ribs, and the long flying strides of the animal as it howled and ran. Still watching, she saw the shadow darken every crack along the wall. She knew by the sounds that the man was trying every standpoint that might help him to see in; but how much he saw she could not tell. She thought of many things she might do to deceive him into the idea that she was not alone. But the sound of her voice would wake baby, and she dreaded that as though it were the only danger that threatened her. So she prayed, 'Little baby, don't wake, don't cry!'

Stealthily the man crept about. She knew he had his boots off, because of the vibration that his feet caused as he walked along the verandah to gauge the width of the little window in her room, and the resistance of the front door.

Then he went to the other end, and the uncertainty of what he was doing became unendurable. She had felt safer, far safer, while he was close, and she could watch and listen. She felt she must watch, but the great fear of wakening her baby again assailed her. She suddenly recalled that one of the slabs on that side of the house had shrunk in length as well as in width, and had once fallen out. It was held in position only by a wedge of wood underneath. What if he should discover that? The uncertainty increased her terror. She prayed as she gently raised herself with her little one in her arms, held tightly to her breast.

She thought of the knife, and shielded its body with her hands and arms. Even the little feet she covered with its white gown, and the baby never murmured—it liked to be held so. Noiselessly she crossed to the other side, and stood where she could see and hear, but not be seen. He was trying every slab, and was very near to that with the wedge under it. Then she saw him find it; and heard the sound of the knife as bit by bit he began to cut away the wooden support.

She waited motionless, with her baby pressed tightly to her, thought she knew that in another few minutes this man with the cruel eyes, lascivious mouth, and gleaming knife, would enter. One side of the slab tilted; he had only to cut away the remaining little end, when the slab, unless he held it, would fall outside.

She heard his jerked breathing as it kept time with the cuts of the knife, and the brush of his clothes as he rubbed the wall in his movements, for she was so still and quiet, that she did not even tremble. She knew when he ceased, and wondered why, being so well concealed; for he could not see her, and would not fear if he did, yet she heard him move cautiously away. Perhaps he expected the slab to fall—his motive puzzled her, and she moved even closer, and bent her body the better to listen. Ah! What sound was that? 'Listen! Listen!' she bade her heart—her heart that had kept so still, but now bounded with tumultuous throbs that dulled her ears. Nearer and nearer came the sounds, till the welcome thud of a horse's hoof rang out clearly.

'O God! O God! O God!' she panted, for they were very close before she could make sure. She rushed to the door, and with her baby in her arms tore frantically at its bolts and bars.

Out she darted at last, and running madly along, saw the horseman beyond her in the distance. She called to him in Christ's Name, in her babe's name, still flying like the wind with the speed that deadly peril gives. But the distance grew greater and greater between them, and when she reached the creek her prayers turned to wild shrieks, for there crouched the man she feared, with outstretched arms that caught her as she fell. She knew he was offering terms if she ceased to struggle and cry for help, though louder and louder did she cry for it, but it was only when the man's hand gripped her throat, that the cry of 'Murder' came from her lips. And when she ceased, the startled curlews took up the awful sound, and flew wailing 'Murder! Murder!' over the horseman's head.

'By God!' said the boundary rider, 'it's been a dingo right enough! Eight killed up here, and there's more down in the creek—a ewe and a lamb, I'll bet; and the lamb's alive!' He shut out the sky with his hand, and watched the crows that were circling round and round, nearing the earth one moment, and the next shooting sky-wards. By that he knew the lamb must be alive; even a dingo will spare a lamb sometimes.

Yes, the lamb was alive, and after the manner of lambs of its kind did not know its mother when the light came. It had sucked the still warm breasts, and laid its little head on her bosom, and slept till the morn. Then, when it looked at the swollen disfigured face, it wept and would have crept away, but for the hand that still clutched its little gown. Sleep was nodding its golden head and swaying its small body, and the crows were close, so close to the mother's wide-open eyes, when the boundary rider galloped down.

'Jesus Christ!' he said, covering his eyes. He told afterwards how the little child held out its arms to him, and how he was forced to cut its gown that the dead hand held.

It was election time, and as usual the priest had selected a candidate. His choice was so obviously in the interests of the squatter, that Peter Hennessey's reason, for once in his life, had over-ridden superstition, and he had dared promise his vote to another. Yet he was uneasy, and every time he woke in the night (and it was often), he heard the murmur of his mother's voice. It came through the partition, or under the door. If through the partition, he knew she was praying in her bed; but when the sounds came under the door, she was on her knees before the little altar in the corner that enshrined the statue of the Blessed Virgin and Child.

'Mary, Mother of Christ! Save my son! Save him!' prayed she in the dairy as she strained and set the evening's milking. 'Sweet Mary! for the love of Christ, save him!' The grief in her old face made the morning meal so bitter, that to avoid her he came late to his dinner. It made him so cowardly, that he could not say good-bye to her, and when night fell on the eve of the election day, he rode off secretly.

He had thirty miles to ride to the township to record his vote. He cantered briskly along the great stretch of plain that had nothing but stunted cotton bush to play shadow to the full moon, which glorified a sky of earliest spring. The bruised incense of the flowering clover rose up to him, and the glory of the night appealed vaguely to his imagination, but he was preoccupied with his present act of revolt.

Vividly he saw his mother's agony when she would find him gone. Even at that moment, he felt sure, she was praying.

'Mary! Mother of Christ!' He repeated the invocation, half unconsciously, when suddenly to him, out of the stillness, came Christ's Name—called loudly in despairing accents.

'For Christ's sake! Christ's sake! Christ's sake!' called the voice. Good Catholic that he had been, he crossed himself before he dared to look back. Gliding across a ghostly patch of pipe-clay, he saw a white-robed figure with a babe clasped to her bosom.

All the superstitious awe of his race and religion swayed his brain. The moonlight on the gleaming clay was a 'heavenly light' to him, and he knew the white figure not for flesh and blood, but for the Virgin and Child of his mother's prayers. Then, good Catholic that once more he was, he put spurs to his horse's sides and galloped madly away.

His mother's prayers were answered, for Hennessey was the first to record his vote—for the priest's candidate. Then he sought the priest at home, but found that he was out rallying the voters. Still, under the influence of his blessed vision, Hennessey would not go near the public-houses, but wandered about the outskirts of the town for hours, keeping apart from the townspeople, and fasting as penance. He was subdued and mildly ecstatic, feeling as a repentant chastened child, who awaits only the kiss of peace.

And at last, as he stood in the graveyard crossing himself with reverent awe, he heard in the gathering twilight the roar of many voices crying the name of the victor at the election. It was well with the priest.

Again Hennessey sought him. He was at home, the housekeeper said, and led him into the dimly lighted study. His seat was immediately opposite a large picture, and as the housekeeper turned up the lamp, once more the face of the Madonna and Child looked down on him, but this time silently, peacefully. The half-parted lips of the Virgin were smiling with compassionate tenderness; her eyes seemed to beam with the forgiveness of an earthly mother for her erring but beloved child.

He fell on his knees in adoration. Transfixed, the wondering priest stood, for mingled with the adoration, 'My Lord and my God!' was the exaltation, 'And hast Thou chosen me?'

'What is it, Peter?' said the priest.

'Father,' he answered reverently; and with loosened tongue he poured forth the story of his vision.

'Great God!' shouted the priest, 'and you did not stop to save her! Do you not know? Have you not heard?'

Many miles further down the creek a man kept throwing an old cap into a water-hole. The dog would bring it out and lay it on the opposite side to where the man stood, but would not allow the man to catch him, though it was only to wash the blood of the sheep from his mouth and throat, for the sight of blood made the man tremble. But the dog also was guilty.

And Women Must Weep

For men must work

She was ready at last, the last bow tied, the last strengthening pin
in place, and they said to her—Auntie Cha and Miss Biddons—to
sit down and rest while Auntie Cha 'climbed into her own togs':
'Or you'll be tired before the evening begins.' But she could not
bring herself to sit, for fear of crushing her dress—it was so light,
so airy. How glad she felt now that she had chosen muslin, and not
silk as Auntie Cha had tried to persuade her. The gossamer-
like stuff seemed to float around her as she moved, and the cut of
the dress made her look so tall and so different from everyday that
she hardly recognized herself in the glass; the girl reflected
there—in palest blue, with a wreath of cornflowers in her hair—
might have been a stranger. Never had she thought she was so
pretty . . . nor had Auntie and Miss Biddons either; though all they
said was: 'Well, Dolly, you'll *do*,' and 'Yes, I think she will be a
credit to you.' Something hot and stinging came up her throat at
this: a kind of gratitude for her pinky-white skin, her big blue eyes
and fair curly hair, and pity for those girls who hadn't got them.
Or an Auntie Cha either, to dress them and see that everything was
'just so'.

Instead of sitting, she stood very stiff and straight at the
window, pretending to watch for the cab, her long white gloves
hanging loose over one arm so as not to soil them. But her heart
was beating pit-a-pat. For this was her first real grown-up ball.

It was to be held in a public hall, and Auntie Cha, where she was staying, had bought tickets and was taking her.

True, Miss Biddons rather spoilt things at the end by saying: 'Now mind you don't forget your steps in the waltz. One, two, together; four, five, six.' And in the wagonette, with her dress filling one seat, Auntie Cha's the other, Auntie said: 'Now, Dolly, remember not to look too *serious*. Or you'll frighten the gentlemen off.'

But she was only doing it now because of her dress; cabs were so cramped, the seats so narrow.

Alas! in getting out a little accident happened. She caught the bottom of one of her flounces—the skirt was made of nothing else—on the iron step, and ripped off the selvedge. Auntie Cha said: 'My *dear*, how clumsy!' She could have cried with vexation.

The woman who took their cloaks hunted everywhere, but could only find black cotton; so the torn selvedge—there was nearly half a yard of it—had just to be cut off. This left a raw edge, and when they went into the hall and walked across the enormous floor with people sitting all around, staring, it seemed to Dolly as if every one had their eyes fixed on it. Auntie Cha sat in the front row of chairs beside a lady-friend; but she slid into a chair behind.

The first dance was already over, and they were hardly seated before partners began to be taken for the second. Shyly she mustered the assembly. In the cloakroom, she had expected the woman to exclaim: 'What a sweet pretty frock!' when she handled it. (When all she did say was: 'This sort of stuff's bound to fray.') And now Dolly saw that the hall was full of *lovely* dresses, some much, much prettier than hers, which suddenly began to seem rather too plain, even a little dowdy; perhaps after all it would have been better to choose silk.

She wondered if Auntie Cha thought so, too. For Auntie suddenly turned and looked at her, quite hard, and then said snappily: 'Come, come, child, you mustn't tuck yourself away like that, or the gentlemen will think you don't want to dance.' So she had to come out and sit in the front; and show that she had a programme, by holding it open on her lap.

When other ladies were being requested for the third time, and still nobody had asked to be introduced, Auntie began making signs and beckoning with her head to the Master of Ceremonies— a funny little fat man with a bright red beard. He waddled across the floor, and Auntie whispered to him . . . behind her fan. (But she heard. And heard him answer: 'Wants a partner? Why, certainly.') And then he went away and they could see him offering her to several gentlemen. Some pointed to the ladies they were sitting with or standing in front of; some showed their programmes that these were full. One or two turned their heads and looked at her. But it was no good. So he came back and said: 'Will the little lady do *me* the favour?' and she had to look glad and say: 'With pleasure,' and get up and dance with him. Perhaps she was a little slow about it . . . at any rate Auntie Cha made great round eyes at her. But she felt sure every one would know why he was asking her. It was the lancers, too, and he swung her off her feet at the corners, and was comic when he set to partners—putting one hand on his hip and the other over his head, as if he were dancing the hornpipe—and the rest of the set laughed. She was glad when it was over and she could go back to her place.

Auntie Cha's lady-friend had a son, and he was beckoned to next and there was more whispering. But he was engaged to be married, and of course preferred to dance with his fiancée. When he came and bowed—to oblige his mother—he looked quite grumpy, and didn't trouble to say all of 'May I have the pleasure?' but just 'The pleasure?' While she had to say 'Certainly,' and pretend to be very pleased, though she didn't feel it, and really didn't want much to dance with him, knowing he didn't, and that it was only out of charity. Besides, all the time they went round he was explaining things to the other girl with his eyes . . . making faces over her head. She saw him, quite plainly.

After he had brought her back—and Auntie had talked to him again—he went to a gentleman who hadn't danced at all yet, but just stood looking on. And this one needed a lot of persuasion. He was ugly, and lanky, and as soon as they stood up said quite rudely: 'I'm no earthly good at this kind of thing, you know.'

And he wasn't. He trod on her foot and put her out of step, and they got into the most dreadful muddle right out in the middle of the floor. It was a waltz and, remembering what Miss Biddons had said, she got more and more nervous, and then went wrong herself, and had to say: 'I beg your pardon,' to which he said: 'Granted.' She saw them in a mirror as they passed, and her face was red as red.

It didn't get cool again either, for she had to go on sitting out, and she felt sure he was spreading it that she couldn't dance. She didn't know whether Auntie Cha had seen her mistakes, but now Auntie sort of went for her. 'It's no use, Dolly, if you don't do *your* share. For goodness' sake, try and look more agreeable!'

So after this, in the intervals between the dances, she sat with a stiff little smile gummed to her lips. And, did any likely-looking partner approach the corner where they were, this widened till she felt what it was really saying was: 'Here I am! Oh, *please* take *me*!'

She had several false hopes. Men, looking so splendid in their white shirt fronts, would walk across the floor and *seem* to be coming . . . and then it was always not her. Their eyes wouldn't stay on her. There she sat, with her false little smile, and *her* eyes fixed on them; but theirs always got away . . . flitted past . . . moved on. Once she felt quite sure. Ever such a handsome man looked as if he were making straight for her. She stretched her lips, showing all her teeth (they were very good), and for an instant his eyes seemed to linger . . . really to take her in, in her pretty blue dress and the cornflowers. And then at the last minute they ran away—and it wasn't her at all, but a girl sitting three seats farther on; one who wasn't even pretty, or her dress either. But her own dress was beginning to get quite trashy, from the way she squeezed her hot hands down in her lap.

Quite the worst part of all was having to go on sitting in the front row, pretending you were enjoying yourself. It was so hard to know what to do with your eyes. There was nothing but the floor for them to look at—if you watched the other couples dancing they would think you were envying them. At first she made a show of studying her programme; but you couldn't go on staring at the programme for ever; and presently her shame at its emptiness grew till she could bear it no longer, and, seizing a moment when people were dancing, she slipped it down the front of her dress. Now she could say she'd lost it, if anyone asked to see it. But they didn't; they went on dancing with other girls. Oh, these men, who walked around and chose just who they fancied and left who they didn't . . . how she hated them! It wasn't fair . . . it wasn't fair. And when there was a 'leap-year' dance where the ladies invited the gentlemen, and Auntie Cha tried to push her up and make her go and said 'Now then, Dolly, here's your chance!' she shook her head hard and dug herself deeper into her seat. She wasn't going to ask them when they never asked her. So she said her head ached and she'd rather not. And to this she clung, sitting the while wishing with her whole heart that her dress was black and her hair grey, like Auntie Cha's. Nobody expected Auntie to dance, or thought it shameful if she didn't: she could do and be just as she liked. Yes, tonight she wished she was old . . . an old, old woman. Or that she was safe at home in bed . . . this dreadful evening, to which she had once counted the days, behind her. Even, as the night wore on, that she was dead.

At supper she sat with Auntie and the other lady, and the son and the girl came, too. There were lovely cakes and things but she could not eat them. Her throat was so dry that a sandwich stuck in it and nearly choked her. Perhaps the son felt a little sorry for her (or else his mother had whispered again), for afterwards he said something to the girl, and then asked *her* to dance. They stood up together; but it wasn't a success. Her legs seemed to have forgotten how to jump, heavy as lead they were . . . as heavy as she felt inside . . . and she couldn't think of a thing to say. So now he would put her down as stupid, as well.

Her only other partner was a boy younger than she was—almost a schoolboy—who she heard them say was 'making a nuisance of himself.' This was to a *very* pretty girl called the 'belle of the ball'. And he didn't seem to mind how badly he danced (with her), for he couldn't take his eyes off this other girl; but went on staring at her all the time, and very fiercely, because she was talking and laughing with somebody else. Besides, he hopped like a grasshopper, and didn't wear gloves, and his hands were hot and sticky. She hadn't come there to dance with little boys.

They left before anybody else; there was nothing to stay for. And the drive home in the wagonette, which had to be fetched, they were so early, was dreadful: Auntie Cha just sat and pressed her lips and didn't say a word. She herself kept her face turned the other way; because her mouth was jumping in and out as if it might have to cry.

At the sound of wheels Miss Biddons came running to the front door with questions and exclamations, dreadfully curious to know why they were back so soon. Dolly fled to her own little room and turned the key in the lock. She wanted only to be alone, quite alone, where nobody could see her ... where nobody would ever see her again. But the walls were thin, and as she tore off the wreath and ripped open her dress, now crushed to nothing from so much sitting, and threw them from her any-where, anyhow, she could hear the two voices going on, Auntie Cha's telling and telling, and winding up at last, quite out loud, with: 'Well, I don't know what it was, but the plain truth is, she didn't *take*!'

Oh, the shame of it! ... the sting and the shame. Her first ball, and not to have 'taken', to have failed to 'attract the gentle-men'—this was a slur that would rest on her all her life. And yet ... and yet ... in spite of everything, a small voice that wouldn't be silenced kept on saying: 'It wasn't my fault ... it wasn't my *fault*!' (Or at least not except for the one silly mistake in the steps of the waltz.) She had tried her hardest, done everything she was told to: had dressed up to please and look pretty, sat in the front row offering her programme, smiled when she didn't feel a bit like smiling ... and almost more than anything she thought she hated the memory of that smile (it was like trying to make people buy something they didn't think worthwhile). For really, truly, right deep down in her, she hadn't wanted 'the gentlemen' any more than they'd wanted her: she had only had to pretend to.

And they showed only too plainly they didn't, by choosing other girls, who were not even pretty, and dancing with them, laughing and talking and enjoying them. And now, the many slights and humiliations of the evening crowding upon her, the long-repressed tears broke through; and with the blanket pulled up over her head, her face driven deep into the pillow, she cried till she could cry no more.

The Carrying of the Baby

Larrie had been carrying it for a long way, and said it was quite time Dot took her turn.

Dot was arguing the point.

She reminded him of all athletic sports he had taken part in, and of all the prizes he had won; she asked him what was the use of being six-foot-two and an impossible number of inches round the chest if he could not carry a baby.

Larrie gave her an unexpected glance and moved the baby to his other arm; he was heated and unhappy, there seemed absolutely no end to the red, red road they were traversing, and Dot, as well as refusing to help to carry the burden, laughed aggravatingly at him when he said it was heavy.

'He is exactly twenty-one pounds,' she said. 'I weighed him on the kitchen scales yesterday. I should think a man of your size ought to be able to carry twenty-one pounds without grumbling so.'

'But he's on springs, Dot,' he said. 'Just look at him, he's never still for a minute; you carry him to the beginning of Lee's orchard, and then I'll take him again.'

Dot shook her head.

'I'm very sorry, Larrie,' she said, 'but I really can't. You know I didn't want to bring the child, and when you insisted, I said to myself, you should carry him every inch of the way, just for your obstinacy.'

'But you're his mother,' objected Larrie.

He was getting seriously angry, his arms ached unutterably, his clothes were sticking to his back, and twice the baby had poked a little fat thumb in his eye and made it water.

'But you're its father,' Dot said sweetly.

'It's easier for a woman to carry a child than a man,' poor Larrie was mopping his hot brow with his disengaged hand, 'everyone says so; don't be a little sneak, Dot; my arm's getting awfully cramped; here, for pity's sake take him.'

Dot shook her head again.

'Would you have me break my vow, St Lawrence?' she said.

She looked provokingly cool and unruffled as she walked along by his side; her gown was white, with transparent puffy sleeves, her hat was white and very large, she had little white canvas shoes, long white suede gloves, and she carried a white parasol.

'I'm hanged,' said Larrie, and he stopped short in the middle of the road. 'Look here, my good woman, are you going to take your baby, or are you not?'

Dot revolved her sunshade round her little sweet face.

'No, my good man,' she said. 'I don't propose to carry your baby one step.'

'Then I shall drop it,' said Larrie. He held it up in a threatening position by the back of its crumpled coat, but Dot had gone sailing on.

'Find a soft place,' she called, looking back over her shoulder once and seeing him still standing in the road.

'Little minx,' he said under his breath.

Then his mouth squared itself; ordinarily it was a pleasant mouth, much given to laughter and merry words; but when it took that obstinate look, one could see capabilities for all manner of things.

He looked carefully around. By the roadside there was a patch of soft, green grass, and a wattle bush, yellow-crowned, beautiful. He laid the child down in the shade of it, he looked to see there were no ants or other insects near; he put on the bootee that was hanging by a string from the little rosy foot, and he stuck the india-rubber comforter in its mouth. Then he walked quietly away and caught up to Dot.

'Well?' she said, but she looked a little startled at his empty arms; she drooped the sunshade over the shoulder nearest to him, and gave a hasty surreptitious glance backward. Larrie strode along.

'You look fearfully ugly when you screw up your mouth like that,' she said, looking up at his set side face.

'You're an unnatural mother, Dot, that's what you are,' he returned hotly. 'By Jove, if I was a woman, I'd be ashamed to act as you do. You get worse every day you live. I've kept excusing you to myself, and saying you would get wiser as you grew older, and instead, you seem more childish every day.'

She looked childish. She was very, very small in stature, very slightly and delicately built. Her hair was in soft gold-brown curls, as short as a boy's; her eyes were soft, and wide, and tender, and beautiful as a child's. When she was happy they were the colour of that blue, deep violet we call the Czar, and when she grew thoughtful, or sorrowful, they were like the heart of a great, dark purple pansy. She was not particularly beautiful, only very fresh, and sweet, and lovable. Larrie once said she always looked like a baby that has been freshly bathed and dressed, and puffed with sweet violet powder, and sent out into the world to refresh tired eyes.

That was one of his courtship sayings, more than a year ago, when she was barely seventeen. She was eighteen now, and he was telling her she was an unnatural mother.

'Why, the child wouldn't have had its bib on, only I saw to it,' he said, in a voice that increased in excitement as he dwelt on the enormity.

'Dear me,' said Dot, 'that was very careless of Peggie; I must really speak to her about it.'

'I shall shake you some day, Dot,' Larrie said, 'shake you till your teeth rattle. Sometimes I can hardly keep my hands off you.'

His brow was gloomy, his boyish face troubled, vexed.

And Dot laughed. Leaned against the fence skirting the road that seemed to run to eternity, and laughed outrageously.

Larrie stopped too. His face was very white and square-looking, his dark eyes held fire. He put his hands on the white, exaggerated shoulders of her muslin dress and turned her round.

'Go back to the bottom of the hill this instant, and pick up the child and carry it up here,' he said.

'Go and insert your foolish old head in a receptacle for *pommes-de-terre*,' was Dot's flippant retort.

Larrie's hands pressed harder, his chin grew squarer.

'I'm in earnest, Dot, deadly earnest. I order you to fetch the child, and I intend you to obey me,' he gave her a little shake to enforce the command. 'I am your master, and I intend you to know it from this day.'

Dot experienced a vague feeling of surprise at the fire in the eyes that were nearly always clear, and smiling, and loving, then she twisted herself away.

'Pooh,' she said, 'you're only a stupid over-grown, passionate boy, Larrie. You my master! You're nothing in the world but my husband.'

'Are you going?' he said in a tone that he had never used before to her. 'Say yes or no, Dot, instantly.'

'No,' said Dot, stormily.

Then they both gave a sob of terror, their faces blanched, and they began to run madly down the hill.

Oh the long, long way they had come, the endless stretch of red, red road that wound back to the gold-tipped wattles, the velvet grass, and their baby.

Larrie was a fleet, wonderful runner. In the little cottage where they lived, manifold silver cups and mugs bore witness to it, and he was running for life now, but Dot nearly outstripped him.

She flew over the ground, hardly touching it, her arms were outstretched, her lips moving. They fell down together on their knees by their baby, just as three furious, hard-driven bullocks thundered by, filling the air with dust and bellowing.

The baby was blinking happily up at a great fat golden beetle that was making a lazy way up the wattle. It had lost its 'comforter' and was sucking its thumb thoughtfully. It had kicked off its white knitted boots, and was curling its pink toes up in the sunshine with great enjoyment.

'Baby!' Larrie said. The big fellow was trembling in every limb.

'*Baby*!' said Dot. She gathered it up in her little shaking arms, she put her poor white face down upon it, and broke into such pitiful tears and sobs that it wept too. Larrie took them both into his arms, and sat down on a fallen tree. He soothed them, he called them a thousand tender, beautiful names; he took off Dot's hat and stroked her little curls, he kissed his baby again and again; he kissed his wife. When they were all quite calm and the bullocks ten miles away, they started again.

'I'll carry him,' said Larrie.

'Ah no, let me,' Dot said.

'Darling, you're too tired—see, you can hold his hand across my shoulder.'

'No, no, give him to me—my arms ache without him.'

'But the hill—my big baby.'

'Oh, I *must* have him—Larrie, *let* me—see, he is so light—why, he is nothing to carry.'

Peronel McCree, and the Sin Called Pride

THE ARCH-SIN

'We should have more Faith in Fate!' Peronel McCree told herself, not two days later when, just as she despaired of all joy, just as she believed her life would flow on, and on, in the drab security of her mother-in-law's rule, something did happen! Actually!

'Of course your dear Mama must accept His Excellency's Invitation. It is a command.'

The Vicar of Mallow's Marsh voiced his agreement with Juliet's impulsive 'Oh! Mama must go! How beautiful she will look!'

Every member of the McCree family was gathered in the shabby morning-room at the Vicarage, into which sunlight was streaming, wholly unimpeded by the threadbare curtains.

Mr and Mrs McCree, their widowed daughter-in-law, Peronel, whom in the sanctity of the maroon fourposter they would sometimes refer to as 'Peronel Proud-heart', and their two grandchildren, Juliet and Donalblain (aged five), were opening the mail, scarcely five minutes back delivered by the red-coated, white-helmeted 'Postie', who was now being regaled with small ale and baps in the kitchen.

Cook Teresa naturally offered sustenance to a man who had walked five miles to deliver two letters; and since every other client on his beat also entertained him with rum, peach-beer, cider, penny-ale, mum, or any other liqueur that came handy, the road that seemed so straight and flat when he started out from

Parramatta at dawn, was apt to seem hilly and curly as he trudged home after a round of fourteen miles.

Today Postie had brought to Mallow's Marsh Vicarage two letters, one of which had a gold crown embossed on the flap of the envelope.

This was addressed (in very bad writing) to Mrs Augustus McCree (who had, 'Oh, my dear, been nobody, nobody at all!') and in it was a gold-inscribed card which begged, in dispirited prose, for the honour of her company at a ball, to be held at Government House, Parramatta, on November the 5th. 'Is it for Guy Fawkes?' Donalblain wanted to know.

Mrs Augustus McCree (who had been nobody) could easily have made a fourth when the three goddesses stood up for judgement on Mount Ida. Paris would certainly have awarded her the apple, for she had less flesh than Juno, less intellectual acidity, less string in her limbs than Minerva (who was never in the running, for she was not his sort, anyway), and her supple figure, her patrician yet delicious face, with its short upper-lip, its cherry-red, bee-stung lower lip, its desolating cheek-bones, which seemed to have known such sorrow, and which quite contradicted the Mona Lisa-like ambiguity of the inviting eyes (so full of sly caresses), certainly outvied the beauty of any known and authentic portrait of Venus herself.

Yes, Peronel McCree was even more beautiful than Botticelli's shell-borne migrant, or Titian's roaring girl, or Giorgione's almost perfect sleeping 'Queen of Love'.

A bloom of ineffable youth far excelling theirs veiling the rose of her cheek, a luminous quality in her milk-white skin causing it to glow as if seen through an alabaster lamp, her rich fan of most curious hair flaming round her small, proudly poised head like a torch, Peronel was altogether lovely.

This young Mrs Augustus McCree had for a Guardian Angel a somewhat battered Custodian of great ability but debatable piety, really rather a Trollop (if female) or Gamin (if male), if the truth must be confessed, who was capable of leading her in any mischief.

'Guardian Angels are bound to vary in merit just as ordinary people do,' Peronel had assured herself in first realising this charming creature's limitations, 'but who am I to expect to have allotted to me the most efficient Angel in High Heaven? I must make do with the one appointed to me.'

And did he (or she?) lead her a dance?

Or she lead him (or her?) a dance?

It was difficult to say.

As for the indeterminate sex of such a heavenly visitant, Peronel called her Guardian Angel 'he', it sounded more dashing.

Mrs Augustus had the habit of standing with wide-open eyes fixed on some spot just beyond the orbit of vision.

With the crested envelope in her hand, so she stood on this sunny morning, her white-spotted muslin wrapper (resented by every woman in the house) clouded by a hundred goffered frills, green bows decking it from neck to instep. Wide bows, these, accentuating at five-inch intervals the titillating undulations of her sweetly inflated body.

The question, of course, was—what should she wear?

About this everyone was most helpful, though 'a drawback, really', as Juliet said, there was absolutely no money to be spent—not a penny.

'If you unpick Juliet's bridesmaid's dress, the cream nun's veiling she wore at dear Aminta Wirraway's wedding, and eke it out with an extra yard or two of red plush, you might contrive a most striking toilette at the cost of a dozen eggs, which I will give you, dear,' Mrs McCree offered kindly.

'I think the curtains off Grandmama's Fourposter would make a unique and magical dress! They are watered silk, of such a beautiful shade of maroon, almost a magenta, really—though one likes to forget about the blood, for I think Magenta comes from the colour of the earth after that battle was fought,' Juliet interposed. 'But you may have my dress if you like, Mama. I can easily re-sew it, without the plush, for my confirmation next year.'

Speculation often glinted in Juliet's eyes when she looked at her radiant Mama. Like the rest of the household she did not quite trust her, though to do her enterprising Guardian Angel justice, the young widow's conduct for the first six months of her widowhood had been exemplary, impeccable; remote, certainly, but as far as the watching women who surrounded her were aware, blameless.

An absence of privacy is the chief drawback of family life.

Remarking on the shifts that the reader of a love-letter may be put to, even Boccaccio has commented on this disadvantage. The unblinking limelight of affection was a sore trial to Peronel and her Guardian Angel. Both, therefore, were delighted when at breakfast, a week after the acceptance of the Governor's invitation had been despatched, Mrs McCree announced that her whole family must attend a party of reconciliation planned by her brother, Dr Boisragon (who had been somewhat estranged from her), in Parramatta. On the strength of her own absence she gave all the servants a holiday.

Peronel, protesting the Penelope-like task of unpicking and re-sewing the nun's veiling, to be her ball gown, stayed at home.

She waved gaily from the front door as the buckboard, the young draught-horse Ruby between the shafts, lurched off down the long, straight road and disappeared behind the turn by the Church tower, the only twist, the only building, between Mallow's Marsh and the metropolis.

How delighted Peronel was to be alone!

For awhile, merely to be in the sunshine, she wandered about without purpose in the garden, and punished the insolence of Nature by stamping on a daisy. From the arbour of Passion-vines from the ripening orchard, the field of green wheat, the drilled rows of corn, the innumerable wooden sheds dedicated to the procreation of domestic life, which had sprung up under the wand of Mrs McCree till they surrounded the Vicarage like mushrooms, right to where the blue, entrancing Razorbacks shaved the sky, the stillness was complete.

The hens clucked not, the cows lowed not, the river chuckled not; all was silence, all was sunshine.

Behind the Vicarage no buxom women laughed with the menservants; indoors no high-piping childish voices argued about this and that. Every window and door in the house stood wide open. 'Not even a thief is to be expected.' Oppressed a little, Peronel strayed inside.

She bent her steps first to this room, then to another, enjoying as she went some intimate and revealing conversations with her Guardian Angel, with whom she was scarcely acquainted (he was new), and whose wings, she now noticed, were slightly singed; but she had no misgivings, they suited each other, they understood one another perfectly.

Both agreed that in this isolated spot, in this barebones of a house, so threadbare, so niggardly with the joys of this life, so lavish in its promises of the next, there was no scope for either of them, no, none at all.

How they laughed together at the absurd picture of Boadicea with her two girls in a chariot on the snuggery wall; at the statue of the Winged Victory in the linoleum covered hall; at the coloured engraving of the Duchess of Devonshire kissing a butcher ('for Political reasons' as the text explained); and at all the smug daguerrotypes and washed out miniatures infesting the drawing-room wall.

The woolwork flowers under the glass dome!

The beaded footstools!

The S-shaped conversation sofa meant for flirtations!

The antimacassars tied on every chair-top on which no bachelor's pomaded head had ever rested!

'Is this to be my home for the rest of my life?' Peronel demanded, dramatically.

'No, indeed!' answered the Guardian Angel indignantly.

'Am I, Peronel McCree, to go to the Governor's ball in my daughter's cast-off clothes? In a perfectly hideous dress?'

'No! No!' The Guardian Angel was positive. 'Indeed you shall not.'

'With no money, and just a dozen pullets' eggs to sell, how can I get a better dress?'

To Peronel this question was purely rhetorical. She had then no hope of getting a better; but her Guardian Angel looked sly: evidently he had something up his wing.

Obviously the house offered her no alternative to re-making her daughter's dress. There were no curtains to be taken down, no hidden lengths of silk to be purloined. But it was three o'clock before Peronel, weak with laughter (Oh, her Guardian had a pretty turn of wit), settled herself at the antique sewing machine in the morning-room that was, so easily, the shabbiest room in the house, to pedal vigorously away at a wrought-iron treadle whose activities depended on a rubber band that slipped continually off its wheel. To snip! To tear! To tack! Though she hated such work she had a genius for it. Since she was one of those people who never give less than their best, the *toilette* (at the word she laughed again) began to assume quite a Parisian air. 'Certainly,' she told her soul-mate, 'it dashes, as well as nun's veiling can ever dash.'

She was standing draped in loops of fabric in the room which faced north-west, so sunlight still streamed into it, and the motes still danced in the yellow beams that fell on her, had she known it, with the dramatic effectiveness of the rays in contemporary pictures of Victoria's Coronation, when, looking across to the door, she saw a young man looking in.

He made a low bow, a most distinguished salutation, his black, low-crowned hat—a shovel-hat with its rough nap, not at all like the headgear worn in Parramatta, sweeping far back as his eyes fixed themselves, with intensity, on his boots.

'Of the Great World!' Peronel realised at once.

She nudged her Guardian Angel to let him know she recognised his handiwork, and he hopped through the window, and flew off to settle on the orchard wall; he was no spoil-sport.

Peronel's visitor wore a red coat cut rather short at the waist in front, but having longer skirts at the back. His waistcoat was of red-and-yellow striped cloth, his breeches were white, with straps buckled below the knees, and his mustard yellow gaiters were buttoned over Wellington boots. Or were they *Hessians*? And were 'Hessians' boots or were they gaiters?

Peronel was vague.

But she was not at all vague in her perception of her visitor's good looks. He was remarkably handsome. The chin that asserted itself above the white stock showed him to be a man of character; he was no mere dandy.

The young widow looked into his blue eyes and thought she had never seen anything so blue. Her caressing gaze took in his aquiline nose, the tanned skin that made his fair hair almost white by comparison.

Peronel had never in her life seen so glorious a being.

Glancing out of the window she perceived that her Guardian Angel looked smug. As she opened her lips in greeting a shower of pins fell on the carpet, but she inclined her head in stately recognition of his civility.

'I could make no-one hear, so I tied up my nag to the verandah-post, and tracked down the whirr of your machine.' He smiled. 'Are you at home?'

'Not at home!' she answered sadly. 'Mrs Augustus McCree is not receiving this afternoon.'

'What a bore,' the young man remarked, as he entered and took a chair beside the sewing-machine, removing, as he seated himself, a froth of flounces. 'I was so looking forward to making her acquaintance.'

'The whole family have driven into Parramatta.'

'I passed them on my way here.'

'Oh?'

Peronel again seated herself at the sewing-machine.

'And what were you looking at so intently on that part of the wall where I see nothing?'

'At my Guardian Angel,' Peronel returned, stooping to place the rubber band on its wheel.

'Is he having the afternoon off?' There was a note of hope in his voice.

'No. I keep him within call.'

'I expect he leads a busy life. What is his name? What is he like?'

'His face is a bit like a swan's—it has that sideways look. He is very fair, a white-winged angel (of the Wyandotte family, I dare say) and he has a magnificent spread of wings—these, unfortunately, are a little singed. My last Guardian Angel left in a hurry. I had not a good word to say for him.' She bit a thread. 'In fairness to others one must be truthful, don't you think, even when writing out a reference for an Archangel?'

'What was the trouble?' The blue eyes met hers.

'Just want of speed on my part. I simply could not keep up with him. However, one hardly realises the troubles an angel may have.'

'Yes?' he prompted.

He was certainly very good looking.

'He said it was hard in this flat, treeless bit of country to find a decent place to perch. He said he had to hover over the clothes line, for there wasn't a safe bough up to his weight in the orchard, and the wall was too low to give him a good take-off. Yes, poor thing! He had to hover so much that it tired his wings, and in that tired, that fatigued state, he found Heaven too far to fly to on his evenings off, so he took to dropping in on Hell. It was sad, really.'

Her vis-a-vis was now holding one end of a flounce while she fed the machine; there was a sociable air of work shared.

'You feel you can trust the present fellah?' He expressed a real anxiety. 'Feel you can depend on him at a pinch, and all that?'

History has not vouchsafed a portrait of Paris. Did he have a perfectly proportioned body which was the acme of masculine strength? Was he endowed with an athlete's grace of movement? Did he have a head like Phoebus Apollo? If so, looking at her visitor, Peronel felt she could guess what Paris looked like. And Hyacinthus, now? There was no authentic portrait of the youth who died for love of his own reflection, but Peronel rather wondered that this self-assured young man could tear himself away from the mirror. Looking at him she had an inkling of what Hyacinthus might have been like.

It has not been customary for poets to hymn the beauty of the male, a strange inhibition, suggestive of what? Of what, indeed!

Few portraits, even those of the heroes of antiquity, are meant to emphasise masculine good looks merely; fewer still portray the wit that may lurk in a wanton blue eye. Exposed in her helpless state to the full appeal of such devastating enchantments Peronel behaved with perfect propriety. Her Guardian Angel would have been disappointed in her.

Her caller, on his part, having felt her eyes caress him, their touch, as they rested with a moth-like lightness on his face seductive as the brush of thistledown, presently went off, bewitched. Pleased with his own sensations, he gave no hint of what he felt, but he booked the first six dances at the coming ball.

'And may I take you in to supper?'

He might.

'And may I drive you home after the dance?'

'Perhaps.' She was demure. 'I must ask my Guardian Angel about that.'

When he had bobbed out of sight behind the pear trees, vanishing as Peronel had watched Dan and Tib vanish, only last week—why! It was only ten days or so back! Three days? How long ago it seemed!—Peronel realised that she did not know his name. But *had he a name*? Had he, in fact, any reality of person? Was he a wraith born of her own imagination? Or had that dismissed Guardian Angel, by way of revenge, sent one of his less reputable friends to lead her astray? He was, she reflected, quite capable of playing her such a trick.

Peronel trembled.

Doubts assailed her.

Temptation followed in the train of her misgivings.

Quite suddenly and with an absolutely firm resolution she decided then and there that nothing—nothing—would induce her to wear the nun's veiling dress at the ball.

What! Be a laughing stock to such people? To such people as *his* friends!

What! See those china-blue eyes rest with amusement on her finery? Her *rustic* finery?

What! Find him cutting *his dances* with her? For shame of being seen with her?

At this last thought Peronel knew she was ready to commit any crime in order to get a dress that would make her the most fashionable, the most alluring siren, in all Parramatta.

Yes! She would sin, if necessary! And when her Guardian Angel rejoined her, a little dishevelled, for a wind had risen, a strange cold wind for a summer evening, she told him so.

He did not seem at all surprised. He was most helpful.

'Yes, yes,' she murmured, listening to him in great excitement, her head bent close to his tempting mouth. 'Yes! I catch your drift! I will finish the nun's veiling as if I meant to wear it, and then—at the very last minute! Yes! Yes! I understand!—*As late as possible*! As late as it would be safe to leave it! Oh, what a marvellous idea!'

There was a further whispered suggestion.

Peronel was shocked.

'Oh, Guardy, I couldn't!' she gasped.

But during the coming night she weakened.

'After all,' she asked herself, 'what harm could come of following one's Guardian Angel's advice?'

Peronel spent most of the night leaning out of her bedroom window and watching the sullied and shrivelled moon slink, sulking, behind banks of cloud, while flocks of curlews flew inland, whistling over the Picton hills. Like the Naxian widow, deliciously disarrayed, her eyes violet-ringed, she watched the sunrise, unaware that she had not slept a wink.

Early in the morning she harnessed Ruby into the sulky and drove herself into Parramatta.

Usually, of late, she had avoided seeing people, but today she stopped to talk to everyone she met, to gossip, to ask questions.

'He is *not* a nincompoop,' Dr Phantom remarked on being questioned. 'They say he fought at Delhi, and Lucknow.'—So the Chemist.

'He was in the Sandbag Battery, in the Crimea.' Dr Boisragon was affable for once, when Peronel encountered him in the Chemist's.

'*His name?*' No-one rightly knew.

'Well, dear,' Mrs Wirraway said, after confessing that she missed Aminta, 'he's staying at Government House. He went out riding this morning with that pretty girl, Lady Mary Something-or-other. The Governor's niece. Such a lovely young creature with a complexion of milk and roses. She wore a bottle green habit, trailing almost to the ground, and a top hat with a flowing veil—yards long, just like the Queen's when she reviews troops. She rode a lively chestnut cob which she managed perfectly.'

'I never saw so handsome a pair,' Miss Loveday Boisragon exclaimed. 'They are perfectly matched.'

Such was the tittle-tattle Peronel picked up.

She spent the price of a dozen pullets' eggs on three-quarters of a yard of cheap plush and drove home—disconsolate!

But she was not long inconsolable. '*He exists*,' she told herself. 'Nameless or not, he is a real person—not a myth, as I feared.'

She was utterly resolved to take her Guardian Angel's advice: she would wear at the ball the most magnificent dress ever seen in Parramatta—oh! in all New South Wales! Sin? What is sin? It is merely an experiment made in pursuit of happiness. And an experiment may be a success, or may not—who said 'The end crowns all'? Ah, who, indeed.

On the evening of the ball, which was to commence at nine o'clock, Peronel dressed herself in the nun's veiling and was duly admired by the whole family at Mallow's Marsh Vicarage.

The dress was beautifully sewn. Everyone allowed that.

It was made with a plain bodice in the hour-glass shape then fashionable. The red plush was folded back, a few inches below the waist in the style called 'a fisher-girl sacque'. Below this frills fell to the instep, and *lissé* pleats showed below them. The neck was cut in a modest square, much frilled. The elbow sleeves were also frilled, and finished with red plush bows. Peronel's sole 'jewel' was a plaited bracelet of her late husband's hair. She flirted a black satin fan on which was painted a kitten looking out of a top hat, rumoured to be the work of Winterhalter. A white woollen cape, flowing from neck to hem, completed her outfit.

Everyone saw Peronel wearing this dress.

Everyone crowded to the gate to see her drive herself off—
a bit early—in the sulky. They watched the young mare, Ruby,
trotting gallantly in the middle of the rut-holed road, the light
vehicle swinging from side to side. They saw the elegant figure of
the lovely Peronel sitting in the centre of the trap in order to crush
her frills as little as possible.

But—*they did not notice the basket under the seat.*

But—they did not see the Guardian Angel behaving with
complete abandon as he swooped, soared and circled in the sky
above his charge.

He was in the highest spirits.

It was a fine night, warm, yet not too warm for dancing. The
moon, free of all cloud, beamed down from a starlit vault.

There was no wind.

The mare knew the road and required no supervision.
Peronel was at liberty to watch her escort, who always charmed
and amused her, and he was in the act of swinging up-sky after a
triple somersault when, in the brilliant moonshine, she saw an
expression of complete dismay overcloud his face.

They were being followed! This Peronel at once realised.

There was that on her conscience which told her, immediately, what her follower would be like. She had not the slightest
doubt that his scarlet garments would be designed to hide a forked
tail and that his peaked cap, with its cock's feather, would be
widened to conceal a horned head.

Fearfully looking round she found her conjecture to be right.
The Foul Fiend himself was hot on her tracks.

'How efficiently his office must be run,' she reflected.

For a sinner, even a sinner poised on the brink of committing
her first really walloping sin, Peronel had plenty of pluck.
Consoling herself with a riddle ('When is a sin not a sin?'—
'When it is merely a peccadillo')—she drove calmly on.

Her competent custodian, having called to his aid several
friends who were enjoying an evening off, soon had a white-
winged bevy circling round her; a cordon of Angels. They kept her

persistent pursuer at bay. Though athletic, musical and good, as all their kind must, of necessity, be, these angelic volunteers came, naturally, from the lowest strata of heaven, they being creatures not quite good enough on the harp, and possessed of voices perhaps a little off-key.

The clop-clop, clup-clup, of old Ruby's hairy heels ringing on the steely road were the only sound to be heard except for the frou-frou of wings and the twitter of a few late, sleepy larks. In that flat, croppy marshland, where not a house or a tree punctuated the miles, the trotting draught-mare assumed gigantic proportions; she looked like an immense chocolate animal, buttered, for the sweat poured down and darkened her quivering flanks. Her name was tied with red tape into scores of double-backed plaits (Donalblain's labour of love), her hearty tail was also rolled double and tied into a blob with tape. Yet the moon shone down as if nothing out of the way was happening when lovely Peronel in her white cape, a choir of angels swooping round her, a devil lurking in the rear, her light vehicle swaying behind the gigantic mare, romped through the great gates of Government House, Parramatta.

But, why, Oh! why, did she immediately turn off the driveway?

But why, Oh! why, did she tie up the sulky, and, dragging behind her the basket she took from under the seat, disappear into a thicket of oleanders?

The angels, naturally, turned their backs.

There was always a difference of opinion at Mallow's Marsh Vicarage as to what time Peronel returned next morning.

Cook Teresa said 'Five o'clock', because she was just getting up, and she always rose at five. (She said.) Juliet said 'Six' because she always woke up at six. (She said.) The Vicar said 'Seven' because he always went across to the Church to conduct a service of prayer and praise at that hour. And he really did. And they all heard, at these stated times, old Ruby's trotting hooves as they rounded the church tower, from which point they would first have been audible.

Peronel herself could not be questioned as she had dropped into bed at once, pulling the sheet over her face. Though everyone dropped in to look at her no-one dared to wake her to ask her how she had enjoyed the ball.

The first gust of the coming gale, the first hint of trouble, came from some words let fall by Miss Loveday Boisragon, who, as her brother had a patient to see in Mallow's Marsh village, had driven over with him; she was anxious to congratulate Mrs McCree on her daughter-in-law's brilliant success at last night's ball.

Sitting with the assembled family in the morning-room, she laid her bouquets at their feet.

'They are all saying that Peronel was the most beautiful woman ever to be seen in that ball room.'

'Did she get all her dances?' Her family had been anxious on that score.

'Every dance! Perpetua Thistledew says there was such a crowd round her the whole time that it was hard to see whom she danced with. His Excellency, apparently, took the first three.'

Juliet, sitting in the arm-chair by the window, had taken her brother on her knee. While listening with half an ear, she was giving Donalblain a lesson in the multiplication table.

She kissed him first on the lips.

'That is *one*! Twice one is *two*.' She kissed him on each cheek. 'Twice two is *four*.' She kissed him on cheeks, chin, and on the tip of his nose.

Donalblain kissed her on the mouth.

'That is "Amen".'

'The kiss to end all kisses.'

Donalblain had been warned against women. He could not think why. For himself he could see nothing wrong with them.

It was at this point in their play that Juliet heard Miss Loveday, a little bewildered, repeat— '*Red Plush*!' She gazed round the circle. 'But no-one mentioned red plush.'

'Mama did have red plush on her dress. Cotton-backed plush, for pullets' eggs fetch so little—'

'This week all the eggs are being pickled—' Mrs McCree broke in.

'Oh, I know! But it was such cheap stuff that I helped Mama to lift the nap with a steaming kettle—'

'I am certain that dear Perpetua mentioned no *plush*!'

Miss Boisragon rose to go. Her brother was waiting and must not be detained; without a word said everyone realised this; and hurried her off.

'I suppose, in that crowd, Perpetua didn't really notice Mama's dress.'

The rest of the family agreed with Juliet; they thought no more of the matter. But that afternoon, while Peronel was still sleeping, Perpetua herself drove over in the Gander's Pond barouche, a coachman and footman on the box.

It appeared that Dr Phantom had also got to see a patient in the village, he had broken his rule. He had brought over a pretty girl, Bathsheba Wirraway, who was so overcome by the adventure that she sat silent the whole of her visit.

'Oh, my dears! Never, never has anyone created such a sensation as Peronel created last night! All Parramatta is talking of nothing else! Her beauty! Her radiant happiness! Dr Phantom said it was more infectious than measles. Wherever she went one noticed there was laughter! Her grace! In the Lancers! In the opening Quadrille! The gallopade! There was a round dance—*not* a waltz, of course—but after supper there was a perfect riot, and we danced "Sir Roger de Coverley". I thought Lady Mary looked down her nose at that. I hardly dare tell you! We ended up with the de Alberts! "As if this was a *barrack-room*!" I heard Lady Mary say! Of course, early on, we had done "The Dashing White Sergeant". That's all the rage! Peronel danced these dances with such enjoyment that half the men in the room stood round the wall to watch her. And *then*!' Perpetua put down her empty cup, 'My dears! Her *dress*!'

The assembled family looked complaisant.

'Dear girl,' murmured Mrs McCree, 'she made it herself, out of Juliet's bridesmaid's dress, the nun's veiling she wore, dear Bathsheba, at your sister Aminta's wedding!'

'And I helped her raise the nap on the red plush.'

'*Nun's veiling? Red plush?*' Perpetua was amazed. 'Peronel wore no nun's veiling or red plush.'

'You cannot have noticed.'

'Notice? Of course I noticed! Peronel's dress was of cream brocade, a most exquisite Italian brocade. I stood quite close to her. I even fingered it.'

'Did it have elbow-length sleeves tied with red plush bows?'

'It had no sleeves.'

'But it had! We saw her!'

'No, indeed. I was standing quite close to her when His Excellency brought her back to the dais after her third dance with him. I heard him say, "I used to believe that a white camellia looked white, dear lady, until I saw one against your snow-white bosom and marble shoulders." And he pressed even closer to her. Peronel backed away, and said (so sweetly), "I look better from a distance, Sir." And she sailed right across the room and His Excellency dashed after her (you know his way, he's a descendant of King Charles the Second), but, *fortunately*, just at that moment one of the *aides* brought up the Mayoress of Doggett's Patch, and Peronel escaped—luckily!'

'But her *dress*!' everyone breathed, astounded.

'Marvellous! Of cream brocade, with a pattern of gold leaves and grapes! Just round her shoulders—which were bare—she wore a circlet of white camellias. Oh, it was exquisite. A full skirt—like those crinolines the Queen wears! Nothing could have been more fashionable. She made every other woman in the room look dowdy. Though Dr Phantom—who danced four dances with her— *did* say that my poor little pink rag looked just as nice on me as her gorgeous raiment did on her! But none of us begrudged Peronel her triumph! It was an honour to the whole sex. I told Dr Phantom we felt like that.'

Perpetua chattered on into a silence as deep as a well.

Mr McCree had been quieter, even, than usual as Perpetua rattled on. Usually he liked the women of his household to sit in dumb adoration round him as he told them about the Hittites or the Jebusites, or elucidated some knotty point, which (he thought) may have been troubling them, in the Apocrypha, then almost a best-seller.

But this afternoon, after listening, as it were, under protest (these women will still be talking), a glint came into his blue eyes, an expression difficult to fathom. It seemed as if he had caught sight of the tail-end of a fabulous monster just whisking round a door. He looked incredulous. He looked horrified. He debated within himself as Nebuchadnezzar may have debated when he saw the writing on the wall.

Presently, with a determined air, he rose, hoisting himself out of his deep arm-chair, and quitted the electrified gathering, which still argued about Peronel's dress.

'*Where could she have got it?*'

Like the Wiltshire farms that lean up against the great house, so narrow a margin separating them from it that, they say, the noise of the threshing-flail is, in the drawing-room, always in the ears, the church had been built up against the Vicarage. A few paved paces, bordered with St Barnabas's Thistles and St John's Wort, brought Mr McCree into the vestry. There was in one corner of an inside wall a chest, a sort of bureau, in which were stored the Church vestments, the one extravagance for which the poor Vicar saved up all his pennies. He opened the top drawer. To his astonishment (he had not expected it), the cope he wore at festivals was there. It was a cope of cream brocade patterned with gold grapes and grapeleaves, and it was said to be a length which rumour elaborated, and once belonged to the Borgias. He had bought it in Italy in his youth. In spite of its origin it was well-behaved; it did not wear out or crumple; but, Mr McCree thought, was all as it seemed? Doubts disturbing him, he shook out the gleaming fabric, and freed it reverently of its silver-paper wrappings.

In the bright light that streamed in through the Gothic windows, which faced west, even the Vicar's tired eyes could see the needle-pricks along the edges of the front panels.

Was that a tacking thread?

He decided it must be.

To all appearances, the cope had been unpicked, re-made, and, yet again, unpicked and restored to its original shape.

It was the sun's last rays that were so generously expending themselves in the vestry. The summer evening was dwindling into night. Every blade of grass in the far-stretching landscape that rolled from Mallow's Marsh to the sea on the one hand, and to the distant Picton Hills on the other, had its gold-tipped shadow. The hens had gone to roost. The men had milked the cows and carried the foaming buckets into the dairy. Except in the old Vicar's heart all was peace.

Life, indeed, was slowing its tempo when Dr Phantom, driving in his smart Hyde Park, rattled up from the village and leaping gracefully out, while his new groom held the horses' heads, ran lightly up the flagged path from the front gate, to stand by the French window, looking into the lamp-lit drawing-room. It is hard to guess for whom his eyes, with so much love in them, were searching.

Coming towards the Vicarage from the Parramatta road, a horseman, who, for the past half-hour might been discerned trotting thitherward—one saw for miles in such a low-lying terrain—arriving just after the young doctor, and just as the sun was staging one of the most spectacular sunsets in all its history—had anyone known it—tied his mount to the fence, and ran, with an ardour equalling Dr Phantom's, to take his stand, at the second French window, peering into the lighted interior. He, too, looked with love-lit eyes at some compelling magnet, not to be identified.

The brocade cope over his trembling arm, Mr McCree had entered a moment or two before the young men took up their stations.

There are, in old Bibles, steel engravings of Sarah standing half in shade, listening, close to the door, while Abraham interviews his angel. So these young men stood gazing in, while Peronel, dressed in her widow's black ('never was under cloud black so fair a star'), entered at the fatal moment when her father-in-law, displaying the brocade cope, was asking Perpetua, 'Is this the pattern you noticed on Peronel's dress?'

'Yes!' Astounded, Perpetua rose to her feet, to finger the rich material. 'Yes! The gold thread! The mellow parchment-like colour! The damascened pattern of grapes and their leaves! Oh, glorious, glorious! Of course it's the same.'

She threw an agonised glance at Peronel.

'I did not mean to be a tell-tale, dear Peronel! The question took me by surprise!'

'Dear Perpetua! Of course you didn't! But, naturally, I meant to explain that I had *borrowed* the cope for the evening—for the honour of the family! How could I possibly have appeared in that brilliant gathering—the élite of Doggett's Patch, Dural, Hornsby Junction, Parramatta, Gander's Pond, and even Little Peeping in the Inlet—Oh, everyone was there! How could I have worn, at such a function, my *daughter's old dress*? One everyone had seen at Aminta's wedding? Everyone would have recognised it—everyone!'

Fairer than Cressida, in her widow's weeds, Peronel looked her loveliest as she spoke. (Though Cressida, possibly, was not expected by an exacting mother-in-law to cover her hair with a widow's cap of white *lissé*.)

Staring in through the two French windows the young men on the verandah had intended to enter, but delight in her beauty held them immobile.

Mrs McCree, in her maroon rep, sitting upright in a high chair, her hair parted and plastered down on each side of her neat head, her hands on her lap, her feet (as directed by the *Young Ladies' Intelligencer* of 1839) laid one across the other at the instep, her usually rosy face white with emotion, could only gasp, 'Oh, what wickedness! Oh, what wickedness! Oh, what desecration! Oh, what sacrilege! Oh, my dear girl, what possessed you?' A murmur that went on like a bee droning, whatever anyone else might be saying.

Juliet, low in her basket chair, clasped the sleeping Donalblain in her arms. It was not for her to criticise her beautiful mother.

But the Vicar, his voice again stuttering, asked, 'D-d-do you mean to say you took this sacred vestment and wore it at a b-b-ball? As a *d-d-dress!*'

'Yes, I did!'

Remembering her triumphs, Peronel smiled.

(But where did that whisper of 'Sin!' come from? Certainly not from her Guardian Angel, whom she saw peeping wistfully in through the side window. He had approved her action! He had advised it! Was that still, small voice her awakening conscience? Oh—she *hoped not.*)

It had lately been ruled by the hierarchy which attends to such matters that it was not necessary for the elder members of the McCree family to have Guardian Angels. A little nightly attention from Matthew, Mark, Luke and John, a few minutes on guard duty round their four-poster, as a compliment, merely, was considered all that was necessary for beings so naturally good as Mr and Mrs McCree.

That Peronel should have needed a mentor was an admission of her frailty. The whole household was aware that she had one; no-one, therefore, was much surprised at her reference to such a personage when she continued, 'I don't admit that I was, person-ally, to blame in any way. I did it on my Guardian Angel's recom-mendation.'

Looking across at the side window she saw that cher confrère nod and smile. He was quite prepared to take the knock himself.

'What!' Mr McCree cried out, warmly. 'Do you mean to tell me that such an act of sacrilege was committed on the recom-mendation of a heavenly Being? I am appalled! What a scandalous charge! How shocked, how surprised, everyone in Heaven must be to hear you!'

'Indeed Heaven will not be in the least surprised! If it was considered wrong of me to borrow a Church vestment—why did Heaven *allot me a Low Church Guardian Angel*? Tell me that now!'

Though Mrs McCree here went off into peals of laughter, though the Vicar smiled a slow smile of appreciation at her neat point, Peronel lost her nerve.

Looking her loveliest, she tore off her widow's cap, with its fluttering lissé lapelles, and threw it on the floor, and crying out in her delicious voice (her eyes full of tears): 'Oh, Darling! Don't let them bully me!' she flung herself through the open French window into the wide-open, the waiting, the welcoming, arms of one of the young men.

Though the lamps were lit in the room, it is a bit tantalising that it was too dark on the verandah for the onlookers to see into whose arms she so gracefully, yet so impulsively, rocketed.

Flight

Constable John O'Shea was an angry man as he rode away from
Movingunda with three little half-caste girls strapped on behind
him.

The only three white men on the station had watched, laughing and slinging off as he mounted and set out, a horde of aboriginal mothers and dogs yelping after him. Most of the native men
were out mustering—thank God, O'Shea reflected—or there
might have been more trouble.

For miles the women and dogs ran behind him, yelling and
screaming; the children yelled and screamed to them. The women
fell back at last, but the children kept on snivelling and wailing.

Constable O'Shea was glad to reach the cover of the scrub and
follow the track over rough, drought-stricken country to Lorgans.

It was a clear day, cold and sunshiny. From the station table-
land, he could see the plains stretching away, grey-blue as the sea
in winter, a wedge of hills darker blue against the distant horizon.
Near by, the mulga looked dead or dying, although recent rains had
left pools beside the track. Fresh green was streaking the red earth
near them, making vivid patches against its mail of black ironstone
pebbles.

Constable O'Shea resented having to pick up half-caste girls
and send them down to government institutions at the request of
the Aborigines Department. He considered it no job for a man
who had to maintain the prestige of the force and uphold law and
order in an outlying district.

But he had received instructions that three half-caste female
children on Movingunda were to be sent down by the train which
passed through Lorgans on the eighth of the month. So there was

nothing for it but to collect the children, and hand them over to the officer who would be on the train.

A rotten business, it had been, removing the youngsters from their mothers. What a shrieking and howling, jabbering and imploring, with attempts to hide the children and run away with them into the bush! One of the gins and her terror-stricken kid had climbed a tree near the creek. It was not until after dark he had got that one, when mother and child crept back and were sleeping by the camp-fire.

Constable O'Shea sweated and swore as he thought of it, and the laughing-stock he had been to the white men on Movingunda, not one of whom would lend a hand to help him. He knew better than to try to make them. Murphy kept the fun going, a father of one of the kids—but not game to admit it. You couldn't blame him. There was a penalty, these days, for cohabiting with native women. But Fitz Murphy had been living with a gin for years, and had several children by her, everybody knew.

McEacharn, at least, made his position clear.

'No,' he said, 'they're not my kids. If they were, you wouldn't get them, O'Shea.'

There had been all the writing to do for official purposes also, giving the kids names, without reference to their parents, black or white—just labels to differentiate them by. Waste of time, O'Shea told himself, since the object of the drive was to separate the children from their aboriginal parents and environment.

Constable O'Shea was at his wit's end inventing names for half-caste brats. This was not the first lot he had had to register. The name a girl was known by in the camp or on the station might be used, but a surname had to be attached. O'Shea cursed the regulations.

This time he had got the native names of the children—Mynie, Nanja and Coorin. Molly, Polly and Dolly were easier to remember, so he put them down as Molly, Polly and Dolly. But surnames—he racked his brains about surnames for the bunch. A girl's father could not afford to be implicated, although occasionally the name of a station or locality might be adopted with certain satisfaction.

'What does Movingunda mean in the blacks' lingo?' he asked McEacharn.

'Ant-hill.'

'That'll do, O'Shea grinned, and wrote 'Anthill' beside 'Molly'. 'How about you chaps,' he continued, 'any of you willing to lend a kid a name?'

'Not on your life,' Murphy blustered.

'Anything you say may be used in evidence against you, eh, Murphy?' O'Shea remarked dryly.

The men guffawed.

'You can name the whole damned lot after me, if you like,' McEacharn growled, 'though God knows I've left the gins alone.'

'Right!'

O'Shea scrawled McEacharn for the next child.

'And the youngest?'

Mick Donovan, the old prospector, who had come into the station for stores, chuckled: 'She's the one gave you such a run for your money, Sarge.'

'Call her Small and be done with,' McEacharn advised.

O'Shea was grateful for the suggestion.

'There,' he said, folding up his report and packing it away with a wad of papers in the breast-pocket of his tunic. 'This batch will start life as young ladies with real classy names.'

The worst of it was, he could not remember which was which, and the kids didn't know which of them was supposed to be Molly, Polly or Dolly. They would only answer to their native names. But, Hell, a man could not be worried about that! The Department would have to sort them out somehow.

Constable O'Shea's temper did not improve as he rode. His charger, a nervous, powerful brute, took some handling at the best of times, and those three stinking kids on his back irritated him. They didn't weigh much more than a bunch of wild pigeons, but their dangling legs and bony little behinds chafed and upset Chief. He had tried to shift them, more than once, shying and pig-rooting whenever he got a chance. The kids stuck like leeches, strapped together though they were. The eldest hung on to O'Shea's belt, the rest to her.

It was hot at midday, the sky bare blue overhead and the sunlight dazzling. When he was thirsty himself, O'Shea gave the kids a drink from his water-bag, and a piece of bread and meat from the crib the station cook had put up for him.

The kids were so scared, they stared, goggle-eyed, when he spoke to them. Not a word would they say. There would be another meal to provide, O'Shea realized, so he rationed supplies carefully.

He had not anticipated this picnic. He had expected that McEacharn would make his car available and drive the kids into Lorgans. McEacharn had intimated, with specious regrets, that he could do nothing of the sort. He had an important engagement on Ethel Creek, a hundred miles in the opposite direction, and the station buggy was out on the mustering camp.

Constable O'Shea understood that if the children were to be dispatched by the train in three days' time, he must be responsible for their means of transport himself. There was no other way but to hoist them up behind him. He would have to sleep out for the night too.

Of course, he could call in at Sandy Gap station and require the manager to put him and his passengers up for the night. But stand another round of laughter and chiacking—not if he knew it! It would be awkward, camping by the track, and keeping an eye on the brats. He had no blankets. They would have to sleep by the fire. He had his rain-coat for a ground-sheet and covering, his saddle for pillow.

At sunset, when he lifted the children down from the big, bay horse, he would have liked to unfasten the straps knotted round their waists; but he knew very well what would happen if they found themselves free. They would be off and away like greased lightning. They knew this country better than he did, young as they were, and would make their way back to Movingunda. Then what sort of a fool would he look, going back after them, with all the business of catching and getting away with them again?

Ordinarily, he would have had his black tracker, Charley Ten, to look after the kids and make the fire; but Charley was giving evidence at a native trial in Meekatharra. There was nothing for it but to keep the kids tied up and make the fire himself.

O'Shea cursed his luck as he hauled a couple of mulga logs together and set them alight. He cursed the hopes of promotion which had brought him to the back-country; cursed Murphy, and every man in the nor'-west, who begot half-castes; cursed McEacharn for making it obvious that he did not intend to facilitate arrangements for removing youngsters from his station; cursed the Protector of Aborigines and the Department for their penurious habit of pushing on to the police in out-of-the-way places, work that should be done by officers of the Aborigines Department; cursed every well-meaning man and woman who believed that the Government ought to 'do something' for half-caste girls, without proper consideration of what that 'something' ought to be.

The three small girls sat on the ground watching him. Three pairs of beautiful dark eyes followed his every movement, alert and apprehensive. The eldest of the children, he had put down as nine years old, the other two at eight and seven.

Part of Constable O'Shea's grouch, though he would not have admitted it, was due to the way the children looked at him. He could not endure children to look at him as if he were an ogre who might devour them at any moment. A good-looking, kindly young man, he prided himself on carrying out his duties conscientiously but without harshness.

A man had to be considered a good sort to get anywhere in a district like this, where he was the only policeman for nearly a hundred miles in any direction, and had to depend on assistance from station-owners and mine-managers in an emergency. This job made him unpopular on the stations and he loathed it. He would rather wade in and clean up a dozen fighting drunks, he

said, than go round collecting half-caste girls on behalf of the
Aborigines Department. Why didn't the Department do its own
dirty work?

O'Shea was disturbed by the thought that it was dirty work he
had been forced to take part in. How would any woman like her
kids being yanked away from her, knowing quite well the chances
were she would never see them again? His own wife, for example?

Constable O'Shea smiled, trying to imagine any man separating his Nancy from her three linty-haired little girls and small
son. But after he had fed the aboriginal children and given them
each a drink of water, he took the precaution of tying their hands
together with strips of rawhide in case they might try to unfasten
the strap round their middles and run away. The children huddled
together and fell asleep, wailing a little, but evidently with no hope
of escape. Constable O'Shea stretched and dozed uncomfortably
on the far side of the fire.

It was evening of the second day when he rode over the ridge
by a back track into Lorgans. He had taken care not to arrive until
dusk so that no one would see him.

For several years Lorgans had been one of those deserted
mining townships, with only the dump and poppet-legs of an old
mine, a pub and the ruins of a row of shops to testify to its former
prosperity. But the railway still ran about a mile away, and with
re-opening of the mine, the township took a new lease of life. Gold
was bringing a good price.

Constable O'Shea's appointment followed a rush on the flat
below the ridge. New shafts were sunk, shops sprouted among the
ruins. Lorgans acquired a population of three or four hundred in a
few months, and O'Shea had brought his wife and family to live in
the smart, new police-station put up for him at the entrance to the
town.

When he reached the gate of the yard behind his house,
O'Shea dismounted, and lifted Mynie, Nanja and Coorin down
from his horse. He did not want his wife to see him with those kids
stuck up behind, and start laughing, as she surely would. She

laughed so easily. Her sense of humour kept her fat and content in this god-forsaken hole, she said; but O'Shea was not going to have her laughing at him if he could help it.

A dog started barking at the sight of him. Mrs O'Shea hurried out of the house as soon as she heard the dog. Her children swarmed about her. A big, fair-haired, youngish woman, she was, Mrs O'Shea, full-bosomed and sonsy. The children were like her, with fair hair and clear rosy skins. All excitement and delight, they ran to meet their father. He swung his son into his arms and the little girls hung onto him.

It was Mrs O'Shea who discovered the three small half-castes, crouched together and staring at her, wide-eyed and woe-begone.

'Oh, Jack,' she exclaimed, 'the poor little things! What are you going to do with them?'

'What do you think?' O'Shea asked impatiently. 'Keep them for pets?'

His daughters guessed just what had happened. They queried maddeningly.

'Did you give them a ride on your horse, Daddy?'

'Why can't we have a ride on your horse, Daddy?'

'Want to sit up behind you on Chief, too, Daddy!'

'Want a ride . . .'

'Can't I have a ride, too, Daddy?'

The half-castes gazed at these other children with amazement. How was it possible for them to talk to the policeman so cheekily and light-heartedly?

'But you can't keep them tied up like that,' Mrs O'Shea protested, still concerned about those wretched little figures.

'They're as wild as birds,' Constable O'Shea declared testily. 'If I gave them a chance, they'd be off back to Movingunda like a shot. And I wouldn't go through all I have had to, to get them again, for quids!'

He put his son on the ground, and walked over to a shed of corrugated iron with barbed wire across a small, square window, unlocked the door and flung it back.

'Come along, you feller,' he called. 'Nothing hurt'm. Missus bring'm tucker, d'reckly.'

Mynie, Nanja and Coorin moved slowly, reluctantly, towards the door, their eyes searching desperately for some way to save them from that dark shed.

It served as a lock-up, but was rarely used except for an unruly drunk or a native prisoner.

'Don't put them there, Jack,' his wife begged. 'They'll be scared stiff—and it's freezing cold these nights.'

'You can't take them into the house,' O'Shea objected.

'What about the room at the end of the veranda?' Mrs O'Shea persisted. 'They can't do any harm there. I'll take them along while you feed Chief.'

'Have it your own way. They'll have to be scrubbed and disinfected tomorrow.'

O'Shea unbuttoned the navy tunic of his uniform, hung it on a post and turned to unsaddle.

'Come on, children,' his wife called cheerily to the half-castes. They trailed behind her as she trundled across the yard. Her own offspring followed curiously.

'Go and finish your tea,' their mother said. 'And Phyll, see that Bobbie doesn't spill his cocoa on the table-cloth.'

Constable O'Shea snapped back the surcingle and girths of his saddle, heaved it on to one arm, and the big bay followed him into the stable. He gave his horse a good hard feed, rubbed him down and ran water into the trough by the stable door before going into the house.

His son was sitting in his high chair, and the three little girls, just about the same age as those half-caste children, chattering gleefully as they finished their meal. Very fresh and pretty they looked, with their hair in neat pig-tails and print aprons over their frocks. Nancy was a wonderful mother; always contrived to have the children looking clean and bonny for the evening meal, and everything bright and pleasant when he came back from one of these long trips across country.

But tonight, as she stood by the fire grilling his steak, Nancy seemed vaguely troubled. Her easy-going, good-natured tolerance of life at Lorgans was overcast.

'I'll be glad when we get a move,' she said, putting a large plate of steak, poached eggs and fried potatoes before her husband. 'It's getting on my nerves—this kidnapping of children.'

'You're not more fed-up with it than I am,' O'Shea replied irritably. 'If the Department wants me to do this job, they'll have to provide me with a car, or a buggy at least.'

'It's a rotten shame, the way these kids are taken from their mothers,' Mrs O'Shea exclaimed. 'The gins will be trailing in from Movingunda for months to ask me what's happened to the children. And what can I say?'

'Tell them they've gone south to be made into young ladies— like you've done before.'

'They don't believe me. You can't lie to an abo. All I know is, they'll never see their children again. The kids won't remember their mothers and the mothers'll lose all trace of them.'

'The great idea,' O'Shea reminded her, 'is that the kids are being saved from leading immoral lives in the native camps.'

'That's all very well,' his wife cried indignantly. 'But how does it work out? The girls learn to read and write, become domestic servants; but more than half of them lead immoral lives in the towns, just the same. Only it's worse for them down there, because they're among strangers. If a half-caste girl has a baby up here, it's taken as a matter of course. But down south, it's a disgrace. And anyhow, why can't the girls be given a chance to come back, work on the stations—and marry? It's because women are so scarce in the back-country that there are half-castes in the first place.'

'It's not my fault.' Her husband swung over and sprawled in an easy chair by the fire. He hauled off his riding-boots and stretched his long legs, with thick home-knitted socks pulled up to the end of his breeches.

'You remember Emmalina from Koolija station,' Mrs O'Shea continued. 'She just sat down by the fence of our yard and wailed for days, after her little girl was sent down. If ever a woman died of a broken heart, she did, Jack.'

'For Christ's sake, Nancy,' O'Shea protested, 'stop fussing about those kids. I've just about had enough of them, and being made to look a fool, hiking across country with the little brutes hanging on to me.'

Mynie, Nanja and Coorin, sitting on the floor of the room nearby, heard the talking: heard for the first time something of the fate before them. They listened intently, staring at the square of window, crossed by barbed wire.

Their quick senses, following every sound of movement and voices, constructed vivid pictures of what was happening in the fire-lit kitchen they had glimpsed as they passed along the veranda. They could see Constable O'Shea having his meal and his woman, standing near, talking to him.

When one of the girls asked for more bread and jam, they could hear the mother cutting the bread, and the small boy get a slap for putting his fingers in the jam. He bawled and his father lifted him out of the high chair and took him to sit on his knee by the fire. The little girls clamoured to sit on their father's knee, too; but he threatened to send them to bed at once if they did not keep quiet and behave themselves.

When her own family had eaten and was satisfied, Mrs O'Shea announced that she was going to take 'those poor little things' something to eat. She turned the key in the lock of the room at the end of the veranda a moment later, and appeared with a plate of bread and jam and mugs of tea on a tray.

Mynie, Nanja and Coorin watched her as she put an enamel mug before each of them and the plate of bread and jam in the middle. No need to share out the portions. They would do that themselves scrupulously, Mrs O'Shea knew.

Each little girl was strapped one to the other. Their wrists were tied together. Mrs O'Shea hovered over them, smiling and motherly, trying to reassure them. She could not bear to see these children so scared and dumb. Such skinny little things, they were, with great brown eyes and curling lashes, blackish-brown tousled hair, and gina-ginas, no more than scraps of faded blue cotton stuff, on their meagre bodies.

The room was a lock-up cell in all but name, kept for more respectable prisoners. There was a chair and table in it and a bed covered with blue-grey blankets. The window had no glass, but was double-crossed with barbed wire.

There was no way the half-castes could get out when the door was locked, Mrs O'Shea told herself. So she took the law into her own hands: knelt down, and with firm white teeth unfastened the leather thongs which bound them: undid the strips of raw-hide biting into those slim brown wrists.

Jack would be furious, she knew, if he found out what she had done. She intended to tie the children up again in the morning, and gambled on no one being the wiser except herself and the children. They could be trusted not to tell.

Anyhow, Mrs O'Shea assured herself, she would not sleep a wink if she thought of those poor little scarecrows sitting there tied up, cold and miserable. She pulled a blanket from the bed and threw it on the floor for them.

'There, now,' she said cheerily, 'you'll be good girls, won't you? You won't try to run away? The Boss'd kill me if you did.'

When she went away, locking the door behind her, Mynie, Nanja and Coorin grabbed the thick slices of bread and jam she had brought them, and guzzled down the warm, sweet tea made with condensed milk.

The room was in darkness, except for that square of starlit sky framed by the window and crossed with barbed wire. When she had eaten her bread and jam and drunk all the tea in her mug, Mynie sidled over to the window.

Stealthily she looked out. Across the yard behind the policeman's house, the stables and the horse-paddock, there was the black wall of the ridge. Mynie could see the track Constable O'Shea had come in by, winding past the mine and the old township until it was swallowed up by a dark mass of trees. One sniff and a quiver of instinctive decision sufficed to inform her companions. The brown eyes communicated, wise and wary.

Leaning against the wall, in the shadow, Mynie began fiddling with the barbed wire. She tried each row where it was held by nails driven into the wooden framework. Her brown fingers curled and twisted, crawled on. It was not until Mynie had tried several rows of wire that she turned to look at Nanja and Coorin with a gleam in her eyes. They crept over, and saw a couple of nails loose in their sockets. The red wood had shrunk, so that the nails could be worked out, and the wire turned back to leave a gap through which a child's body might squeeze.

The three slunk back to their place on the floor and sat watching and waiting. Coorin fell asleep. Her head drooped on Nanja's shoulder; but Nanja and Mynie listened, tense and alert, to all that was going on in the kitchen.

Mrs O'Shea put the boy to bed. She shooed the little girls off to wash and brush their hair. They didn't want to go to bed. The policeman told them a story about three pigs. Then they kissed him, saying, 'Goodnight, Daddy!' over and over again, and ran away laughing and chattering.

'Don't forget your prayers,' Mrs O'Shea called.

One after the other, the little white girls talked as if they were remembering the words of a corroboree song:

> Gentle Jesus, meek and mild,
> Look upon a little child;
> Pity my simplicity,
> Suffer me to come to Thee.

Mrs O'Shea trotted into their bedroom, kissed the girls and put out the light. Then there was the washing up to do. She hustled about, clearing away dishes and chatting to her husband in a brisk, jolly way. He yawned and stretched a good deal.

At last, he exclaimed:

'Cripes, I'm dead tired! How about a bit of shut-eye?'

They went to a room at the front of the house. Mynie and Nanja heard them moving about as they undressed. The bed creaked as they got into it. For a while, the policeman and his wife talked softly together. Now and then Mrs O'Shea's little laugh flew out. Then all was quiet.

Nothing more than the sound of regular breathing vibrated through the thin partitions, the sound of two people sleeping heavily, tranquilly, with an occasional puffing sigh or long-drawn snore.

Mynie and Nanja did not need to talk. They wakened Coorin. She understood immediately why they had done so. One passion dominated all three. They did not know whether to believe the policeman would kill his woman if he found out she had untied their hands and unfastened the strap. They could not think of that.

Their only instinct was to escape, to make their way back over the hills and plains to the miahs of their own people. It was rough, strange country they would have to pass through. They were on the far side of the hills which had been the boundary of their world. Those mysterious blue hills where, Wonkena said, the gnarlu lived, the gnarlu who came hopping out of the darkness like a frog when there was a corroboree on Movingunda.

They had heard the women singing to scare him away, and seen old Nardadu herself stand up and hurl a burning stick at him when he came too near the camp-fire. They were terrified at the thought of having to cross the gnarlu's territory at night; but they were so little and insignificant, Mynie thought, they might find their way back to Movingunda without being noticed. Anyhow their fear had to be overcome if they were not to be taken away, never to see their mothers or the back-country again.

Mynie slid over to the window and worked on the nails. She drew them out. Her eyes searched the yard. There was nothing moving. She turned back the wire where she had untwisted it. The hole in the barbed screen was just big enough for her to squeeze through. Nanja lifted Coorin. Mynie pulled her through and put her on the ground. Nanja stuck and struggled before she joined them.

For a moment they clung to the shadow of the house, afraid to stir in case the dog might fly at them, his barking arouse Constable

O'Shea and his woman. Then they crawled under the veranda to the far side. Stepping carefully, they crossed the shingly ground to the road, scarcely stirring a pebble.

Swiftly, silently, on bare hard feet, they streaked along the track to the ridge. In a few minutes the township lay behind. As they climbed the ridge, trees closed round them; mulga, dark and creaking, whispering with strange voices, thorn-bush and minnereechi casting black shadows, shadows that sprawled and clutched, sliding away with dry cackling laughter.

Nanja and Coorin kept close to Mynie as they went on. All three shrank together when the gaunt arms of a dead tree swayed out towards them. They scudded off through the scrub. The scrub became denser. Writhing shapes peered and leered at them from every bush. Thin, bony fingers grabbed at and scratched their legs, tore their gina-ginas. They ran on, coming at last to a gorge between two great hills.

A pool lay at the bottom of the hills, but Mynie steered away from it, knowing the worst jinkies lurk beside shadowy water. A sinister '*wauk, wauk!*' came from the pool, and sent them scrambling up the hill. The great weather-beaten rocks were less fearsome than the trees; but they crept from the shadow of one rock to another, stopping with wildly beating hearts to listen and gaze about them before stealing on.

Then the moon rose, a worn silvery plate, thrusting itself up behind the back of the hillside. It had scarcely risen half-way when a squat, unwieldy shape moved across it, hopping and flopping towards them.

It was the gnarlu, Mynie, Nanja and Coorin were sure—the dreaded evil spirit they had seen hopping and flopping, just like that, up to the camp-fire in a corroboree. They did not wait to see whether this gnarlu had the same white markings. There was no Nardadu, now, to scare him away with her fire-stick. Mynie turned and fled, with Nanja and Coorin after her, back along the way they had come, through the gorge and the dark scrub again, coming at last to the track that led to the mines, the township, and the police-station.

The sky was dimming in the false dawn before they got there, slipped under the fence, crossed the shingly ground beside the house and crawled under the veranda to the further side. The barbed wire gaped over the window, just as they had left it. Mynie squirmed through. Nanja lifted Coorin, then hoisted herself through the window.

When they were sitting huddled up on the floor again, their eyes met and conferred. Without a word spoken, they agreed that their fear of the future was nothing to the terrors they had passed through. It was a comfort even to hear the policeman and his wife sleeping peacefully, with a puffing sigh and a long-drawn snore now and then.

Mynie stole over to the window, found the nails on the ledge where she had left them, fitted them into place and twisted the wire round. That done she went back to Nanja and Coorin, stretched on the floor, and drew the blanket over them.

When Mrs O'Shea brought in some porridge and milk a few hours later, they were still asleep, lying curled up like chrysalids in the dingy blanket.

'That's good girls,' she said, gaily. 'I knew I could trust you. You feller only little bit blackfeller. Little bit white feller, too.'

'Yukki!' Mynie breathed, wondering if that was why they had come back to the white man's house.

Mrs O'Shea found the strap and fastened it round their waists again. Painstakingly, a little apologetically, she knotted the strips of raw-hide round their wrists.

MARJORIE BARNARD

The Persimmon Tree

I saw the spring come once and I won't forget it. Only once. I had
been ill all the winter and I was recovering. There was no more
pain, no more treatments or visits to the doctor. The face that
looked back at me from my old silver mirror was the face of a
woman who had escaped. I had only to build up my strength. For
that I wanted to be alone, an old and natural impulse. I had been
out of things for quite a long time and the effort of returning was
still too great. My mind was transparent and as tender as new skin.
Everything that happened, even the commonest things, seemed to
be happening for the first time, and had a delicate hollow ring like
music played in an empty auditorium.

I took a flat in a quiet, blind street, lined with English trees. It
was one large room, high ceilinged with pale walls, chaste as a cell
in a honeycomb, and furnished with the passionless, standardized
grace of a fashionable interior decorator. It had the afternoon sun
which I prefer because I like my mornings shadowy and cool, the
relaxed end of the night prolonged as far as possible. When I
arrived the trees were bare and still against the lilac dusk. There
was a block of flats opposite, discreet, well tended, with a wide
entrance. At night it lifted its oblongs of rose and golden light far
up into the sky. One of its windows was immediately opposite
mine. I noticed that it was always shut against the air. The street
was wide but because it was so quiet the window seemed near. I
was glad to see it always shut because I spend a good deal of time
at my window and it was the only one that might have overlooked
me and flawed my privacy.

I liked the room from the first. It was a shell that fitted without touching me. The afternoon sun threw the shadow of a tree on
my light wall and it was in the shadow that I first noticed that the
bare twigs were beginning to swell with buds. A watercolour,

109

pretty and innocuous, hung on that wall. One day I asked the silent woman who serviced me to take it down. After that the shadow of the tree had the wall to itself and I felt cleared and tranquil as if I had expelled the last fragment of grit from my mind.

I grew familiar with all the people in the street. They came and went with a surprising regularity and they all, somehow, seemed to be cut to a very correct pattern. They were part of the *mise-en-scène*, hardly real at all and I never felt the faintest desire to become acquainted with any of them. There was one woman I noticed, about my own age. She lived over the way. She had been beautiful I thought, and was still handsome with a fine tall figure. She always work dark clothes, tailor made, and there was reserve in her every movement. Coming and going she was always alone, but you felt that that was by her own choice, that everything she did was by her own steady choice. She walked up the steps so firmly, and vanished so resolutely into the discreet muteness of the building opposite, that I felt a faint, a very faint, envy of anyone who appeared to have her life so perfectly under control.

There was a day much warmer than anything we had had, a still, warm, milky day. I saw as soon as I got up that the window opposite was open a few inches. 'Spring comes even to the careful heart,' I thought. And the next morning not only was the window open but there was a row of persimmons set out carefully and precisely on the sill, to ripen in the sun. Shaped like a young woman's breasts their deep, rich, golden-orange colour seemed just the highlight that the morning's spring tranquillity needed. It was almost a shock to me to see them there. I remembered at home when I was a child there was a grove of persimmon trees down one side of the house. In the autumn they had blazed deep red, taking your breath away. They cast a rosy light into rooms on that side of the house as if a fire were burning outside. Then the leaves fell and left the pointed dark gold fruit clinging to the bare branches. They never lost their strangeness—magical, Hesperidean trees. When I saw the *Firebird* dance my heart moved painfully because I remembered the persimmon trees in the early morning against the dark windbreak of the loquats. Why did I always think of autumn in springtime?

Persimmons belong to autumn and this was spring. I went to the window to look again. Yes, they were there, they were real. I had not imagined them, autumn fruit warming to a ripe transparency in the spring sunshine. They must have come, expensively packed in sawdust, from California or have lain all winter in storage. Fruit out of season.

It was later in the day when the sun had left the sill that I saw the window opened and a hand come out to gather the persimmons. I saw a woman's figure against the curtains. *She* lived there. It was her window opposite mine.

Often now the window was open. That in itself was like the breaking of a bud. A bowl of thick cream pottery, shaped like a boat, appeared on the sill. It was planted, I think, with bulbs. She used to water it with one of those tiny, long-spouted, hand-painted cans that you use for refilling vases, and I saw her gingerly loosening the earth with a silver table fork. She didn't look up or across the street. Not once.

Sometimes on my leisurely walks I passed her in the street. I knew her quite well now, the texture of her skin, her hands, the set of her clothes, her movements. The way you know people when you are sure you will never be put to the test of speaking to them. I could have found out her name quite easily. I had only to walk into the vestibule of her block and read it in the list of tenants, or consult the visiting card on her door. I never did.

She was a lonely woman and so was I. That was a barrier, not a link. Lonely women have something to guard. I was not exactly lonely. I had stood my life on a shelf, that was all. I could have had a dozen friends round me all day long. But there wasn't a friend I loved and trusted above all the others, no lover, secret or declared. She had, I supposed, some nutrient hinterland on which she drew.

The bulbs in her bowl were shooting. I could see the pale new-green spears standing out of the dark loam. I was quite interested in them, wondered what they could be. I expected tulips, I don't know why. Her window was open all day long now, very fine thin curtains hung in front of it and these were never parted. Sometimes they moved but it was only in the breeze.

The trees in the street showed green now, thick with budded leaves. The shadow pattern on my wall was intricate and rich. It was no longer an austere winter pattern as it had been at first. Even the movement of the branches in the wind seemed different. I used to lie looking at the shadow when I rested in the afternoon. I was always tired then and so more permeable to impressions. I'd think about the buds, how pale and tender they were, but how implacable. The way an unborn child is implacable. If man's world were in ashes the spring would still come. I watched the moving pattern and my heart stirred with it in frail, half-sweet melancholy.

One afternoon I looked out instead of in. It was growing late and the sun would soon be gone, but it was warm. There was gold dust in the air, the sunlight had thickened. The shadows of trees and buildings fell, as they sometimes do on a fortunate day, with dramatic grace. *She* was standing there just behind the curtains, in a long dark wrap, as if she had come from her bath and was going to dress, early, for the evening. She stood so long and so still, staring out—at the budding trees, I thought—that tension began to accumulate in my mind. My blood ticked like a clock. Very slowly she raised her arms and the gown fell from her. She stood there naked, behind the veil of curtains, the scarcely distinguishable but unmistakable form of a woman whose face was in shadow.

I turned away. The shadow of the burgeoning bough was on the white wall. I thought my heart would break.

CHRISTINA STEAD

The Old School

The brick school in its yellow playground lay south west from and below Lydham Hill. One morning the wind-break on the knoll half sank to the horizon like a constellation wheeling; the house lay close to the breast of clay, shawled in pines. It turned out that there were trees in the school ground too—a Moreton Bay fig, a pepper tree with outstretched arms and in the lower part, near the headmaster's house, some flower beds for the infants.

The rumour about the school among the very small children who had never been there, was that children were beaten there and prisoned, 'caned and kept in, even the babies'. Mistrial and injustice were common at home, but there never was any particular conclusion, while in this new yellow earth, there were strange administrators, and things had a beginning and an end, the end at four o'clock, the conclusion liberty, sometimes delayed 'kept in half an hour'.

Cause and effect were much clearer than at home, effect often unlooked for, doomful and needing analysis. Cause and effect mostly concerned the boys. A boy who jumps over the fence in the evening and shouts while playing stolen football, who picks a pansy from the infants' garden, who takes a pear from the Jollys' fruit stall, will soon be seen at the headmaster's table waiting for six cuts. There are even trusties, worthy little boys who do not seem to earn much respect, who are willing to take him there. And it is known pretty soon that the boy who stays away a whole week, a truant (that is a terrible word) in the hot silent gully, hidden by trees, paddling in the shallow creek, will go to the reformatory. The shadow of the reformatory was steep and dark. The informants—there are always a number of small sages about—know all about it. It had barred windows, food was bad, beatings the usual thing and you only came out of there to go to prison. In any

113

case, in there they wore blucher boots. Blucher boots were stiff work-boots with heavy soles, cheap and long wearing. It was accepted that children who came to school in blucher boots would leave school early and do rough work. They might even work on the road alongside their fathers, who, too, wore blucher boots. The very word was socially significant: 'he's wearing blucher boots!' The nice girls looked down and away in shame, the dirty girls grinned. Nevertheless there was Tom Biggar, a fleshy chest-nut and rose boy often good at drawing. Mr Roberts put upon the varnished table a blucher boot to draw and beside it some pota-toes. There were protests from the girls and the nice boys. They also did not want to draw potatoes. Tom's were very good though. Mr Roberts said he might be an artist. Tom laughed. 'I'm going to work on the road with father, when I can.' He did not mind the prospect at all: he would earn money like his father.

All the outside information, these certitudes, were spread by the informants, natural moralists, two or three to a class and as far as I knew, all little girls. There were girls and boys in each class, but in their own society, that is in the playground, they did not mix. There was one moral little boy, though: he was called after one of the greatest English poets and had a good memory. Once the whole school was assembled in the long room to hear of a most serious crime. 'Who did it? It is a mistake to think you must be loyal to your classmates, when such a thing has been done.' The headmaster marched up and down and called 'Speak out'. Many moral questions were debated by the girls in large circular evasions but this was an obsolete law never debated. (The informants knew that someone had scandalously coupled the names of male and female teachers in stolen chalk on the boys' outhouse.)

In all the school assembled, only one child had the moral courage to tattle, Dryden Smith himself, an undersized clerkly boy of ten; 'It was Snowy Thorne.'

This delation froze the school in lessons and caused the playgrounds to move with wagging heads and hands, as a fern-slope under wind; whatever the verdict, Dryden was left alone, contaminated: such a lesson in public morality lasts through life. Even the informants dared not become informers.

At the end of the year, Dryden won a prize *From Log Cabin to White House* given by Mr Roberts, a man who protected children, and Dryden recited before the parents and the minister 'Horatius at the Bridge', standing up trembling but brave. I can still see his pale serious round face as it rose, twice, once for the denunciation, once for the poem. And I saw him once more, at Christmas, at the old Anthony Hordern's with his little face just above the counter, where they sold men's ties. We saw each other but made no sign. He was at work. I was at school. I too had won a prize, 'Feats on the Fjord', which struck me as second best and I recited 'There was a sound of revelry by night'. I could see, as I proceeded, that the parents were stupefied with boredom and good manners.

The informants, our moralists, had clean dresses, pink, blue or sprigged, patent leather shoes and white socks, and curls natural or rag. They did clean school work too, even when we got to pen and ink. Goodness alone knows how, with their pink cheeks and shiny curls and neatly dressed brisk little mothers, they got all this news about jails, reformatories, judges and sentences, lashings, canings, bread and water.

When wrongs took place in school or grounds, the informants instantly knotted together, a town moot: they discussed, debated and delivered an opinion. What the teachers said was brought forward but only as hearsay. I never had an opinion to give; in one way I did not understand and then I was always puzzled. I thought then that cruelty and injustice were natural and inevitable during all of a poor creature's life.

Now Snowy Thorne, the accredited bad boy of the school, a ten-year-old orphan with straw hair, tear-stained face, a good Norfolk suit given him by his aunts and blucher boots—if the little girls picked him out for gossip and innuendo it was because the teachers had picked him out first. The headmaster, a grey haired small-headed socialist, a mild moderate mediocre fellow, thought he had been slighted in being sent out to this distant suburban school, a revenge for his opinions. He hated Snowy Thorne. Some iniquity discovered, Mr Fairway would call together the three upper classes (fifth was top class then), pack them into the long room which was built in a court house style, and make Snowy Thorne walk up and down, up and down, all the length of the room, by the three blackboards, up and down from the desk where he got his canings to the door to the yard through which he could escape (but Mr Roberts stood there), in his neat but yellowing Norfolk suit and his dull black boots. What annoyed Mr Fairway was that Snowy Thorne would not admit all of his crimes, until after being baited and exhibited and worn down he cried and was caned; and even then no one was sure. But who else threw ink into the new fish pond that Mr Fairway had just put in at his own expense to cheer up the boys' playground? Who else wrote certain symbols on the wall, for example, a rooster and a strange eye with long lashes? Whose pale poll was seen at evening star time alone in the playground and whistling to itself? Where had the toffee apples gone from the IXL shop? It could only have been the butter ladies' boy (his aunts sold butter). I do not know what became of Snowy Thorne. Poor Mr Fairway! The school was given more classrooms, a better grade; and a new assistant head, smart, conceited and lively and, worst of all, with a BA degree, came to push the aging man about.

When we first came to school, we sang a pretty song about the old bell,

> I was hung in my place when the village was young,
> And the houses were scattered and few,
> In the old dingy belfry for ages I've swung.
> But my song is the same as when new.

Though I knew it was about another place, it also seemed to be to be about Bexley, where the houses were scattered and few; but by the time Mr Bobsley BA came, closer settlement had begun, many old paddocks were closed to us.

The first teacher I knew was a confident pretty neat woman, married, with two young children at home. She told us about them almost every day: luckily for her in these children she had met her ideals. She had large blue eyes and crinkled hair; and her children were fair, too. The school children called her 'very strict', not a slur. This was another moral issue often debated—who was the better teacher, the strict or the slack?

'If I hear a single sound you won't go home to lunch, you'll stay in all day and I'll make rabbit pie out of you and eat you,' she said. This threat caused some of the infants to sob out of hunger in prospect; others sobbed out of fear. We were very young. Each shiny morning she looked up and down the ranks as they marched in and standing at her desk would cry, 'Millie fall out, Jack Dodger, Will Hill, Polly—fall out' and by the time the class stood at its desks there would be on the floor a ragged line of the guilty, surveyed by the others with interest and guilt. It was not always possible to understand why they were guilty. It was easy to note some, torn jacket, hair 'like a birch broom in a fit', and Maidie Dickon of course, for truancy, though she hid in no sunny gully. We sang the first song, 'Good morning to you, glorious sun', sat down and the moment came, the review of the sinners, more exciting to the teacher than to them. Some after a homily would be sent back to their seats, two or three were left to tramp up and down. Then a general explanation of the law. If parents could not afford boots they must send a note explaining; but if children had boots and came without them, then—and so forth. Children had the duty of asking their parents for boots and shoes; if the soles were worn out, they themselves must take them to the boot-mender's. I myself stood there once in broken boots, but was saved. As I stood there with flushed cheeks and resentful, the class sang its second song, with the chorus, 'Shoo, shoo, go out black cat'. At this moment the headmaster appeared twinkling (he was younger and happier then). He pretended to be a black cat and ran out: the delinquents were sent back to their seats. When the class set to work, Maidie Dickon would be called to the desk and her case gone into. She had been away eight days, say, and only returned in response to the teacher's note. She must now go home and bring a note of excuse from her mother. The dark haired little girl went out silent, passive. As she clumped to the door, one of the informants, the censors (who felt themselves enabled to speak in class) remarked that Maidie was wearing boys' boots, blucher boots. So she was. Presently another who had been sent to the head with a message, returned to say that Maidie was sitting in a corner of the shed, doing nothing. So she was, she could even be seen from our doorway, quite still, head drooping. A willing messenger was sent to tell her to go home. The next day she did not come; but at mid-morning on the following day someone saw a motionless bundle there, with her two bare legs in the boots, crouched in the infants' shed: she had no note.

For a few days after, she sat in her desk in front, clumsily doing lessons with a book and pencil from the school cupboard. In those days, new books and pencils from the cupboard were given out sparingly: you had to bring your own. The censors were indignant (though well provided with books and pencil cases). There was a considerable outcry, 'It isn't fair' they exclaimed. Usually a new book was given as a sort of prize, for very good work. Maidie would begin a new exercise book and then stay away for so long that the book would belong to someone else by the time she returned. She came without any property at all, no pencil box, sponge box, slate pencil, pencil, school bag, lunch, handkerchief, forlornly destitute.

The censors (the informants) were astonishing news-gatherers. How could they know?—but they did—that Mr Dickon was a road worker who had been on strike (for them a criminal thing), that Mrs Dickon was a washerwoman, never home in the daytime. When she got a query from the teacher, Mrs Dickon always answered at once, on odd pieces of paper, bills or newspaper, which were exhibited and read out to the class by the clean gold haired teacher. These notes would say 'Maidie had to help me,' and once she said 'I have a new baby and Maidie had to stay at home to help.' Maidie knew a brief popularity then: the informants loved new babies.

Monday mornings were bank mornings. Children with prudent parents brought each a shilling or a sixpence and went to the headmaster who wrote down in each bank book the sum brought. He complained about it—how did we know that?—and we could not understand his complaint at such a privilege: a moaner, evidently. I also banked one shilling a week and one Monday the shilling was missing. Neighbours and busybodies (informants should I say) helped me look for it, said it was stolen. Knowing how confused I was, how I always lost things at home, I thought I had lost it myself. We turned out the little lunch case, poked at its seams and everyone studied the floorboards. 'Who stole it?' very soon became 'Maidie Dickon stole a shilling.' 'How do you know?' 'She must have, she's poor.' Even the teacher was shaken. Maidie Dickon remained as before, silent, forlorn. I felt guilty. I felt sure it was I. Justice without evidence took its course. The following Monday when I opened my case a shilling piece lay on top. 'Maidie Dickon must have put it back' they cried. As for me, I believed that I had overlooked it, that it had fallen out of a seam, a pocket. That notion of Maidie Dickon climbing up all those stairs (I was at the back in a banked classroom), opening cases, taking out, putting in and all with such cunning and stealth, she who never moved, was always late, did not fit. Even now, she never spoke, never volunteered word or action. There she is though, the little girl in white, with her bowed heavy shoulders and black eyes, in my mind; and with her, the horror of money.

She was sitting there one morning hunched more than usual because of the dress. Someone was reading the lesson, 'A man in a land where lions are found was once out late in the day far from home' (a phrase I have never forgotten), but the little girls' interest was glued to a topic right at home and they interrupted the fascinating lion story (I remember that the man hid in a hole under the cliff and the lion leaped right over him into the gulf), to remark to the teacher that Maidie was wearing a new dress made out of a sheet. 'No, it's a flour bag, her mother hasn't got any sheets.' This was a serious argument without malice. 'Mrs Taylor, she shouldn't come to school in a dress made out of a sheet'—craning, inspecting, deciding. They had been simmering with this news, waiting for the moment to let it out. Before school, she had pulled away from their inquisitive puzzled fingers and eyes, little sparrows pecking at the odd-feathered one, her large opaque black eyes on them and then away—with what feeling? Even in the lines that morning, they, the good, had been disorderly, fluttering. And now, when the bright haired woman settled them all, they told her she had been obeyed. Maidie had only stayed away the last time because she had no dress to wear. Now she had a dress, 'It's made out of a sheet.' 'Flour bags?' 'No, it's sheet.' The teacher, curious, went right up to Maidie's desk and studied the dress.

It was soft old thick cotton, made in fashion, with a deep yoke, long sleeves into wristbands, several inch wide pleats into a waistband, tucks and a wide hem to let down. It was white and remained white, though certain marks (which had made them say flour bags) had faded with washing.

Maidie never had any lunch. During the lunch recess she sat by herself at the far end of the wooden seats which ran round under the high brick walls. The rest of the girls in groups in the noonday shade of the buildings occasionally glanced her way, during a lull in their busy colloquies, condemning her for her misery, some, perhaps, curious about her life. If a newcomer, a wandering casual, not yet incorporated socially or perhaps even kind-hearted, approached her, the playground leaders at once dispatched a messenger, 'You mustn't talk to her: she hasn't any lunch,' and some other parts of the indictment might be added, if the wanderer hesitated.

Some hungry children ate their lunches in snatches under the desks during school hours and had none left when noonday came. Some of these grasshoppers cast eyes on their friends' lunches and even begged; but they got little if anything. They too had the sin of lunchlessness, though it was understood they were more weak than sinning. Was it one of those who in the morning poached another's lunch? In the middle of the morning Dorothy (a sweet little girl who was not an informant) found her lunch gone. 'The thief—the thief' a word they liked to shrill and who could it be? Yes, Maidie it might be—but for some reason the informants had grown a little careful since the episode of the shilling. They must have had doubts, too. But what a din!

She listened at her desk, motionless: she sat in the shed or playground. At last, the lunchless one, Maidie wept, but no one pitied her. They sang the midday song, 'Home to dinner, home to dinner, hear the bell, hear the bell, bacon and potatoes . . .' etc. Dorothy lived too far away to go home and the teacher gave her money for the IXL shop.

It is a hard cruel knot that has gathered in the shade at the top of the yard, looking over their shoulders fiercely at the girl in the white dress, a bundle of submission in the sun sometimes shaking her black basin-crop which she scratches ('she has nits') and glancing mildly round her: perhaps she is shortsighted. 'Thieves oughtn't to be allowed in school,' and they bring into their talk the reformatory, these pink and blue girls, whispering secrets, boasting and harsh; and yet all are afraid. The reformatory for Maidie, there with coarse dishes, coarse clothes, sleeping on sacking or planks, there children are flogged, though it serves them right, there is the cat o' nine tails, there they are put into cells alone, there are iron bars on the windows and if they escape the police catch them. The little girls in pink and blue know the names of the jails—Long Bay, Parramatta, Bathurst. Where do the charming little balls of fluff, their mothers' happiness, gather this awful lore? Mrs Taylor, the teacher, comes round the corner of the infants' building where Maidie sits in the midday sun, close to the side gate leading into the headmaster's dark snug cottage. Mrs Taylor speaks,

'Are you hungry, Maidie?'

'Yes.'

'Have you any lunch?'

'No.'

'Don't you ever bring any lunch?'

'No.'

'Come and have lunch with me.'

She takes her by the hand. They go round the corner towards the infants' building where the teacher has her packet lunch, done up in a white damask serviette, on her desk.

The teacher does not acquire merit by this action. How set back the informants are now! 'She oughtn't to do it!' Yes, morality has got a black eye. The teacher has fallen from grace. 'She shouldn't give her lunch when she never brings any.' What Mrs Taylor does will henceforth be debated with less than latitude: she has sided with the luckless, rebuffed the righteous. I was there. I was never able to make up my mind about things; and so it is still there, clear to me, the ever burning question of good and bad which (to be fair to the informants) so greatly occupied their minds. I always thought it strange that adults do not notice how profoundly little children are engrossed and stirred by moral debate. They are all the time sharpening their awareness of the lines and frontiers.

Twenty Strong

DELLA PARKINS, THE TEN-MILE FARM, BRANCH CREEK, VIA WOONGANATTIE, was painted in thin black lettering on the tin trunk. Della looked downward at it from the high seat of the buggy on which she sat, the lettering blurring and distorting through her tears.

'Here,' said the driver of the buggy, who was also the mail-man, and who was at present unwillingly escorting Della to school in Woonganattie, it being shearing and no one else having time, 'put your feet on it.' He juggled the trunk into position with his foot and she rested her black buttoned boots on it, placing them sadly and sedately side by side. 'Aren't you going to give your folks a wave?' he asked.

She turned and waved forlornly through the flap at the side. Her mother on the back steps, her father by the foot-scraper, waved back. A flannel-singleted shearer washing his face in an enamel dish on a tripod outside the shearer's hut raised his arm and waved too. Other shearers smoked outside the shed, filling in the moments before they must go inside. She could still feel the throb of the engines from the shed as the engines heated up. The sheep were restless in the yards. A bird note trembled intolerably in the air; the pumpkin vines flaunted yellow flowers and the clover was tenderly green beside the smooth silver of the dam. It made her feel sad as she drove away from it all in the clear bright light of the early spring morning. A tear pressed from under one eyelid and slid slowly down her cheek. She turned her head away from the white-painted house, the gently rolling paddocks, and resolutely faced the road ahead, a grey road, soft with the dust of a rainless winter, winding away for ever across the plains. With one hand she smoothed her green crepe dress over her thin, hunched-up knees. It was a smart frock. She had picked it herself from the catalogue. 'In shades of olive, rose, saxe and navy,' Mother had read out to her. 'Olive', she had said. And now here she was riding to the end of the world in the stiff new dress, and watering it with her tears. Was this the outcome of picking a dress in which to be happy? It showed you never could tell. How many other girls were riding up or down Australia at this very minute, weeping down the front of their Sunday finery?

The mailman's name was Tom. He was a thin, old man, with tea-stained whiskers and brown neck hanging in folds above his collarless, striped shirt. He glanced at Della uneasily. 'People haven't any right,' he thought, 'sending a kid out done up like that. Them buttoned boots. Not worn any more, buttoned boots aren't. Won't she have a time of it, landing at school in buttoned boots.'

'Don't you want to go to school?' he asked.

'No,' she answered.

'Come now. You've got to be learned you know. Lessons aren't so bad once you get the hang of them.'

'Oh, I can do lessons,' Della replied loftily.

'What have you got to go to school for?'

'I'm too bad to stop home any longer,' she told him mournfully.

'Bad! You don't look bad to me.'

'Don't I? Well, I am. I'm awful bad. I've given Mother nerves.'

'You don't say! What was it you did that was so bad?'

'Oh, everything—'

'For instance now?'

Della stopped crying to pick and choose amongst her misdeeds. 'I nearly got drowned in the dip last week,' she said.

'Pooh! Did that once myself,' replied Tom.

'Did you? What did everyone say?'

'Didn't say anything. They didn't know.'

'But how did you get out?'

'Brother of mine. Big bloke. Pulled me up the side.'

'Maybe if I'd had a brother——'

'They're handy when you're a kid,' admitted Tom.

'Then I fell in a tank through a hole in the top. Gee, it was terrible wet and dark——'

'You seemed to be set on getting yourself drowned.'

'I've nearly been drowned most ways,' replied Della modestly. 'In the creek and in the dam and once in the horse-trough.'

'Kind of slimy,' murmured Tom.

'Ugh.' Della shivered, then looked at Tom suspiciously. 'How do you know?'

Tom nodded his head. 'Me too, once.'

Della's eyes were bright with interest. 'Have you ever been bitten by a snake?' she asked.

'No. Have you?'

'Not quite, but I pulled one out of a log by its tail one day.'

'How was it it didn't bite you?'

'The devil looks after his own, Father said.'

'I don't know as how that was a nice thing to say to a little girl,' replied Tom thoughtfully. 'Not that I'm any judge. I was never a hand with children.'

'Didn't you have any children?'

'Lord love us. I had ten.'

'Well, how was it you never got your hand in?'

'I can't rightly remember. It was a long time ago and I was only home Sundays. A mail run used to be a mail run in those days.'

'They couldn't have been bad like me.'

'No worse or no better if you ask me. All kids are the same. Not good and not bad.' His hands tightened on the reins and the horses came to a stop. 'You just take a squint back that way. See them tin roofs. That's the last you'll see of your place for a few months. Now take a look over this way, across what we used to call the Prairie. That's McAlistars' stockrails in the distance. Shift your eyes a little to the north, that belt of timber, that's Munros'. And in front here, where the road curves by the river, that's Ryans'.

Big places, all of them. In the old days large families were reared on them. Nine kids here, ten kids there, twelve somewhere else and so on. Fine kids, too. What they didn't know about sheep and cattle and horses, wasn't worth knowing either. You couldn't ride this way this time of the morning then and see the plains empty on every side of you. Shut me eyes now and I can see them mad McAlistar boys galloping straight for me, putting their horses at the fences, standing straight in the stirrups, their black hair waving upright in the wind. Many's the time I threatened to tell their father of their wild ways. And what did they do? Laugh at me till the morning echoed, and I guess I deserved it.' Tom lapsed into silence and sat quietly looking at the reins in his thin calloused hands. Della watched him covertly. She'd heard tell of the McAlistar boys, too, but most of them had been dead before she was born.

'You were telling me something,' she said politely after a long time.

'Was I?' asked Tom and jogged up the horses. They ambled forward and broke into a brisk trot, spiralling the dust softly into the sunny air. 'I'm an old man and I forget.'

'About all the children who used to be around here once,' prompted Della.

'They're here no more,' said Tom.

'There's me. But I'm bad.'

'I guess I'd be bad too if I were the only little person for miles around.'

'Would you?' asked Della delightedly.

The buggy swept down a slope and clattered over the bridge. Murphy's lay behind them, its roof burnished silver under the sun. 'Time was,' said Tom sorrowfully, 'as five little girls used to wave at me over the bridge railing. They used to wear pigtails and pinafores.'

'I guess it was a long time ago.'

'It was, but it weren't so quiet. Australia's a quiet place these days. I'm not the kind to want to tell the young people anything. The young people always know best, I reckon. But it's sort of funny.'

'What's funny?'

'You, for instance. You're the only little girl for miles around. Four places that reared families and now among them all there's only you. What happens? You've got to be sent to school because you give your mother nerves, and your father—'

'I give him a headache.'

'There! Don't you think it's funny?'

'No,' said Della puzzledly. 'It's not funny. Not at all.'

Tom sighed. 'Perhaps you're right,' he said.

They went on endlessly over the winding road. Now and then a stunted gum flaunted its twisted trunk and abandoned curved leaves by the roadside, or a log hollowed greyly among the riotous spring grasses; they passed over culverts, and bridges that spanned waterless creeks. There was a wayside post office, into which Tom disappeared for three minutes, and a wayside pub that held him captive for fifteen. He came back wiping his whiskers. 'They want to put a car on this run now, but it's going to be over my dead body they do it,' he told Della boastfully.

Della wasn't interested.

'What's school going to be like?' she asked.

'School. Oh, school's all right. There's singing comes from there in the daytime. And at night the kids laugh and skylark on the lawns till bedtime. The sound floats across the creek and into the township. Look, that's the township, down there, Woonganattie. A good little town, Woonganattie. As up to the minute as they're made. My, the kids are going to laugh when you hit Woonganattie in those buttoned boots.'

'What's up with my boots?' asked Della ominously.

Tom looked at her. For the first time he noticed the set of her mouth and the light in her green eyes.

'I guess I was wrong,' he muttered. 'It's not the boots.'

'What's up with my boots?' repeated Della.

'Nothing. Nothing.' Tom averted his eyes hurriedly and whipping up the horses they fled along the curve that led into Woonganattie, drawing up with a flourish in front of the school. Della Parkins, of the Ten-mile Farm, Branch Creek, via

Woonganattie, had arrived at school. No princess of old was ever delivered with more aplomb to the austere way of learning, tin trunk, green crepe dress, buttoned boots and all. 'What's up with my boots?' said the light in her eye. She was twenty strong. The kids everyone should have had, but hadn't.

Under the House

'If you don't wait under the house,' said Rhoda to me, 'she won't come at all.'

Sybil, at Rhoda's side, jumped up and down and said, 'She won't come at all if you don't.'

'And for all we know,' said Rhoda, 'another visitor might come with her. So go on, Bea, wait under the house.'

'Go on, Bea.'

At the foot of the wooden steps, which jutted like a ladder from the verandah of the house, the three of us stood in the solid heat. We all wore dresses of brown and white checked cotton made by our mother. Rhoda, who now took me by the shoulder, was ten, Sybil was six, I was four. I deduce these ages from my knowledge that when I was five we left that house, which, with its land, was known as Mooloolabin, having been called after Mooloolabin Creek, the secreted stream on its northern border, to which our brother Neal, the eldest of us all, was allowed access, and we girls were not.

Rhoda's long greenish eyes, as I pleadingly sought them with my own, did not regard me with her usual love, her almost maternal concern, but were made remote and pale by the projection of herself into her intention, by the heat of her imagination. I had had much delight from my sister Rhoda's imagination, but that day I was resistant. I felt she and Sybil were deserting me. 'I want to wait here,' I said.

'Not in the sun,' said Sybil. When Sybil asserted herself, she sought the backing of our mother. 'Mum would be angry if we left you in the sun.'

'And you would go to the gate and peep. I know you,' said Rhoda, turning me by the shoulder. 'You can't peep from under the house.'

Rhoda could be coaxing and implacable at the same time. She kept hold of my shoulder as she and Sybil walked me alongside the cool breath of ferns under the steps, and then beneath the floor of the verandah. In the vertical slats encompassing that area which is still called, in Queensland houses, the under-the-house, there were two gaps, back and front, and through the front gap I was now ushered, or pushed.

'And no coming out and looking down the front paddock,' warned Rhoda, as she and Sybil hurried away.

I could never go alone into the under-the-house at Mooloolabin without an uneasiness, a dogged little depression. Unless it was raining, no lines of washing hung there, and nor did my father use that space for his workbench, as he would do in the suburban house to which we were soon to move, for at Mooloolabin all such needs were filled by the Old Barn, the first shelter my father's parents had put up on their arrival with their family from Ireland.

So, in the under-the-house at Mooloolabin, there was no extension of the busy house above except the meat safe hanging from a rafter, the boxes of wood cut for the stove, and the tins of kerosene used for the lamps. These objects, dull and grey in themselves, left dominant to my eyes the sterile dust at my feet, the rows of tall sombre posts with blackened bases, and the dark vertical slats splintering the sunlight outside. Broken cobwebby flowerpots were piled in one corner. From a nail in a post hung the studded collar of the dog Sancho, who had had to be shot, and from another hung the leg irons dug up by my grandfather, relic of 'some poor fellow' from the days when Brisbane was a penal colony.

Feeling imprisoned, put away, discarded, I stood where Rhoda and Sybil had left me, waiting for them to get too far away to detect me when I ran out and peeped through the garden gate. Above my head, in the big front bedroom where the three of us slept, I heard Thelma crossing the floor, slow as ever in her clumsy boots. Thelma came in from one of the nearby farms to help my mother. By the brief muffling of her footsteps, I knew when she passed over the red rug beside my bed. My discontent with the dust and husks of the under-the-house made the bedroom upstairs seem packed with colour and interest, increasing the attractions of the embroidered bedcovers, the lace valances over the mosquito nets, and that particular red rug, so memorable because of that dawn when Rhoda had plucked it from the floor and flung it over my shoulders.

We had both been wakened by the silence, the cessation, after so many days, of the hammers of rain on the iron roof. Warning me to hold the edges of the rug together, Rhoda took me by the other hand. We crept down the front steps, stealthily opened and shut the gate dividing garden from paddock, and ran splashing down the broad rutted track towards the road. It was a quarter of a mile (my brother Neal has since told me), but memory, woven tight though I know it to be with imagination, insists that it was longer, showing me, beyond correction, a flat extended prospect crossed by those two running figures, one backed with red wool, the other with her long tangled brown hair.

I had no goal in mind. My elation in the expanding daylight was enough. But when we reached the road, a goal was provided. Heard before seen, the gutter was running with water, a miniature torrent, over stones a cascade. Instructed by Rhoda, I squatted beside it. Still holding the edges of the rug together, I put the other hand, cupped, in the torrent. I shouted to find myself holding a ball of live water. I was amazed, enraptured by such resilience, freshness, softness, strength. I had never seen a swiftly running stream, had never seen the sea. Rhoda took no part, but stood at my side, satisfied with my delight, with the rewards of the entertainer, until she judged it time for the scene to change.

'Come on. Come back. Quick. Or they'll catch us.'

Who would? I didn't ask, but gleefully connived, adding my own hints of danger. The sun was prickling the tops of the uncropped grass as we ran back.

Now I heard my mother enter the bedroom above my head, her footsteps also muffled for a moment by the red rug. I could not distinguish the words she said to Thelma, yet could hear the swishes and soft bumps as they gathered up the mosquito nets and tossed them on top of the valance frames, out of the way before mattresses were turned and beds made.

My mother's presence in the bedroom stopped me from running out and peeping through the gate. The bedroom window overlooked the front garden and the paddock beyond, and if she happened to look out and see me peeping, she would call to me in her pleasant commanding voice and ask why I had been left alone. Rhoda, when delegated to mind me, was gravely warned never to leave me alone, because of the creek.

So I fidgeted and waited while her footsteps crossed and recrossed the floor above my head, brisk and staccato above the indecisive steps of Thelma. She wore neat black or brown shoes (polished by Neal) laced over the instep. Her parents had emigrated from England when she was three. Both she and Thelma wore aprons, Thelma's of opened-out sugar bags, hers of checked cotton.

They went at last, together, but left me in indecision by standing talking in the corridor near Neal's room. I would feel safe once they were in there, working. Neal's room, like the creek, was forbidden to me, though in this case the risk was to him. I had drawn a margin of red crayon round a page in one of his exercise books, in emulation of his own neat margins ruled in red ink. The consequent hullaballoo he raised is my strongest memory of Neal at Mooloolabin. Visually, all that reaches me is the misty outline of a thin figure, not much less than man-sized, standing in profile, with the hump of a school satchel on his back.

Neal and Rhoda went to the local school, where the teaching was deplorable and they were likely to get nits in their hair. 'Are we to bring up our children among ignorant cow cockies?' my mother sorrowfully asked my father, by lamp-light. They owned half an acre of suburban land, near a 'good' school. They could sell here and build there. But my father, though agreeing about the teaching and the nits, was reluctant to leave his father's meagre acres. From an office in Brisbane he instructed others how to farm, how to treat disease in stock and crops, but still hankered to return to farming himself, so that sometimes he would respond to my mother, 'Better a cow cocky than an office johnny.'

As soon as I heard my mother and Thelma go into Neal's room and begin work, I ran out from under the house and stood at the gate, looking through the palings. But no visitors were approaching, neither by the track across the paddock nor through the long grass from the clump of the she-oaks to one side.

But suddenly, under the she-oaks, I caught a movement, a flash of shining blue. I jumped to the bottom bar to get an unimpeded glimpse between the pointed tops of two pickets, eager to see again the exotic high gloss of that blue.

Instead, I saw a boy emerge, in grey and white. For a moment he stood uncertainly in the sun, then ran back into the she-oaks. As he was about the size of Curly Moxon, from the adjacent farm, who was moreover the only child within range, I thought that Rhoda and Sybil had been diverted, the game of visitors abandoned, myself forgotten.

The sun beat on my back and penetrated my green-lined sun-hat. I went back under the house and wandered drearily about. In Neal's room work was still going on. I passed beneath our parents' bedroom (which I remember only as white, starchy, insipid, and often locked) and wandered about beneath the other side of the house, longing for solace and company, tempted by the red and blue medallions on the kitchen linoleum, the blue and white crockery on the dresser. In the windowless living room, dimness would make magnetic the forbidden objects—the dark books on the higher shelves, the shining violin in its red velvet nest, the revolving top of the music stand. But the books on the lower shelves were permitted, and beyond the glass doors, on the verandah, stood canvas chairs with sagging mildewed seats wide enough to contain entirely my curled body.

Thelma and my mother crossed the corridor into the kitchen. I saw myself standing at the table (spoken to, tended, receiving something on a plate) and considered wandering out to the foot of the back steps and having a fit of coughing. Yet when I heard Thelma come out of the back door and embark on the stairs,

I instantly took off my hat and slipped behind the nearest post, my heart beating in that manner so interesting when Rhoda was with me.

Thelma took a plate of meat from the hanging safe. I was much thinner than the post I stood behind, and I held my hat crushed against my chest, but I must have moved; she must have glimpsed me as I had glimpsed that flash of blue under the she-oaks.

'Hey, who's that?' she called out. 'Beatie? Syb?'

Behind my post, I did not move.

'One of you, anyway,' concluded Thelma.

She turned and started up the steps. With one eye, I watched her feet rising between the treads. Then I ran over and seized the tennis ball lying among the boxes of wood and, by the time my mother's feet appeared between the treads, I seemed engrossed in bouncing the ball against a rafter, and catching it and bouncing it again.

'Beatie?'

My mother stood in the gap in the dark slats, behind her an expanse of sun-yellowed green and the weathered silvery timber of the Old Barn. The horse Pickwick was moving into the gap with his usual slow intent, cropping grass.

'Beatie, where are Rhoda and Syb?'

I resumed my game, saying they had just gone off for a while. She came and took the ball from my hand. 'Gone off where?'

'You'll spoil it.'

'Spoil what?'

'It's a game.'

'What kind of game?'

Did she know about our visitors? She had sometimes stunned Rhoda and me (though not Sybil) with her knowledge of our secrets. 'I have to wait here,' I said with crafty vagueness, 'till they come.'

She looked dubious, but gave me back the ball. 'You *will* wait here?'

'I promise.'

'And not go wandering off to the creek?'

'I promise. God's honour.'

'Your promise is quite enough,' she said with a tartness I noted but did not yet understand. She twitched straight the hat I had put on in such a hurry. 'And that sandal is loose. Here.'

As she had crouched, I extended a foot and submitted to this service I could have done for myself. Her hair was already grey, making her olive skin look fresh and polished, and kindling her eyes beneath their dark brows. At that time she must have been in her early forties, about the age at which Rhoda died. She rose to her feet to go. 'Mum?' I said.

'Yes, dear?'

'Ro won't get into trouble for leaving me?'

'Rhoda has been told again and again.' My mother turned and started up the stairs, adding, 'We will have to see.'

'We will have to see' meant that it was important enough to consult my father. I crushed the tennis ball between my palms, hoping that Rhoda would get off with a reprimand, chastisement being the alternative. As soon as my mother's feet disappeared, I dropped the ball and ran towards the front of the house. Warnings must be carried. But when I reached the ferns under the steps I heard the high affected voice of a visitor, and I stepped back under the house and waited.

Rhoda and Sybil came in from the sunlight. Rhoda wore a floppy-brimmed hat of shining blue crinoline and carried a little petit-point bag. Her cheeks and lips were pink with cochineal and her face white with what could only have been talcum, for our house was as unprovided with face powder as it was with lipstick and rouge. She held the bag at a dainty distance and swung her hip-less body from side to side, while Sybil, dressed as a boy in grey pants, white shirt, and a tweed cap, tried to trudge.

'You are Beatrice, I believe?' said Rhoda, in a high, bored drawl.

But I could not rise to my part. I was distracted not only because I had betrayed Rhoda's dereliction to our mother, but also by the evidence which Rhoda and Sybil presented of other punishable acts. It did not matter that the clothes Sybil wore were Neal's, made to fit by many pins and tucks, nor that the tweed cap was my father's. Forgivable also were Rhoda's apricot silk dress, court shoes stuffed with paper, and little handbag; all were play property, donated by my mother's youngest sister, who was modern. And Rhoda's hair was not really cut, but looped and pinned to the top of her head, so that beneath the crown of the blue hat it approximated the look of the bobbed hair she longed for, but which was denied to her though granted to Sybil and me.

No, it was the hat itself that alarmed me, the hat, the hat. Not even the modern aunt would have worn it. It was the type called by Rhoda a 'see-through' or 'actress' hat. It was in fact by these descriptions of hers that I recognised it as utterly foreign, and certain to fall into the category of the forbidden. It looked brand new, too, and attached to its band was a bright pink rose of stiffened cloth. And then, to divert my attention (if anything could) from the scandal and mystery of the hat, were the military medals and regimental colours pinned to Sybil's shirt.

Rhoda's body was moving from side to side in a stationary sashay. 'The little girl must be shy,' she remarked to Sybil.

'Why don't you answer, little girl?' gruffly demanded Sybil.

I cried out at Rhoda, 'Where did you get that hat? It's brand new. And those are Neal's medals.'

'Oh, no, no, no,' said Rhoda with a laugh. 'Those are Johnny's father's medals. But goodness, I quite forgot to introduce us. I am your sister Rhoda's rich friend Maisie Lemon. And this is Johnny Pumper.'

Overhead, Thelma clanked a bucket down on the bathroom floor. By my mother's footsteps I could locate her in the kitchen. Under compulsion not to shout, I wailed instead. 'It's not Johnny Pumper. It can't be. And where did the hat come from? It's *new*. And those are *Neal's medals*.'

On my forbidden forays into Neal's room I had seen how he kept those Anzac decorations in little separate boxes, each laid out on a piece of card, with a border ruled in red ink. I was aghast at

Rhoda's sheer nerve in having gone in there and simply grabbed them.

But Rhoda was looking at me with mild adult surprise. 'Who is Neal, little girl?' she asked. Sybil frowned and folded her arms.

'You'll get into awful trouble,' I said.

'What a silly little girl,' remarked Rhoda to Sybil. Sybil shook her head in wonder at my silliness. Rhoda turned again to me.

'Johnny's father was a war hero, killed at Gallipoli.'

For a moment I was arrested. At the nitty school there were many fatherless children. But the attraction of the word 'hero' could not conquer my distress, my confusion at having been presented with too many problems at once, so that I did not know which to tackle first. I said, trying to be calm, 'That is not Johnny Pumper. And how will you know the right boxes to put the medals back into?'

Sybil gave a gasp and turned shocked eyes on Rhoda. For a moment Rhoda's eyes responded in kind, but in the next moment she had converted her shock into the energy with which she patted her hair and thrust forward her painted face.

'Little girl,' she said with clarity, 'you are not very polite. I introduce Johnny and myself, and instead of saying how-do-you-do, you go on with all that bunkum. I will give you one last chance.' She indicated Sybil, who again folded her arms and set her feet apart. 'This is Johnny Pumper, and I am your sister's great friend, Maisie Lemon.'

Also with my feet apart, I flailed my arms around like a windmill. This reduced my impotence and anxiety, and enabled me to say, 'Those are stupid *stupid* names.'

Rhoda did not move nor speak. The hand with which she had indicated herself remained suspended in graceful limpness near her chest, a hostage to the game behind which she could withdraw into brief consultation with herself. For of course I was right. The names were stupid. Rhoda had reached that point in her creation where her characters had slipped away from her first flippant choice of names and now needed rechristening.

'It is true,' she said at last, 'that I am not Maisie Lemon.'

I pointed vehemently. 'And that is not Johnny Pumper.'

For very near the heart of my offendedness was Sybil's imper-sonation, which deprived me of the original Johnny Pumper, a foolish pigeon-toed redhead who resided in the sky and was often in serious trouble with his father. Whenever it thundered Rhoda said that Mr Pumper was roaring at Johnny, and demonstrated the terrified tumbling gait at which Johnny tried to escape his father.

'No,' admitted Rhoda, 'it's not Johnny. That's true, too.'

'Then why did you say it was?'

Rhoda's eyes were narrowing, her tone becoming threat-ening. 'I had an important private reason. It is something to do with the government. And now, dear—'

'And the hat!'

'And now, dear,' said Rhoda, in steady and overt threat, 'I have a little present for you.'

I was silent at once. After giving me a glare of warning, she opened the petit-point bag and took out a small parcel. Unwrapped, it disclosed three big lollies, tenderly pink, perfectly globular. We were seldom allowed sweets, and these looked as desirable as the kind bought in shops. I put my hands behind my back and stared at them. Sybil shuffled closer, licking her lips. I said, through my watering mouth, 'Where did you get the hat?'

'You may take one, little girl.'

Suddenly Sybil and I both plucked with greedy little hands at Rhoda's palm. Rhoda took the remaining sweet, raised her eye-brows as she examined it, then slowly and fastidiously put it into her mouth. With my own sweet still melting in my mouth, I flung both arms round Rhoda and clutched her tight.

'Ro! Tell me about the hat.'

'I shall never tell you about the hat,' said Rhoda blithely.

'Ro!'

'I shall carry the secret of the hat to my grave.'

One of Rhoda's eyes had a cast. It was extremely elusive. Like that flash of blue under the she-oaks, or the movement Thelma glimpsed of the child behind the post, you saw it, then doubted that you had. Even at her photographs I must look closely to detect it.

She can't have been physically punished—chastised—for leaving me unguarded, or I would have remembered it. At that time illness was taking hold of my father, stiffening and hollowing out his big frame, and sometimes, after he had made the long journey home from Brisbane, his coughing and exhaustion left my mother room for no other concern. In any case, it was certainly not one of those occasions when Rhoda, her face wet with tears, would hug me and whisper that she was going to run away, and would give me as a memento her cinnamon brown handkerchief with the clown embroidered in one corner. How we bawled and clung! The next day she would take the handkerchief back.

As for the medals, I recall only my mother saying, with absent-minded benignity, that no great harm had been done, and Neal could put the medals back himself, though Rhoda must promise not to take them again.

Maisie Lemon evaporated, as characters will when untimely exposed, and so did both Johnny Pumpers, the fake drawing the original with him. Rhoda's attempt to reinstate the original during the next thunderstorm met with my absolute stubborn and insulted resistance. Later, an attempt was made to bring on a Christabel Someone and a Cyril Somebody-else, but before they would take hold, we moved to the suburban house.

As soon as we moved from Mooloolabin it became Old Mooloolabin, by the same process as, when our paternal grand-parents moved from their first stout unornamented shelter, it became the Old Barn. At the new house we had less need of outright fables. Relations and our parents' friends could easily visit, other children lived nearby and could be asked home, and we could see, passing in the street or standing behind counters in shops, persons of sufficient familiarity, yet sufficiently strange, for Rhoda and I to graft upon their lives our frequently outrageous speculations.

And in a bush gully at the straggling end of the street ran a creek frequented by children my mother would have called rough or even undesirable. We did not have that child-tracking device, the telephone; I would say I was going to Betty's or Clare's and would go instead to hang around at the creek, keeping a slight distance, shy yet fascinated. I kept the creek secret even from Rhoda, feeling that it would lose value if it were not all my own. Rhoda, now that she had friends of her own age, also had her secrets, but in spite of our different preoccupations a special fidelity to each other remained, and for me, the hat remained a marvellous apparition, ever blue, shining, and brand new. At first I continued to beg Rhoda to tell me where she got it, losing my temper and pummelling her when she wouldn't; but she would only give her former answer, or would smile as if at private knowledge as she fended off my fists. And after a few months, though I continued to ask, my question—Where did you get the hat?—became cabalistic, something to sing into a silence, to murmur for the mystification of cousins, or to whisper for reassurance if we found ourselves isolated in uncongenial company.

Only once did the ground of our tacit deceit shift a little. Now that we lived near shops we managed to get more manufactured sweets than before, but I continued to remember as so excellent those three pink lollies that one Saturday afternoon, when my mother was out visiting, attended by Sybil, and Neal was helping my father in the garden, I persuaded Rhoda to show me how to make them. I watched closely as she mixed icing sugar, milk, coconut and cochineal, and as she rounded the mixture between sugared palms. She covered it briefly—a magician's gesture—before presenting it. And I saw that it was imperfectly round and slightly grey with handling. Yet there was Rhoda's face, as confident and triumphant as at Old Mooloolabin.

I took the lolly, put it in my mouth, and twirled away through the house until I reached the front verandah. Here I rotated quickly and silently, the better to meditate on what I had just learned. Rhoda came out and twirled nearby. The wide verandahs and smooth boards of the new house had set us dancing, and a Christmas play had given us our models.

Coming to a stop beside Rhoda, my speculation complete, my decision made, I advanced my right foot, curved my right arm above my head, and gazed upward at my hand. Rhoda, the backs of her hands forward, bowed low to the audience. Beneath our feet, in the under-the-house, the leg irons hanging from one nail, and Sancho's collar from another, were seldom noticed among all the stuff from the Old Barn. Outside in the garden Neal, now clearly defined as a tall youth with dark curls and a meritorious frown, walked in a strenuous slope behind a lawnmower. Gazing upward at my primped hand, I said to Rhoda, 'That hat wasn't new.'

'It's true,' she said, 'it wasn't *new*.'

Undefeated, she contrived to imply, by that slight inflection, that its lack of newness was a distinction, adding mystery, extending possibilities. Filled with delight, I flung myself twirling away down the length of the verandah. Once again, as when we ran back from the marvellous torrent, I fully connived, this time by silence, so that together, twirling at different parts of the verandah, we put my new-found cleverness in its place.

The Christmas Parcel

Christmas in 1935 would have been a dreary affair for the Churchers but for a parcel, more like a small crate, sent from the eldest, Maxine, in Sydney.

Maxine was eighteen, and had been away two years. The first Christmas she sent a card, and the Churchers were delighted with this and stood it against the milk jug on the table for Christmas dinner, which was baked stuffed rabbit, for they were plentiful, but money was not.

The next Christmas Eve the driver of the mail car gave several long blasts on the horn passing the paddocks where the Churcher children were standing, spindly legged among the saplings and tussocks, trying to invent a game to ward off disappointment that there would be no presents.

Their mother had warned them. Sometimes she cried softly as she told them, sometimes she was angry and blamed their father for his inability to find work, sometimes she was optimistic, indulging in a spasm of house cleaning, washing curtains and bed clothes, whitewashing the fireplace ready to fill with gum tips, and scrubbing the floorboards until they came up a grey white, like sand on some untouched beach.

Who knows, something might turn up, she would say as she worked. Her better off sisters in distant towns might send a ten shilling note in their Christmas cards, which would buy lollies, cordial, oranges, bananas, and raisins for a pudding, and be damned to Fred Rossmore who would expect it paid off the account, owing now for half a year.

The clean house gave her spirits a lift, as if they were cleansed too, and she would finish off the day by bathing all the children in a tub in front of the stove, adding a kettle of hot water with each one, washing their heads as well, and sending them out to sit on the edge of the veranda and share a towel, very threadbare, to dry.

Their old skimpy shirts and dresses were usually not fastened properly; it didn't matter, it would be bedtime soon.

The young Churchers would feel lighter in spirit too, sniffing at the soap lingering on them, although it was the same Mrs Churcher used to wash the clothes. They would look forward to fried scones for tea, and some stewed peaches, a small greenish variety, sour near the stone, eaten bravely while trying to avoid thinking of the sugar and cream that would make them so much more palatable.

Mr and Mrs Churcher were sitting on the woodheap when the mail car driver blew the horn through a cloud of dust.

'And a Merry Christmas to you too!' Mrs Churcher shouted. She was in a black mood, and Mr Churcher feared it and feared for the children, soon to trail home, not giving in readily to the futility of hanging stockings. While she angrily shuffled a foot among the chips, he looked at the children like stringy saplings themselves, some like small scarecrows, for they were playing a game with arms outstretched, their ragged old shapeless clothes flapping in the wind that had sprung up, kindly cooling the air after one of the hottest days of the summer.

Mr Churcher watched as one of them suddenly tore off to the track that led to the road. It was Lionel, racing hard and soon lost to sight where the track disappeared into a patch of myrtle bush. Mr Churcher was surprised at the energy with which Lionel ran. He worried about the children's not getting enough to eat, but perhaps they were doing better than he thought. Anyone who could run like that after tearing about all day must be suitably fuelled. He felt a little happier, and looked at Mrs Churcher, surprised she was not sharing this feeling. She looked over the top of their grey slab house at some puffed up clouds, but not seeing them, he was sure, for the clouds had a milky transparency and he foolishly thought they would have a softening effect upon her. But her face wore a cloud of another kind, dark and thunderous. There was mutiny in her dark eyes, creased narrowly, not wide and soft, not even her body was soft, but gone tight in the old morrocain dress, practically the only one she owned.

'I'll chop the head off the wyandotte,' Mr Churcher said. He was proud of his knowledge of poultry, and they had a cross breeding in their meagre fowl run, comprising cast offs from other, fussier, farmers who pitied the impoverished state of the Churchers.

They rented their old place from the Heffernans, who had built it as their first home when they settled on the land fifty years earlier. Heffernan bought an adjoining property as fortunes improved and used the old place to run cattle. Since the house wasn't fenced in it was difficult, due to wandering steers, to grow produce to feed the eight children, or seven, now that Maxine had gone.

Mr Churcher was in constant conflict with Jim Heffernan. He (Mr Churcher) considered the five shillings a week rent unreasonable; he was actually doing the Heffernans a favour living there in a caretaking capacity, stopping the house from falling into ruin. He never tired of pointing out the work he put into the fowl run, although he had actually stolen some wire netting from a bundle delivered to the roadside for the Heffernans to extend their kitchen garden. Mr Churcher saw the heap and sent Lionel for pliers to snip a length from a roll, which he was sure would escape the notice of the Heffernans.

Mrs Churcher was distressed to see the children a witness to theft, but put those feelings to one side when she saw Mr Churcher had made a good job of the pen and more eggs appeared, since the fowls did not continue to lay in obscure places like inside blackberry bushes and up hollow logs.

Mr Churcher was thinking now of making some reference to the fowl pen to expose (once again) a more commendable side of his character and get him into his wife's good graces, although he did not think there was much chance of this. He took up the axe and spat on the blade, rubbing the spittle along the edge.

'I'll chop off its head before they get here,' he said, seeing the ragged little army, still several hundred yards off.

'It'll be tough as an old boot,' Mrs Churcher said looking at his. Her own feet were bare.

'It'll make good gravy and there's plenty of 'taters,' he said, injecting cheer into his voice.

Mrs Churcher was going to say the dripping to roast the fowl in was needed for their bread, for they had not eaten butter in weeks, when a shrill cry made her look towards the myrtle patch on the rise.

Lionel came screaming out of it, like a brown leaf bowling along, aided by a strong wind, his feet beating so hard upon the earth, Mr and Mrs Churcher expected the vibrations to be felt at the woodheap. They stood up.

'He's bitten! A snake's got him!' she cried out. (Her mood would not allow for anything but the worst news.)

But Lionel had stopped yelling to fly towards the woodheap, with the other children breaking into a run and shouting wildly too.

Lionel flung himself upon his father. He was a skinny boy of eight, so red of face now his freckles had disappeared in what looked like a wash of scarlet sweat. His brown straight hair, in need of a cut, was standing upright in spikes or plastered to his wet ears. His chest, no bigger it seemed than a golden syrup can, heaved and thudded and his little stick-like arms were trembling.

'It's a parcel! The biggest I've ever seen! With Dad's name on it! Mr Barney Churcher, it says. And there's a million stamps!'

That was as much as he could say. He breathed and puffed and held his father's waist for support.

'Barney Churcher! That's me!' Mr Churcher said. He stroked down his front and looked up the track. 'That's me alright!'

Lionel sat panting on a block of wood. 'Oh, it's big, it's so big!'

The other children, all six of them, had reached the woodheap by this time. Ernestine was first. She was thirteen, and fairly fleet of foot too. 'The mail car left us a parcel!' she called back to the running knot.

'Big!' Lionel cried now, with enough breath back to stand and throw his arms wide. 'Take the slide for it!'

'Hear that boy!' said Mr Churcher looking at Mrs Churcher, watching for the film of ugliness to slide from her face. He's a smart boy and he's ours, was the pleading message in his eyes.

'Go and get whatever it is, and I'll stoke the stove, for God knows what we'll eat,' Mrs Churcher said, walking off. Mr Churcher told himself her body was softening up a little and that was something.

'Come on!' he called, sounding no older than Lionel, and seizing the rope attached to the slide standing on its end by the tank-stand. The slide flew wide with the great tug Mr Churcher gave it, and the children laughed as they jumped out of its way.

'Lionel should get a ride!' Ernestine cried. She was brown haired and slender like Maxine, and would be a beauty too.

'He should and will!' Mr Churcher shouted and steadied the slide while Lionel climbed on and made a small heap of himself in the middle. Raymond, who was fifteen, took a part of the rope, and like two eager horses with heads down, father and son raced ahead, the slide flying over the brittle grass, barely easing its pace up the rise.

The parcel was from Maxine. They knew her writing. The contents were enclosed in several sheets of brown paper, then the lot wedged into a frame of well spaced slats. Mr Churcher's name and their address was written on a label nailed to one side. Above the writing was a line of stamps, some heavily smudged with the stamp of the post office through which it was sent.

Mr Churcher and the children crowded around it, sitting by the slip rails, the gate long gone, unhinged by the Heffernans and used on their new property. All of them, even four year old Clifford who had ridden to the road on Ernestine's back, bent over the parcel, stroking the paper, patting the wood, jumping back to keep their eyes on it, as if it might disappear. How different the road, the sliprails, the deeply rutted track leading to the house, looked with it there. Leave it, leave it! cried part of the minds of the Churchers. Take it away and the emptiness will be more than we can bear!

'Come on!' called Mr Churcher, as if he too had to discipline himself to break the spell. He flung the parcel onto the slide and put Clifford beside it.

'Not too fast!' cried six year old Josephine, who was not as sturdy as the others and suffered bronchitis every winter. Ernestine took her on her back for she was no heavier than Clifford. She whispered into Ernestine's neck that the parcel might be opened before everyone was there, for Mr Churcher and Raymond were flying down the track with the wind taking all of Clifford's hair backwards.

'No, no!' cried Ernestine, breaking into an energetic jog. 'We'll all be there!'

Mrs Churcher was watching the track. 'There's Mum!' Clifford shouted.

'We got it!' screamed Lawrence, who was nine and between Gloria and Lionel in age. (Which accounts for all the Churcher children.)

Mrs Churcher watched, as if mesmerized, the parcel sliding to a stop at the edge of the veranda. Mr Churcher took his eyes off it to fasten them on her face. A crease at each corner of her mouth kept any threatened softness at a distance.

'From Maxine,' Mr Churcher said, pleading. He looked down on it beside Clifford, who was still on the slide reluctant to climb off.

'The stamps,' Mr Churcher said, touching them with his boot. 'Look what it cost even to send it.'

'It's a parcel for us for Christmas, Mum!' Ernestine said, brown eyes like her mother's begging with some impatience for her excitement.

'There'll be nothing to eat in it,' Mrs Churcher said. 'Toys and rubbish, I'll bet.' She looked hard at it, perhaps to avoid the eyes of the children, every pair on her she felt.

'I'll knock the old chook's head off!' Mr Churcher said.

'Not Wynie!' came in a chorus from most of them.

Gloria, who had wild red hair, sat on the edge of the veranda and held her bare feet. 'We can eat anything,' she murmured dreamily.

'Anything you'll be eating too!' Mrs Churcher said.

'It's soft,' Lionel said. 'So I reckon it's clothes. Clothes.' The light in his eyes ran like a small and gentle fire setting alight the eyes of the others.

'It's heavy, even for Dad,' Ernestine said. 'There's something in there for you Mum, I reckon. New plates, like you want.'

'Plates! They'd smash to smithereens. We'll be sticking with the tin ones!' Her eyes rested briefly on Mr Churcher. It's your fault they're only tin, they said.

Mr Churcher looked down on his hands wishing for a cigarette to use them, but he had no tobacco. There might be tobacco in the parcel. Yes! A packet of Log Cabin and papers. Two packets. Maxine used to sit on his knee and watch him roll cigarettes when she was a little thing, no more than two and the only one. They thought there would be no more and life would be fairly easy with the Great War finished and not too many joined up from Cobargo, thank heavens, to show him up. (He had no sense of adventure where war was concerned, no inclination to join in fighting.)

They had rented a little place in the town for six shillings a week (one shilling more than this and a palace in comparison, as he was always threatening to inform Jim Heffernan) and he had work, stripping bark, cutting eucalyptus, navvying on the road now and again. But the Depression came, and so did the children. Sometimes he went away for work, down as far as Moruya, coming home with his clothes in one sugar bag and some produce in another, oysters one time which the children had never tasted and passionfruit, which had been growing wild on the side of a mountain cleared for a new road. Mrs Churcher waited hopefully for him to produce some money, but there was always little of this. Once there was a pound note which the children looked upon as a fortune. It was a terrible disappointment to them when Mrs

Churcher gave it to Fred Rossmore to ensure credit for a few more weeks.

Mr Churcher was thinking of past homecomings now, looking at the parcel, still on the slide with Clifford, irrelevant thoughts, for they concerned Maxine, not likely to come home herself, spending all that money on things for them. The children saw. They found other things to look at momentarily, but in a while their glances strayed back.

'Did any of you find any eggs today?' Mrs Churcher said. (For the fowls had found means of escaping the pen and were reverting to former laying habits.) They had not, it seemed. They stared at the parcel, as if the remark had insulted it.

'Then what do we eat?' Mrs Churcher said. She did not look at Mr Churcher, who turned his face towards the paddocks, hard and dry like his throat.

'You'll find something, Mum,' Ernestine said. 'You always do.'

'There comes a time when you don't!' Mrs Churcher said. 'It's come at Christmas. A good time to arrive!'

Her voice, hard as the baked, brittle paddocks, gave the words a ringing sound like an iron bar striking earth it couldn't penetrate.

Mr Churcher longed for an early evening, for long striped shadows to bring a softness to the hard, harsh day.

'Will we have nothing for Christmas dinner?' Clifford said, huddled and dreamy on the slide. The others felt their bodies twitch, hungrier suddenly than they were before.

'Remember last year?' Gloria said. 'We had baked rabbit and Maxie's card.'

'This year is better,' Lionel said. 'We got the parcel.'

'If Mum will let us open it,' Gloria said.

Mr Churcher looked at Mrs Churcher's set face.

'It's not addressed to me,' she said.

Mr Churcher slapped a top pocket as if tobacco were already there. 'It's not Christmas yet,' he said. They looked at the setting sun filling the sky with salmon and peach jam and beaten egg white.

'We'll go into town and ask Fred Rossmore for some stuff!' He put his hands down and his face away. 'We can pay after Christmas.'

'With the endowment money I want for something for the kids to wear back to school!' Mrs Churcher cried.

The children wondered briefly which of them might have got something new.

'There might be things in here we could wear,' Lionel said, with a gentle toe on the brown paper.

'Come on!' Mr Churcher said, and began to walk rapidly off. He was taking the short cut through the bush, cutting off a quarter of a mile of road. Lionel ran to him and they both stopped and looked back to see who else was coming. Even with distance Mr Churcher's face showed he wanted Ernestine.

'I'll get my shoes and carry them!' she said, and was in and out of the room where the girls slept before Mr Churcher turned his head towards the track again. She ran to her father, not looking back.

Raymond, after standing with legs apart for a moment, holding his braces with fingers hooked in them, let the braces snap back into place and followed, racing past the little group to sit on a log some hundred yards ahead and wait, picking up bits of dead wood, rabbit dung and anything big enough to throw at nothing.

After a while they were lost to sight of those on the veranda, the gums and wattles and grey white logs, their roots exposed like a mouthful of rotten teeth, swallowing them up.

'I wonder what they'll bring back?' murmured Gloria. Clifford stood up and jumped off the slide, a very small jump he tried to make big. Lawrence moved along from his place on the veranda and put both feet on the slide.

'I'll stay with the parcel and mind it,' he said.

Mrs Churcher padded to the kitchen, opening the stove door and shutting it with a clatter of metal so loud Gloria came uneasily inside.

'Did you see that?' Mrs Churcher said, sitting with her knees spread, stretching the morrocain until you saw through it.

Gloria did not know what she should have seen.

'Him!' Mrs Churcher said.

That meant Mr Churcher. That much she did know.

'Do you know why he made Ernestine go?'

No, Gloria didn't. Her chest went tight. Perhaps Ernie was his favourite. She (Gloria) was ugly (she thought). She and Lawrence were the two heavily freckled and with bright red hair. She had only sandshoes and could not have gone to town on Christmas Eve. Not that she would cry about it. There might be shoes in the parcel for her. She sat forward in her chair so that she saw a corner of it, watched by Lawrence, Josephine and Clifford, close together on the veranda edge. She was sorry she had come inside. Her mother strode to the stove now and put in a piece of wood Gloria thought too big and green to burn properly.

When Mrs Churcher went back to sit by the kitchen table she put her head on her arm and began to cry. 'Rotten men!' she said, sitting up suddenly and wiping her eyes with her fingers.

A thin smoke began to bathe the log in the stove and some of it ran out of the stove door. 'You need some chips,' Gloria said, anxious that her father should not be blamed too harshly for the wood he had brought in. Perhaps it was the smoke that sent more tears running down Mrs Churcher's cheeks.

'He took her with him to get stuff easier from Fred Rossmore!' Mrs Churcher said. 'I know Fred Rossmore!'

Of course, Gloria thought. Everyone in Cobargo did. Even children knew he was a powerful man in the town.

'He's fond of girls,' Mrs Churcher said. That seemed alright in Gloria's view, except for the tone of her mother's voice (like an iron bar on hard dry earth it couldn't penetrate).

'Huh!' Mrs Churcher said, which would be interpreted as meaning that Gloria knew precious little about Fred Rossmore's character. 'Not for their good, but for his!' Mrs Churcher said.

Gloria pondered this. It appeared to mean that with Ernestine there, Fred Rossmore would not be handing out goods from his shelves. Her heart was troubled for her father coming in empty handed.

'He touches diddies if you let him,' Mrs Churcher said. 'And up here.' She touched the morrocain stretched across her chest.

Gloria considered this a small price for butter, bacon, tinned peaches and biscuits, but dared not say so.

'And that parcel,' Mrs Churcher said. 'I wonder about that.'

Gloria bent forward again to see it, the most innocent thing in all the world.

'To start with, a man would put it in a frame like that. Not her.'

I wish she wouldn't say her, Gloria thought. Maxine had the nicest name of them all. Ernestine was next. After that it seemed Mrs Churcher's selection of names was clouded by her worries at feeding and clothing them all. Gloria had been told an aunt, a sister of her father, had named her after the film star Gloria Swanson. Gloria felt a deep shame that she failed to turn out looking anything like Miss Swanson.

The green wood was filling the kitchen with smoke and Mrs Churcher got up and rubbed it into the hot ashes for it to burn quicker.

'For all we know a man might have bought what's in it. I reckon he did.'

'For touching her diddie?' Gloria said.

Mrs Churcher was across the room in a second with a slap across Gloria's face so violent, Gloria lost her balance on the chair, and the noise brought the three from the veranda running to the door. They returned almost at once.

'Only Mum whacking Gloria,' Clifford said, sitting down even closer to the parcel.

'There!' Mrs Churcher said, working the legs of the chair into the floor as she sat down. Gloria lay her face on her knee and cried softly. Mrs Churcher also cried. She allowed the tears to run in a great hurry down her cheeks, and when Gloria lifted her head she was surprised to see her mother's eyes quite bright and her face quite soft. She left her chair and went and sat on her knee. The fold of her stomach was soft as a mattress, and her shoulder a pillow, a fragrant fleshy pillow.

Mrs Churcher began to rock Gloria and this appeared to set them both crying without sound. When the others came in, tired of waiting by the parcel, Gloria lowered her face and Mrs Churcher turned hers. But they saw enough to make their eyes water too, so they moved together in a little bunch and stood giving all their attention to the stove fire.

Lawrence went off and returned with his old hat full of peaches. Gloria brought in some spindly wood that helped the green piece burn. Josephine asked if she could set the table, and Gloria, frowning on her, said to bring in some clothes from the line. The peaches were not as small and hard as those usually found, and when they had rolled to a stop on the table and Gloria brought a saucepan and a knife, Mrs Churcher said: 'You'd better let me.'

The four of them pressed their small chests against the edge of the table as they watched the peeling. It was a miracle of thinness, the furry skin falling from the knife like pale green tissue paper. Look at our Mum, said their eyes to each other. If only there was sugar to shake on some spoonfuls, without spilling a grain.

Mr Churcher brought some. Clifford, going out to check on the parcel, saw them come out of the bush and start their troop across to the house. He yelled as loud as Lionel when he found the parcel.

'They've got something!' he cried, flying inside then out again. The others followed except Mrs Churcher, who went to the stove with the saucepan of peaches and stayed there, making sure the lid was tight and they were on the right part of the stove to cook gently. Gloria allowed herself a brief look at the returning party, then when her mother had hung up the hessian oven rag, she went and hooped both arms around her and lay her face in the hollow of her breasts.

'They're coming,' Mrs Churcher said, not actually pushing her off.

'Sugar, Mum!' Lawrence cried, as Mr Churcher put the little brown bag on the table with two tins of herrings in tomato sauce, some cheese, cut into such a beautiful triangle it would be a shame to disturb it, and a half pound packet of tea and some dried peas.

'And look what Ernie's got!' Lionel cried, stepping aside from in front of her to reveal her holding clasped against her waist a paper bag. Everyone knew, by the little squares and rolls and balls making little bulges in the paper, it could be nothing else but sweets.

'Lollies!' screamed Clifford, and Mrs Churcher turned to the stove again and they saw by the neck showing under the thick straggling bun of her grey and black hair that she was crying.

'Stop crying, Mum,' Josephine said. 'Ernie will give you one.'

'They're for all of us to share,' Raymond said, in case anyone should begin to think differently. He sat on the doorstep with a glance backwards at the parcel, the afternoon sun making diamonds of the tacks holding the label in place.

'Mum's not well,' Mr Churcher said. He was standing in the middle of the room, one hand near his waist, the fingers spread as if a cigarette was there. 'She's having another one.'

Mrs Churcher sat and found the hem of her petticoat to wipe her nose.

'It'll be the last,' Mr Churcher said.

The eyes of the children said this might or might not be so. Ernestine put the bag of sweets at the end of the top shelf of the dresser and snapped the glass doors shut. She moved to the table and put the other things from Fred Rossmore's inside the food safe. Mrs Churcher's wet eyes followed her. Ernestine's old sleeveless print dress showed her round tanned arms, and her hair heavy as a bird's nest showed bits of her neck, pure white inside dark brown slits. She brought out flour to make fried scones, holding the bag between breasts beginning to pout. Tears ran over Mrs Churcher's cheeks as Ernestine lowered the flour to the table and took a mixing bowl from the crude shelf above her head.

'There's four boys and four girls in this family,' Lionel said. 'So the next one can be anything it likes.'

Mr Churcher was on a chair with his elbows on his knees. 'Well said, Lionel. A smart boy that.' He longed to be brave enough to look into Mrs Churcher's eyes. 'You're all smart, all of you,' he said.

Raymond looked at the kitchen floor boards between his feet. He had left school a year ago, and still had no job except for trapping rabbits in the winter and selling the skins, a great pile of them for only five shillings. The tips of his ears were very red.

'Next year things are going to be better,' Mr Churcher said. Everyone half believed it, and Mrs Churcher, as if her mind were on something else, took out the sugar, and carrying it to the stove tipped a little onto the peaches. They also watched her fold the top of the bag down letting nothing escape.

'Yes, I reckon next year will be better,' Mr Churcher said, putting a hand to a back pocket and moving it around there, as if making room for a packet of tobacco.

'And there's the parcel!' he said, throwing back his head suddenly like a terrier about to bark.

Josephine flung herself on Ernestine, as if the excitement was too much to bear alone. Raymond drew himself into a tight ball with his face crushed between his knees.

Lionel and Lawrence went to the veranda to each put a light foot on the parcel. Clifford climbed onto his father's knee, and Gloria leaned against her mother, with the cheek still red from the slap rubbing gently into her morrocain shoulder.

'And it's Christmas tomorrow!' Mr Churcher said, with his head back again and the words coming out like a terrier's bark. Out of the corner of his eye he saw Mrs Churcher's face start to go soft, then tighten again. She stood, taller than normal, he thought and looked across at him. Her eyes swept the children to one side. She might have sent them from the room, though all were there, faces tipped up at her, eyes begging for harmony.

'That parcel was sent from the place where the bad girls are,' she said.

There was a rush for the veranda to look at the parcel again. Even Mr Churcher screwed his head towards it, but turned it back almost at once. His face did not believe it.

Gloria had a vision of a great mass of girls with pinched and sorrowful faces and their skirts dented deeply in the region of their diddies. She looked at Ernestine, who was measuring flour into a bowl with lowered eyes, but there was nothing to be seen past her waist, which was level with the table.

'Make sure you sift that flour properly,' Mrs Churcher said. Then she sat on a chair with her head up, not looking at Mr Churcher. 'You can see on the stamps where it was sent from.'

'She could have given it to anyone to post. It's a great thing to lug herself,' Mr Churcher said.

'She never writes,' Mrs Churcher said.

'She was saving up for all those stamps,' Mr Churcher answered. He got up and went and pulled the label from the parcel, looking at the stamps and postmark.

'You see it? Kings Cross! That's where she is!' Mrs Churcher took the bowl of flour from Ernestine and buried her hands in it. She began to cry again.

Mr Churcher put the label in the dresser next to the lollies from Fred Rossmore.

'Now it doesn't matter where it came from,' Lionel said. Mr Churcher's eyes told Lionel this was wisely said.

Josephine went to Ernestine to cry into her waist. 'We'll never know what's in the parcel!' she wailed.

'That's right!' Mrs Churcher was mixing dough fast with a knife, her tears temporarily halted. 'We'll send it back!'

Josephine wept louder and Ernestine, checking that her mother's hands were covered with dough, and Josephine seemed safe from a blow, held her very tight.

Raymond went pale, and the freckles stood out on Gloria and Lawrence for their faces had a pallor too. Lionel, sitting suddenly beside Raymond, turned the sole of one foot up and looked long and intently on it.

'You're a cruel woman, Maudie,' Mr Churcher said.

The children were not as frightened by his words as they might have been. He called Mrs Churcher Maudie in the soft moments.

Mrs Churcher, her face clear of tears, tossed her head high and banged the frying pan on the stove. It was not a terribly loud bang though.

'I know my Maxie,' Mr Churcher said. He was seated with his elbows on his knees. He held two fingers near his face and the children looked hard to be sure he had no cigarette.

'Your Maxie!' Mrs Churcher said.

'Our Maxie!' Mr Churcher said. 'A good girl!'

'Yes, yes, yes!' came in different voices, Josephine's the strangest, for she was laughing as well as sobbing. Ernestine wandered outside, still holding Josephine, and Gloria followed.

Under the old apricot tree, from which the fruit had been early and hungrily stripped, they put their backs to the trunk.

'I'm frightened,' Gloria said. 'If there are gold and jewels in that parcel, what will we do?'

Ernestine tried to shrink the parcel in her vision. Mr Churcher came to the back door and filled the opening. Ernestine, Gloria and Josephine went and sat at his feet on the slabs laid on the earth to make a rough veranda.

Ernestine bound her body in her arms and rocked herself a little while, looking away to the mountains gone black to show the sunset up all the brighter.

She lifted her face, no less lovely, to her father. 'You open the parcel, Dad. Like Mum said, it's addressed to you.'

'By jove I think I might!' Mr Churcher said, loud enough to swing Mrs Churcher's face from the food safe to which she was returning the flour.

'I'm setting the table here,' Mrs Churcher said. 'Without any help as usual!'

'Leave the table setting!' Mr Churcher said. 'I'm bringing in the parcel!'

He didn't go through the kitchen but strode around the house with Ernestine, Gloria and Josephine clinging to him.

Raymond, Lawrence, Lionel and Clifford were around the slide when they reached it. Mr Churcher lifted the parcel as if it were a pillow.

'Our Dad's so strong!' cried Lawrence. They stepped back like a guard of honour for him to go to the kitchen. He laid it on the table end.

'Don't break the box!' Lionel said. 'It'll be handy for something!'

'A doll's cradle!' Gloria said. 'If there's a doll in there for Josie!' Her eyes then sent an agonized apology to her mother.

There was no doll in there. But Josephine forgot her disappointment when the paper was pulled away and Ernestine held up a quilt, a snowy white fringed quilt with the honeycomb pattern broken up with a design of roses as big as cabbages, and trailing stems and leaves.

'Look at that!' someone cried.

'For Mum's bed!'

'And Dad's!'

Ernestine put it tenderly on a chair.

'Towels!' shrieked Gloria as four were found inside and four sheets with only a little fraying at the hems.

After that came a tablecloth, heavy and white, a beautiful thing for Christmas dinner, and several tea towels.

Ernestine held them up against the open doorway and there was hardly any wear showing.

'Give them all to Mum!' Gloria cried.

Mrs Churcher was on a chair, hands on her thighs, trying to keep the hardness in her eyes.

Mr Churcher sat on the door step where Raymond had been. He was watching Ernestine, Gloria and Lionel come to the end of the parcel.

Lionel shrieked when he held up a single page with Maxine's writing on it.

'I hope you like these things,' she wrote, 'I work for these people called Pattens. Mr Patten has a shop. He brought home some new sheets and things, all in colours which is the new fashion now. Mrs Patten decided to give me the old ones, or some of them, to send to you. She is not paying me this week, but says she has a Christmas present for me. They are having roast pork for Christmas dinner here, but I would rather be having what you are.'

Lionel read the letter and everyone hearing it was quiet.

Mrs Churcher bent down to look into the stove fire, which was smoking again, so she needed to find her petticoat hem to wipe her eyes and nose.

Mr Churcher stared at his hands as if for the first time he realized they were holding nothing.

Mai

(BLACK BEAN)

Mai was the maker of flour which the women of her tribe used for the cakes they baked on the hot stones. She would travel far and wide looking for the seeds she pounded to make the flour.

One day, when Mai was out searching, she saw an old woman chattering and screeching to herself. Mai noticed that the old woman was carrying many seeds; she asked if she might have some of them. But the old woman was selfish and mean. She would never share with anyone outside her own tribe. All her tribe were like herself; and they did not gather their seeds, as Mai did, but stole them from the other tribes. They would paint themselves with many colours to blend with the surroundings, so that no one would see them when they came to steal.

Again Mai asked the old woman for some of her seeds, and again the old woman screeched at her and drove her away. Mai decided she would make a plan to punish the old woman. She watched where the old woman hid her seeds, and when she was asleep, Mai went to the place and took them away. Then she asked the honey ants to sit where the seeds had been.

When the old woman awoke and went to the place where she had left her seeds, she found the ants and became very angry. Screeching as loud as she could, she picked up the ants and bit them in half.

Then the ants punished both the old woman and Mai for stealing. They turned the old woman and all her many-coloured tribe into birds; and Mai they turned into a tree. Now, the old woman's tribe, still screeching, searches the blossoms of that tree for the lost seed which Mai stole from the old woman so long ago. And the flowers of the black-bean-tree are the same colours as the plumage of the mountain parrots that tear at them in their search for food.

ELIZABETH JOLLEY

My Father's Moon

Before this journey is over I intend to speak to the woman. *Ramsden*, I shall say, *is it you?* The train has just left the first station, there is plenty of time in which to contemplate the conversation; the questions and the answers and the ultimate revelation. It is comfortable to think about the possibilities.

The woman sitting on the other side, diagonally opposite, could be someone I used to know. A long time ago. In another place. Her clothes are of the same good quality, the same materials, even the same colours. It is the tilt of the head which is so remarkably similar. She looks like someone who is passionately fond of the cello. Fond of listening to the cello. I look at her hands and feel sure she plays the piano. When I look at her hands it is as if I can hear her playing a Mozart sonata or practising something from Bach. Repeating and repeating phrases until a perfection is achieved. I am certain, as I go on looking, that she plays Cyril Scott's *Water Wagtail*.

For some time now I have travelled by suburban train to and from the places where I work. This evening I am on the earlier train. I caught the earlier train on purpose even though, because of this, I arrive too soon . . .

The unfamiliar early train travels, of course, through the same landscape, the familiar. There is nothing remarkable in this. It is my reason for taking this train which makes the journey remarkable. The train stops at the same stations but naturally the people getting in or out are not the same people as those on the later train.

I sit staring out of the window at the same meeting places of unknown roads, at the backs of the same shabby houses and garden fences, at the same warehouses and the same smash repair yards and at the now well-known back of the metropolitan markets.

About once a week I catch the earlier train for a special reason. Every week it is the same. Every week I think that this time I will speak to her. This week I am on this train in order to speak to her. I always sit where I can see her from the side and from the back and I sit close enough to hear her voice if she should speak. I long to hear the voice, her voice, to know whether it is the same voice. Voices and ways of speaking often remain unchanged.

This time I almost brought the violin case with me though I am not now accustomed to carrying it when I go out. If Ramsden saw the violin case, if the woman saw it, she would remember.

'They're both in good condition,' the man in the shop said, 'both the same price. Choose your pick,' he said. 'Take your time.'

I could not make up my mind, and then I chose the violin case, the following week I went back for the camera case but it had gone. The violin case had once been lined with some dark red soft material, some of it was still left. I only opened it once and it was then I saw the remains of the lining. I carried the case whenever I went out.

The first time I saw Ramsden the sentry at the hospital gates had his bayonet fixed. He looked awkward and he blushed as he said; 'Who goes there!' Surprised, I told him my name and my identity card number, it was the middle of the morning and we were challenged, as a rule, only after dark. I supposed the rule must have been changed. A despatch from HQ, I thought, seeing in my mind the nimble motor cyclist arrive.

Ramsden, on her way out, gave a small smile in the direction of the violin case and I was pleased that I had bought it. On that day I had been at the hospital for seven weeks.

Two people sitting behind me are talking in German. I begin to listen to the animated conversation and grope for meanings in what they are saying in this language which was once familiar. I begin to recognize a few words: *eine Dame … keine Ahnung … langsam … Milch und Tränenbäche … mein Elend … zu grosser Schmerz … und so weiter*. But I want the words of cherishing spoken in German. I want those first words the child remembers on waking to the knowing of language. I wish now in the train to be spoken to as *du …*

The woman sitting on the other side is looking calmly out of the window. Naturally she sees the same things that I see. It is quite comfortable to know that I have only to lean over and touch her sleeve.

I never worked with Ramsden. I saw her sometimes in the dining room. There are several little pictures of her in my mind. The doctors called her Miss Ramsden. She did the penicillin syringes too. One nurse, usually a senior, spent the whole day cleaning and sterilizing the syringes and the needles, setting up the trolley, giving the injections and then clearing the trolley and cleaning and sterilizing and checking all over again. Whenever I passed the glass doors of the ward where she was I saw her in the sterilizing room seriously attending to the syringes and needles for the three hourly injections.

'Ramsden,' I said, 'this is the part we like isn't it? This part, this is it, we like this——'

'It's the anticipation,' she replied, 'it's what is hoped for and then realized,' she was sitting on the edge of her bed.

'This part, this——' I said once more. I pointed with one finger as if to place the cello somewhere in the space between us. 'This going down part,' I said, 'is the part we like best.'

Ramsden nodded. She was mending a stocking. Her stockings were not the usual ones, not the grey uniform stockings which were lisle and, after repeated washing, were hard to mend. Ramsden's glistened like honey. Dark, honey coloured stockings. Ramsden's stockings were silk stockings. She was oversewing a run at the ankle. Her sewing was done so carefully I knew the repair would be invisible. She had invited me into her room to listen to a record.

'Do you know why you like it?' she repeated an earlier question. The cello reminded me of her. How could I tell her this. I shook my head. Staff nurse Ramsden, she was senior to me. When she listened to music she sat with her legs crossed over and she moved her foot very slightly, I could see, in time to the music.

How could I speak to her about the downward thrust of the cello
and about the perfection in the way the other instruments came up
to meet the cello. How could I say to her that I thought someone
had measured the movement of the notes controlling carefully the
going down and the coming up in order to produce this exquisite
mixture. There were other things too that I could not speak about.
How could I say to her what I thought about the poet Rilke, about
his face and about how I felt when I looked at his photograph in the
book she had. She knew his poems, understood them. I wanted to
tell her that when I looked at Rilke's face I felt clumsy as if made of
wood. Even the way he stood in the photograph had something
special about it and when I read a poem of his to myself I wanted
to read lines aloud to her. 'Listen to this, Ramsden,' I wanted to
say, 'listen to this.'

> But hand in hand now with that God she walked,
> Her paces circumscribed by lengthy shroudings
> uncertain, gentle, and without impatience.
> Wrapt in herself, like one whose time is near . . .

There were other things too from *Orpheus*, but she knowing his
poems might have felt I was intruding. When I read Rilke everything I was trying to write seemed commonplace and unmusical,
completely without any delicacy and refinement. I never told
Ramsden I was trying to write because what I wrote was about
her. I wanted to write about Ramsden. How could I tell her that.

Later when she talked about the music she said the soloist was
innocent and vulnerable. She said the music was eloquent and that
there was something intimate about the cello. She was very dignified and all her words seemed especially chosen. I wanted her to
say them all again to me. The word intimate, I had never before
spoken to anyone who used this word. She said the cello, the music
of the cello, was intimate. Ramsden's discipline prevented her
from repeating what she had said. She continued to oversew her
stocking and we listened once more to the second movement.
When I listened to a particular passage in this movement I seemed
to see Ramsden walking ahead of me with great beech trees on

either side of her. Magnificent smooth trees with their rain soaked branches darkened and dripping. Then we were walking together, I imagined, beneath these trees, with the wet leaves deep round our ankles. Ramsden, I thought, would have small ribbed socks on over her stockings . . .

Lyrical, she said, the music was lyrical and I was not sure what she meant. She said then that, if I liked, I could borrow her records.

When I played the record at home my father, not knowing the qualities of the cello, asked if I could make the music a bit quieter. It was my day off, most of it had been wasted because I slept and no-one woke me. My father asked was there a piano piece. He said he liked the piano very much. I told him that staff nurse Ramsden played the piano and my mother said perhaps Miss Ramsden would come some time and play the piano for us. She said she would make a fire in the front room and we could all sit and listen . . .

Because I caught the earlier train I have an hour to spare before it is time for the clinic to open. The people who attend this clinic will be setting off from their houses in order to keep their appointments.

I walk to a bus stop where there is a bench and, though I am in a familiar place, I feel as if I have come to a strange land. In one sense there is a strangeness because all the old houses and their once cared for gardens have gone. In their place are tall concrete buildings, floor upon floor of offices, all faced with gleaming windows.

Some lit up and some dark. The buildings rise from parking lots all quite similar but unrecognizable as though I have never seen them before. Small trees and bushes planted as ornaments offer a few twigs and leaves. The new buildings are not at peace with their surroundings. They are not a part of the landscape, they are an imposition. They do not match each other and they have taken away any tranquillity, any special quality of human life the streets may have had once.

The Easter lilies, uncherished, appear as they do every year with surprising suddenness, their pink and white long lasting freshness bursting out of the brown, bald patches of earth at the edges of those places which have been left out from the spreading bitumen.

If I had spoken in the train I could have said, 'Ramsden,' I could have said, 'I feel sad. Lately I seem unable to prevent a feeling of melancholy which comes over me as soon as I wake up. I feel nervous and muddled and everything is accompanied by a sense of sorrow and futility.' Should I join a sect? I could have asked her. A cult? On TV these people, with a chosen way, all look light hearted. They dance carrying bricks and mortar across building sites. They jive and twist and break-dance from kitchens to dining rooms carrying wooden platters of something fresh and green neatly chopped up. Perhaps it is uncooked spinach. Perhaps it is their flying hair and their happy eyes which attract, but then the memory of the uneasiness of communal living and the sharing of possessions and money seems too difficult, too frightening to contemplate. In real life it won't, I could have told her, it won't be the same as it is on TV. Probably only the more sparkling members of the sect are filmed, I could have said this too, and something is sure to be painted on the spinach to make it look more attractive. Food in advertisements, I could have been knowledgeable, food in advertisements is treated before being photographed. I left the train at my station without another glance in her direction.

Perhaps the lilies are a reminder and a comfort. Without fail they flower at Easter. Forgotten till they flower, an unsought simultaneous caution and blessing.

It seems to me now, when I think of it, that my father was always seeing me off either at a bus stop or at the station. He would suggest that he come to the bus or the train just as I was about to leave. Sometimes he came part of the way in the train getting out at the first stop and then, waiting alone, he would travel on the first train back. Because of the decision being made at the last minute, as the train was moving, he would have only a platform ticket so, as well as all the waiting and the extra travelling, he would be detained at the other end to make explanations and to pay his fare for both directions. All this must have taken a lot of time. And sometimes in the middle of winter it was bitterly cold.

The strong feeling of love which goes from the parent to the child does not seem a part of the child which can be given back to the parent. I realize now with regret that I never thought then of his repeated return journeys. I never thought of the windswept platforms, of the small smouldering waiting-room fires and the long, often wet, walks from the bus to the house. I simply always looked ahead, being already on my journey even before I set out, to the place to which I was going.

The minutes which turned out to be the last I was to have with my father were at a railway station. When it was time for my train to leave even when the whistle was being blown my father went on with what he was saying. He said that if we never saw each other again I must not mind. He was getting older he said then, he was surprised at how quickly he was getting older and though he planned to live a long time it might be that we should not be able to make the next journeys in time. It is incredible that I could have paid so little attention then and the longing to hear his voice once more at this moment is something I never thought of till now.

He had his umbrella with him and when the train began to move he walked beside the moving train for as long as he could waving the umbrella. I did not think about the umbrella then either. But now I remember that during the years he often left it in trains and it travelled the length and breadth of England coming back at intervals labelled from Liverpool, Norfolk, St Ives and Glasgow to the lost property office where he was, with a kind of apologetic triumph, able to claim it.

The huge Easter moon, as if within arm's length, as if it can be reached simply by stretching out both hands to take it and hold it, is low down in the sky, serene and full, lighting the night so that it looks as if everything is snow covered, and deep shadows lie across pale, moon whitened lawns. This moon is the same moon that my father will have seen. He always told me when I had to leave for school, every term when I wept because I did not want to leave, he told me that if I looked at the moon, wherever I was, I was seeing the same moon that he was looking at. 'And because of this,' he said, 'you must know that I am not very far away. You must never feel lonely,' he said. He said the moon would never be extinguished. Sometimes, he said, it was not possible to see the moon, but it was always there. He said he liked to think of it as his.

I waited once for several hours at a bus stop, a temporary stop on a street corner in London. There was a traffic diversion and the portable sign was the final stop for the Green Line from Hertford. It was the long summer evening moving slowly into the night of soft dusty warmth. A few people walked on the pavement. All of them had places they were going to. A policeman asked me if everything was all right.

'I'm waiting for someone,' I told him. I waited with Helena for Ramsden.

In the end, in my desperation, I did write my letter to Ramsden asking her to help me to leave Fairfields, the school where I had gone to live and work taking Helena with me. It was a progressive boarding school. There was not enough food and I was never paid. In my letter I told Ramsden everything that had happened, about my child, about my leaving home, about my loneliness, about my disappointment with the school. I had not expected, I told her, such fraudulent ways. My poverty, I thought, would be evident without any description. After writing the letter I was not able to wait for a reply from Ramsden because, when I went to give notice that I wanted to leave in a fortnight, Patch (the headmistress) replied in her singing voice, the dangerous contralto in which she encouraged people to condemn and entangle themselves, 'By all means but please do go today. There's a bus at the end of the field path at three o'clock.' Neither she nor Miss Myles, after exchanging slightly raised eyebrows with one another, said anything else to me.

I sent my letter to the last address I had from Ramsden almost five years earlier. She was, she said then, still nursing and had a little flat where I would be welcome. Five years is a long time.

I told her in my letter that I would wait for her at the terminus of the Green Line. As I wrote I could not help wondering if she was by now playing the piano in concerts. Perhaps on tour somewhere in the north of England; in the places where concert pianists play. I tried to think of likely towns and villages. As I wrote I wept, remembering Ramsden's kind eyes and her shy manner. Staff nurse Ramsden with her older more experienced face—as someone once described her, and her musician's nose—someone else had said once. She had never known what there was to know about the violin case I carried with me in those days. It has been my intention always to tell her but circumstances changed intentions.

I begged her in the letter and in my heart to be there. Five years is a long time to ignore a kind invitation from someone. A long time to let pass without any kind of reply. With failing hope I walked slowly up and down the pavement which still held the dust and the warmth of the day. I walked and waited with Helena who was white faced and hungry and tired. Sometimes she sat on our heavy case on my roughly folded school winter coat. I tried to comfort myself with little visions of Ramsden playing the piano and nodding and smiling to Helena who would dance, thump-thump, on the carpet in the little living room. I seemed to remember that Ramsden said in the letter, sent all those years ago, that her flat was tiny.

'You'd best be coming along with me.' It was the policeman again. He had passed us several times. Helena was asleep on the folded coat and I was leaning against the railings at the front of an empty house.

The woman in charge of the night shelter gave me a small huckaback towel and a square of green soap. She said she had enough hot water if Helena and I could share the bath.

'She's very like you,' the woman said not trying very hard to hide her curiosity behind a certain sort of kindness. She gave us two slices of bread and butter and a thick cup of tea each. She handed me two grey blankets and said Helena would be able to sleep across the foot of the bed she was able to let me have for one night. The girl who had the bed, she explained, was due to come out of hospital where she had been operated on to have a propelling pencil removed from her bladder.

'The things they'll try,' the woman said, 'I or anyone, for that matter, could have told her she was too far gone for anything like that. All on her own too poor thing. Made herself properly poorly and lost her baby too.' She looked at Helena who was eating her bread and butter, crusts and all, neatly in what seemed to me to be an excessive show of virtue.

'There's some as keeps their kiddies,' the woman said.

'Yes,' I said avoiding her meaning looks. The night shelter for women carried an implication. There was more than the need of a bed. At St Cuthbert's the nurses had not been too sympathetic. I remembered all too clearly herding ATS girls into one of the bathrooms every evening where they sat naked from the waist down in chipped enamel basins of hot water and bicarbonate of soda. In her lectures the Sister Tutor reminded often for the need to let patients be as dignified as possible. The hot basins defied this. Many of the girls were pregnant. Some women, the Sister Tutor said, mistook the orifices in their own bodies. All this, at that time, belonged to other people.

Later my own child was to be the embodiment of all that was poetic and beautiful and wished for. Before she was born I called her Beatrice. I forgot about the ATS.

Grateful for the hot bath and the tea and the promised bed I addressed the woman in charge as Sister.

Did the Sister, I asked her, ever know a staff nurse called Ramsden. The woman, narrowing her eyes, thought for a moment and said yes she thought she had—now she recalled it. There was a Ramsden she thought, yes she was sure, who joined the Queens Nurses and went to Mombassa. I tried to take comfort from the doubtful recollection. Yes, went to Mombassa with the Queens Nurses. Very fine women the Queens Nurses. And one night, so she'd heard, the cook in the nurses' quarters was stabbed by an intruder. Horribly stabbed, a dozen or more times in the chest, the neck and the stomach. Apparently the murder was justified, brought on by the cook's own behaviour—him having gone raving mad earlier that same day. But of Ramsden herself she had no actual news.

I understood as I lay under the thin blanket that she had been trying to offer some sort of reply to my stupid and hopeless question. Perhaps the cook in Mombassa was often murdered horribly in these attempts to provide answers.

I tried to sleep but Helena, accustomed to a bed to herself, kicked unbearably all night.

Being at a bus stop, not waiting for a bus, and with the dusk turning quickly to darkness, I think of my father's moon. This moon, once his moon and now mine, is now climbing the warm night sky. It hangs in the branches of a single tree left between the new buildings.

The journey to school is always, it seems, at dusk. My father comes to the first stop. This first journey is in the autumn when the afternoons are dark before four o'clock. The melancholy railway crawls through water logged meadows where mourning willow trees follow the winding streams. Cattle, knee deep in damp grass, raise their heads as if in an understanding of sorrow as the slow train passes. The roads at the level crossings are deserted. No-one waits to wave and curtains of drab colours are pulled across the dimly lit cottage windows.

At the first stop there is a kind of forced gaiety in the meetings on the platform. Some girls have already been to school and others, like me, are going for the first time. My father watches and when the carriage doors are slammed, one after the other, he melts away from the side of the train as it moves slowly along the platform gradually gathering speed, resuming its journey.

I sink back at once into that incredible pool of loneliness which is, I know now but did not understand then, a part of being one of a crowd. I try to think of the moon. Though it is not Easter, my father said before the doors had all been slammed, there will be, if the clouds disperse, a moon. He pointed as he spoke towards the dome of the railway station. Because he pointed with his umbrella I felt embarrassed and, instead of looking up, I stared at my shoes. I try to think about his moon being behind the clouds even if I cannot see it. I wish, I am wishing I had smiled and waved to him.

In the noisy compartment everyone is talking and laughing. We are all reflected in the windows and the dark shadowed fields slip by on both sides.

The school bus, emblazoned with an uplifting motto, rattles through an unfamiliar land. The others sing songs which I have never heard before. There is no moon. The front door of the school opens directly on to the village street. Everyone rushes from the bus and the headmaster and his wife stand side by side in a square of light to receive us.

'Wrong hand, Veronica. It is Veronica, isn't it?' he ticks my name on a list he has. 'Other hand, Veronica. We always shake hands with the right hand.'

When I unpack my overnight bag I am comforted by the new things, the new nightdress, the handkerchiefs and the stockings folded carefully by my mother. Especially my new fountain pen pleases me.

Almost at once I begin my game of comparisons, placing myself above someone if more favourable and below others if less favourable in appearance. This game of appearance is a game of chance. Chance can be swayed by effort, that is one of the rules, but effort has to be more persistent than is humanly possible. It is a game of measuring the unfamiliar against the familiar. I prefer the familiar. I like to know my way, my place with other people, perhaps because of other uncertainties.

I am still on the bench at the bus stop. My father's moon is huge and is now above the tree in a dark blue space between two buildings. A few cars have come. I have seen their headlights dip and turn off and I have seen the dark shapes of people making their way into the place where my clinic is. They will sit in the comfortable chairs in the waiting room till they are called in to see me. Unavoidably I am late sometimes but they wait.

At the other place where I work there is a scent of hot pines. The sun, beating down on a near-by plantation all day, brings into the warm still air a heart lifting fragrance. There is a narrow path pressed into the dry grass and the fallen pine needles. This is the path I take to and from the railway station. Sometimes I suggest to other people that they walk on this path. The crows circling and calling suggest great distance. Endless paddocks with waving crops could be quite close on the other side of the new tall buildings. The corridors indoors smell of toast, of coffee and of hot curries. It is as if there are people cooking at turning points on the paths and in corners between the buildings. It is as if they have casually thrown their saris over the cooking pots to protect them from the prevailing winds.

From where I sit it seems as if the moon is shining with some secret wisdom. I read somewhere that it was said of Chekhov that he *shows us life's depths at the very moment when he seems to reflect its shimmering surface*.

My father's moon is like this.

But the game. The game of comparisons. Before meals at school we have to stand in line beginning with the smallest and ending with the tallest. The room is not very big and the tallest stand over the smallest. We are not allowed to speak and our shoes and table napkins are examined by the prefects. It is during this time of silence and inspection that I make my comparisons. Carefully I am comparing my defects with those of my immediate neighbours. I glance sideways at the pleats of their tunics and notice that the girl next to me bulges. In my mind I call her Bulge, her pleats do not lie flat, they bulge. She is tall and awkward, taller than I am and more round shouldered. I try to straighten my back and to smooth my tunic pleats. I can be better than Bulge. She has cracked lips and she bites her nails. I try not to chew my nails but my hands are not well kept as are the hands of the girl on the other side of me.

She has pretty nails and her hair is soft and fluffy. My hair is straight but not as greasy and uneven as Bulge's. Fluffy Hair's feet turn out when she walks. My feet are straight but my stockings are hopelessly wrinkled and hers are not. We all have spots. Bulge's spots are the worst, Fluffy Hair's complexion is the best. She is marred by a slight squint. We all wear spectacles. These are all the same except that Bulge has cracked one of her lenses. My lenses need cleaning.

It is the sound of someone closing a case very quietly in the dormitory after the lights have been turned off which makes me cry. It is the kind of sound which belongs to my mother. This quiet little closing of a case. My night dress, which she made, is very comfortable. It wraps round me. She knitted it on a circular needle, a kind of stockinette she said it was, very soft, she said. When she had finished it she was very pleased because it had no seams. She was telling our neighbour, showing her the night dress and the new clothes for school, all marked with my name embroidered on linen tape. The cabin trunk bought specially and labelled clearly 'Luggage in Advance' in readiness for the journey by goods train produced an uneasy excitement. My mother, handling the night dress again, spoke to me:

> *ein weiches reines Kleid für dich zu weben,*
> *darin nicht einmal die geringste Spur*
> *von Naht dich drückt—*

'Shut up,' I said, not liking her to speak to me in German in front of the woman from next door. 'Shut up,' I said again, knowing from the way she spoke it was part of a poem. 'Shut up,' I crushed the night dress back into the overnight bag, 'it's only a nightgown!'

When I stop crying I pretend that the nightdress is my mother holding me.

On our second Sunday afternoon I am invited with Bulge and Fluffy Hair and Helen Ferguson and another girl called Amy to explore a place called Harpers Hill. Bulge is particularly shapeless in her Sunday dress. My dress, we have to wear navy blue serge dresses, is already too tight for me and it is only the second Sunday. Fluffy Hair's dress belongs to her Auntie and has a red lace collar instead of the compulsory white linen one. The collars are supposed to be detachable so that they can be washed.

I wish I could be small and neat and pretty like Amy, or even quick like Helen Ferguson who always knows what's for breakfast the night before. Very quickly she understands the system and knows in advance the times of things, the difference between Morning Meeting and Evening Meeting and where we are supposed to be at certain times, whose turn it is to mop the dormitory and which nights are bath nights. I do not have this quality of knowing and when I look at Helen Ferguson I wonder why I am made as I am. In class Helen Ferguson has a special way of sitting with one foot slightly in front of the other and she sucks her pen while she is thinking. I try to sit as she does and try to look as if I am thinking while I suck the rounded end of my new pen.

During Morning Meeting I am worrying about the invitation which seems sinister in some way. It is more like a command from the senior girls. I try and listen to the prayer at the beginning of Meeting. We all have to ask God to be in our hearts. All the time I am thinking of the cross roads where we are supposed to meet for the walk. Bulge does not stop chewing her nails and her fingers all through Meeting. I examine my nails, chew them and, remembering, sit on my hands.

Between Autumn-berried hedges in unscratched shoes and new stockings we wait at the crossroads. The brown ploughed fields slope to a near horizon of heavy cloud. There are some farm buildings quite close but no sign of any people. The distant throbbing of an invisible tractor and the melancholy cawing of the rooks bring back the sadness and the extraordinary fear of the first Sunday afternoon walk too vividly. I try not to scream as I screamed that day and I try not to think about the longed for streets crowded with people and endlessly noisy with trams. It is empty in the country and our rain-coats are too long.

The girl, the straw coloured one they call Etty, comes along the road towards us. She says it's to be a picnic and the others are waiting with the food not far away. She says to follow her. A pleasant surprise, the picnic. She leads us along a little path across some fields to a thicket. We have to bend down to follow the path as it winds between blackberry and under other prickly bushes. Our excited talk is soon silenced as we struggle through a hopeless tangle of thorns and bramble. Amy says she thinks we should turn back. Bulge has the most awful scratches on her forehead. Amy says, 'Look, her head's bleeding.' But Etty says no we shall soon get through to the place.

Suddenly we emerge high up on the edge of a sandy cliff. 'It's a landslide!' I say and, frightened, I try to move away from the edge. Before we have time to turn back the girls, who have been hiding, rush out and grab us by the arms and legs. They tie us up with our own scarves and rain-coat belts and push us over the edge and down the steep rough walls of the quarry. I am too frightened to cry out or to resist. Bulge fights and screams in a strange voice quite unlike any voice I have ever heard. Four big girls have her by the arms and legs. They pull her knickers off as she rolls over kicking. Her lumpy white thighs show above the tops of her brown woollen stockings.

'Not this man but Barrabas! Not this man but Barrabas!' They shout. 'She's got pockets in her knickers! Pockets in her knickers!' The horrible chant is all round Bulge as she lies howling.

As quickly as the big girls appeared they are gone. We, none of us, try to do anything to help Bulge as we struggle free from the knotted belts and scarves. Helen Ferguson and Amy lead the way back as we try to find the road. Though we examine, exclaiming, our torn clothes and show each other our scratches and bruises the real hurt is something we cannot speak about. Fluffy Hair cries. Bulge, who has stopped crying, lumbers along with her head down. Amy, who does not cry, is very red. She declares she will report the incident. 'That's a bit too daring,' I say, hoping that she will do as she says. I am wondering if Bulge is still without her knickers.

'There's Etty and some of them,' Helen Ferguson says as we approach the cross roads. It has started to rain. Huddled against the rain we walk slowly on towards them.

'Hurry up you lot!' Etty calls in ringing tones, 'we're getting wet.' She indicates the girls sheltering under the red-berried hawthorn.

'I suppose you know,' Etty says. 'Harpers Hill is absolutely out of bounds. So you'd better not tell. If you get the whole school gated it'll be the worse for you!' She rejoins the others who stand watching us as we walk by.

'That was only a rag. We were only ragging you,' Etty calls, 'so mind you don't get the whole school gated!' Glistening water drops fly from the wet hedge as the girls leap out, one after the other, across the soaked grass of the ditch. They race ahead screaming with laughter. Their laughter continues long after they are out of sight.

In Evening Meeting Bulge cannot stop crying and she has no handkerchief. Helen Ferguson, sitting next to me on the other side, nudges me and grins, making grimaces of disgust, nodding in the direction of Bulge and we both shake with simulated mirth, making, at the same time, a pretence of trying to suppress it. Without any sound Bulge draws breath and weeps, her eyes and nose running into her thick fingers. I lean away from her heaving body. I can see her grazed knees because both her stockings have huge holes in them.

Before Meeting, while we were in line, while two seniors were practising Bach, a duet on the common room piano, Bulge turned up the hem of her Sunday dress to show me a large three cornered tear. It is a hedge tear she told me while the hammered Bach fell about our ears. And it will be impossible, when it is mended, she said, for her mother to lengthen the dress.

I give another hardly visible but exaggerated shiver of mirth and pretend, as Helen Ferguson is doing, to look serious and attentive as if being thoughtful and as if listening with understanding to the reading. The seniors read in turn, a different one every Sunday. It is Etty's turn to read. She reads in a clear voice. She has been practising her reading for some days.

'Romans chapter nine verse twenty one,' her Sunday dress is well pressed and the white collar sparkles round her pretty neck.

> 'Hath not the potter power
> over the clay, of the same lump
> to make one vessel unto honour
> and another unto dishonour?

And from verse twenty,' Etty looks up smiling and lisping just a little,

> 'Shall the thing formed say to
> him that formed it, Why hast
> thou made me thus?'

Etty minces from the platform where the staff sit in a semi-circle. She walks demurely back to her seat.

'These two verses,' Miss Vanburgh gets up and puts both hands on the lectern, it is her turn to give the Address, 'These two verses,' she says, 'are sometimes run together.'

'Shall the clay say to the potter why hast thou made me thus . . .'

Bulge is still weeping.

Miss Besser, on tiptoe across the creaking boards of the platform, creeps down, bending double between the rows of chairs and, leaning over, whispers to me to take Muriel.

'Take your friend out of Meeting, take her to . . .'

'I don't know her. She isn't my friend,' I begin to say in a whisper, trying to explain, 'she's not my friend . . .'

'To Matron,' Miss Besser says in a low voice, 'take Muriel.' I get up and go out with Bulge who falls over her own feet and, kicking the chair legs, makes a noise which draws attention to our attempted silent movement.

I know it is the custom for the one who leads the other to put an arm of care and protection round the shoulders of distress.

I know this already after two weeks. It is not because I do not know . . .

I wait with Bulge in the little porch outside Matron's cottage. Bulge does not look at me with her face, only with her round and shaking shoulders.

Matron, when she comes, gives Bulge a handkerchief and reaches for the iodine. 'A hot bath,' she says to Bulge, 'and early bed. I'll have some hot milk sent up. Be quick,' Matron adds, 'and don't use up too much hot water. Hot milk,' she says, 'in half an hour.'

I do not go back into Meeting. Instead I stand for a time in a place where nobody comes, between the cloakroom and the boot-room. It is a sort of passage which does not lead anywhere. I think of Bulge lying back if only for a few minutes in the lovely hot water. I feel cold. Half an hour, that is the time Matron has allowed Bulge. Perhaps, if I am quick . . .

The lights are out in our dormitory. I am nice and warm. In spite of the quick and secret bath (it is not my night), and the glass of hot milk—because of my bed being nearer the door the maid brings it to me by mistake—(it has been sweetened generously with honey) in spite of all this I keep longing for the cherishing words familiar in childhood. Because of the terrible hedge tear in the navy blue hem and, because of the lumpy shoulders, I crouch under my bed-clothes unable to stop seeing the shoulders without an arm round them. I am not able to weep as Bulge weeps. My tears will not come to wash away, for me, her shoulders.

At night we always hear the seniors, Etty in particular, singing in the bathroom. Two of them, tonight, may have to miss their baths. Etty's voice is especially noticeable this night.

> *Little man you're crying*, she sings.
> *Little man you're blue*
> *I know why you're crying*
> *I know why you're blue*
> *Some-one stole your Kiddi-Kar away from you*

The moon, my father's moon, is too far away.

The Easter moon is racing up the sky. The stunted ornamental bushes look as if torn white tablecloths have been thrown over them and the buildings are like cakes which, having taken three days to ice, are now finished.

Tomorrow is Good Friday.

Next week I shall take the earlier train again and, before the journey is over, I shall speak to the woman.

Ramsden, I shall say, *is it you? Much water has gone under the bridge*—this is not my way—but I shall say it carelessly like this—*much water has gone under the bridge and I never answered your letters but is it you, Ramsden, after all these years, is it?*

It's Raining in Mango

The day Billy Mumbler was released from gaol where he had done six weeks with hard labour for tax evasion, he had only the clothes he stood up in. They were jeans, a t-shirt, a torn cotton zip-through windbreaker, and thongs. He realised he would have to walk back to the coast. Seven months before he'd gone west past Flystrike for mustering in one of the stations. His earnings for the five months he was there amounted to only a few thousand dollars, but the taxation people were charging him provisional tax and he didn't understand.

How could Billy Mumbler be a tax dodger?

Boong, no-hoper, river-tribe layabout.

But while Billy was a boong, he was none of the other things.

After the mustering was over, the station boss offered him a few weeks' work fencing. He was a hard worker and the rest of the men liked him.

Billy had never seen a tax return form until the arresting copper showed him one and even though he could read and wasn't as stupid as whites wanted to believe, he was troubled by the questions.

The elastic clauses of the form stretched to mind's breaking point.

'It's like this, Billy,' the copper said patiently. And he tried to explain.

'Don't give me no explanation,' Billy said. 'Them buggers rooked me anyway.'

'What buggers?'

'Them station people. Shoulda been a whole lot more. A whole lot.'

'Well, I don't know about that,' the copper said. 'But you earn, you pay. It's the law. Anyway you must have something tucked away.'

'Sent it all home,' Billy said. 'Well, most, anyway. Anyway, how'd they know?' He marvelled. 'How'd they know about me way down there?' He meant Canberra or Brisbane or any big town he'd never seen.

'Gawd knows!' the copper said. 'They've got these computers now.'

Billy didn't know what a computer was. He asked other people. How'd they know?

He asked the visiting parson who came to him in the remand cell.

'Not a sparrow falls,' the parson said. He was low-Church Anglican and the answer was only what might have been expected.

At the magistrate's hearing Billy raised his hand before sentence was pronounced.

He was ignored for two minutes. His arm ached.

'Yes?' the magistrate snapped finally, looking at Billy over the tops of his glasses.

'How'd they know?'

'The computer,' the magistrate said.

Later a cellmate explained. They were jogging round the exercise yard of Flystrike gaol, melting in the vivid heat.

'Not a sparrow falls,' Billy said bitterly.

Now the copper was asking him, 'Got your bus fare? Train?'

Billy could not be bothered answering. He scowled into the hot morning.

'Guess you'll have to walk then,' the copper said, pleased with something in the day. 'It's illegal to hitch, mate, but maybe I'll turn me other eye.' He winked, showing how his eye would turn. 'Okay then, Billy. On yer way. You got a long walk.'

The sky was heavy with unshed rain. The morning lay over the town like a plastic skin.

Billy wandered down the road from the gaol and squatted under a tree to read again the one letter he'd received since he'd been inside. It had arrived only a few days before and already was grimy with rereading. He could see the copper standing back at the lock-up watching him.

> Dear Billy, his mum wrote, when you get out that place you better get back soon, you dads on a drunk charge at Eldon done workin on the raleway, no ones hear but me an Mable an we finding it hard no man about, enyway you Loo sez she not goin wait to long you come back, all reddy she got eyes goin fast that big Garfeel from the ilans. Not much fish in river till las week, plenty then you should see. Water come up real high. Them white folks other side was cut off. You come soon, you homes hear, its rainin in Mango.

He read it again. And then again. An ant started crawling across the paper. He crushed it neatly, folded the letter and shoved it back in his jacket pocket, wiggled his toes and contemplated the blacktop running out of town. Miles and miles and miles. Jesus, he thought, all that bloody way. While he sat there wriggling his toes and slapping at flies, the copper came sauntering along the road to him.

'Don't want to leave us, Billy?' The irony was as leaden as the weather. 'Sticking around, eh? Waiting for something to turn up? That's the trouble with being nice to you Murris. Never know when it's time to leave the party.'

Billy shrugged and looked at his feet and wiped flies away.

The copper frowned. He didn't want to start anything. He wasn't a bad fellow, it was just the bloody climate, and Billy had been no trouble. 'You'd better get going,' he advised, or they'd have to throw another charge at him, loitering, being without means of support.

'Get you on a vag charge, eh? I don't want to do that, not right now, not when you've just left us.'

'I'm goin' home,' Billy said. 'It's rainin' in Mango.'

The copper looked at Billy sitting there, a natural part of the dusty sidewalk. The morning sun munched ravenously at them both. 'Try the garage, mate, the last one as you leave town. There's a bloke going through to the Taws. Maybe he'll give you a lift.'

Billy uncurled and wandered off along the street past the hot little shops and the drinkers who'd started already because it was thirsty country, and was overtaken by the copper in his police car just before he came by the last houses. By the time he reached the garage, the copper was arguing with a truckie whose fridgemobile was pulled in at the bowser.

Billy stood back a little and the truckie kept looking over at him and he could tell his colour was being hated.

'Ah, come on, mate,' the copper was saying. 'He's a good black. Not a real crim. Just a tax dodger like the rest of us.' He winked. 'Never gave any trouble and anyway we want him out of town. Got enough on our plates already with Christmas coming up and the rodeo. Don't want any extra. You'll be doing us a favour. It won't go unnoticed, mate.'

The truckie strode over to Billy and fixed him with a hard stare. His eyes travelled up from Billy's thongs to his curly skull and then slowly travelled to the feet again.

'Okay,' he said at last. 'You can hop up. But no trouble, mind. First bit of trouble and you're off. I don't care where it is. Get it?'

'Thanks, mister,' Billy said. He moved round to the passenger side of the cabin and began to open the door.

'Wait a sec,' the copper said as Billy got one foot on the step. 'Jesus, I must be getting soft. Here, take this. You'll need some tucker.' He handed Billy a two dollar note.

The truck reached the Taws in under eight hours. The driver was a large hard-bodied man of few words. He drove relentlessly fast through claypan and bulldust country boring past coast-bound traffic as if it weren't on the road. Billy kept quiet. It was always best to keep quiet. Country and western tunes screamed out of the cassette player. The cabin throbbed.

As they drew near the Taws, rain began spitting on the windscreen, becoming increasingly heavy until it challenged the wipers. In the main street, gutters were awash.

'I'd take you on,' the truckie said, speaking round his cigarette, 'but I'm stopping off here for the night. Got to pick up another load of carcases. You'll be right here. There's plenty of stuff moving up the coast. Try at one of the pubs.'

Billy squeezed the note in his pocket and scuttled through the rain to a hotel directly across the road. On the veranda a couple of old-timers sat drinking and speculating on the weather, gummy men who watched him all the way up the steps and into the bar. Inside there were a couple of blacks down one end playing darts and four or five pensioners propped against the polished wood in the high malt-stinking gloom.

The barman paused in his wiping and regarded Billy.

Then he looked past him and spoke to the truckie who had come in behind, shaking water from his hair like a dog. 'What'll it be, mate?'

Billy waited patiently, rubbing one thonged foot against the other, practising easily the humility he had known all his life. When the truckie had taken his beer off to a corner, giving the tiniest of nods, Billy gave his order to the back of the barman's head.

The next minute he found a beer planked down in front of him and an extended hand open on the length of towelling dampcloth that stretched along the bar counter. The barman's hand seemed not to belong to his body, for his head was turned indifferently while he chiacked with a lounger at the other end.

Billy put his note in the hand, which closed over it, clamlike. He drank slowly. The room seemed filled with eyes. He licked his dark lips nervously. Finally he addressed the room at large. 'Any trucks goin' up the coast tonight?'

There was nothing but the violence of rain slamming the iron roof.

Then the mumbling resumed, aged quacks, grating coughs, nasal suckings, and the barman turned up the radio.

Billy gulped his beer down.

'What about me change, mister?' he called to the barman.

The barman pivoted slowly and fixed him with an outraged eye.

'You talking to me, mate?'

'I said what about me change?'

'I put it there, mate, right in front of you.'

They both inspected the sodden towelling.

'No you didn't.'

The barman turned back to the radio and began twiddling knobs.

'No you didn't,' Billy shouted. 'You didn't give me no change.'

The barman's eyes swept the room, gathered them all in and then rested on Billy.

'You calling me a liar?'

'Ain't no change there,' Billy persisted. 'You never put no change.'

The barman walked slowly over and leaned both hands on the bar and stuck his face up close to Billy.

'Think you better go, boy,' he said softly. His breath smelt of steak and Quickeze.

'I want me change,' Billy said.

'You know what you are?' the barman asked slowly and clearly. 'You're a troublemaker. A real troublemaker. You get yourself out of here quick-smart or I'll have the police in.'

Billy looked wildly around the room. The other blacks dropped their eyes. 'He never!' he cried. 'He never put no change there. You see him put me change?'

Unfriendly eyes regarded him. The truckie rose from his table and wandered over, casually, and took Billy's arm in an iron grip.

'Come on now,' he ordered. 'You better get going.' He steered Billy across the room and onto the veranda. The rain was so dense it screened the shops across the street. 'You won't win, mate,' he advised confidentially. The empty town was weeping in their faces.

'No way. You know what these places are. Better get going and write it down to experience. You'll pick up a hitch all right.' He gave Billy a friendly little shove. 'You get going before there's any trouble.'

Billy yanked his arm angrily away and walked into the rain.

It was storm-dark outside and the road out of town rippled like a river.

Billy swore, but under his breath, hitched his jeans, took off his thongs and stuffed them into his back pocket, and began walking.

The circle might be perfect, containing its own finality.

The nobility of the forward line his great-grandfather Bidiggi had advised in the tribal language he had almost forgotten now except as sounds that picked at his dreams. The forward line.

He was travelling that way through the rain to Mango.

Cars and trucks raced past his paddling figure and splashed him from head to foot. Not that it mattered. The rain had already obliterated the meaning of his thin clothes. Head down, eyes on sloshing feet, he merely slapped one bare foot after another.

No matter what, Billy thought angrily, no matter what he did! There was only this paralysing sense of effort in an imprecise landscape, like the heights of failure he'd clambered over and over again from the primary school where he never did well enough, to high school, for one year. His uniform fell to bits. Everyone laughed at him. 'Me mum hasn't an iron,' he explained to an uninterested form master. 'She got to wash me stuff in the river.' How the kids roared. Like animals, he hated, like fuckin animals, the lot of us, jus livin like animals, remembering his uncle gone rotten with the trembles, hands clutched round the flagons dropped illegally outside the mission grounds and sneaked in at night. His mum with her eyes blacked fighting that Loo, not a full-blood mum, once a pretty quarter-caste working round the hotels in Reeftown cleaning the rooms, and then got into trouble and went back up the coast, a kind of punishment till Charley Mumbler became her man, legally spliced by the minister and everything, one of them hearties with God-given muscle and strength and moral purpose that pervaded the should-be idyll of beach and jungle clearing like a holy stain. Billy knew about that stain. Just like the purple dye they used in the harbour to show where the crap flowed. He couldn't help grinning.

The grin cheered him. After two hours he understood only the technology of feet. His face ran like a beach.

About eight miles out a bunch of coast-bound hippies pulled up beside him in their van and took him on board, made space for him amongst the junk of tools, old timber and a dead bed-base that cluttered the tray. They took him all the way up the coast to Reeftown, huddled with three of them under their canvas tarp, and set him down on the esplanade in a night fluid with frogs and mosquitoes.

His big splayed toes met the sodden turf with the same indifference with which he'd padded through bulldust slush along the highway. He made his way to the public toilets, stripped off his soaking clothes and hung them over the cubicle wall to dry, and fell asleep in a coiled-up ball on the filthy cement floor.

Later, a hammering on the door woke him. The sound separated itself from the noise of the rain and he dragged on his wet jeans and pulled the door open to a brotherly bottle thrust in his face. There was a group of black men under one of the figs near the water and he sat with them and drank and slept again, curled up this time between the buttresses of the tree, a disturbed sleep of brawls and shouts and whacked flesh and curses and a police round-up from which he woke in a summer-sick cell, the bucket knocked over, the stench rising and a Palm islander moaning on the other board bunk. His windcheater and shirt were rolled up in one corner.

'Not good enough, Billy,' the sergeant in the cell doorway pronounced. 'We know all about you. Flystrike said you'd be on your way. There's nothing we don't know.'

'Like God, eh?'

'Now don't be cheeky,' the sergeant said, the morning at his back, throwing his shadow long and menacing over the concrete floor and the urine puddles. 'Come and get a mop and clean up that stinking mess.'

Later, sick with belly cramps, Billy walked out of town, cutting through cane fields to the railway line in the foothills. The morning rail-motor had already gone up the range and he had the track to himself. He still had his mum's letter in his pocket, unreadable now, the ink run and the paper wadded, but he could remember it by heart. Bits kept talking to him. *Not much fish in river till las week . . . water come up real high . . . its rainin in Mango.*

Halfway up the range, his thighs aching from striding sleeper to sleeper, the rain started again. A goods train lumbering by to Tobaccotown slowed enough near tunnel nine for him to slip over the side of one of the cars and when he finally reached the whistle stop near the settlement the afternoon had turned black with storm-cloud.

As he trudged up the track from the little station, guinea grass dragged at his knees. Behind him the river snarled white and the wind kept turning over the raggy banana leaves outside the shacks as if it were reading them. He wavered outside his own doorway, seeing lamp-flicker in the gusty air, hearing the kids screaming themselves stupid with delight at his homecoming, feeling the arms hugging and the hands touching, smelling his wife's hot familiar smell and his mother screeching, 'You got me letter? Got me letter?'

He pulled the damp wad of paper from his pocket and put it down on the table and wanted to howl.

'I got it,' he said.

Three days before Christmas late afternoon he was walking into Mango township with his father, the two of them head down to the blustering weather, when old Will Laffey from the place upriver overtook them and gave them a lift. The steam from their bodies rose in a fug in the closed space of the van. Wind spun branches and leaves across the road. The windscreen wipers tore at glass.

'Hello Charley, hello Billy,' Will Laffey said pleasantly. 'Christmas shopping?'

'Christmas drink more like it,' Billy said. He grinned.

'I hope you'll have one with me,' Will said.

'Okay,' Billy said. 'Loo's in town with the kids. She been shoppin'. I'm goin' to give her a hand, put her on the train back. Then I'm stayin' on a bit.'

The top pub was jammed with drinkers. Television screamed above the racket. They walked down the road to the bottom pub where Loo waited patiently, an old pram piled high with groceries. The two boys chased each other endlessly up and down the footpath. Will insisted that Loo join them, at least for one drink. She wheeled her rickety pram into a corner near the door and the three of them crammed in at a table amongst the timber workers and concreters from the new shopping complex.

'What'll it be?' Will asked. 'Beers all round?'

Outside the kids kept dodging up and down, squealing shrilly as the rain swiped at them, catapulting into the doorway and hurling themselves against their mother's hip.

'Them kids,' Loo complained.

The noise of the rain made talk difficult. The air was curdled with breath and steaming clothing. Billy tried to tell Will about the fencing job and gave up. He sat next to his father and stared gloomily into the rainwashed street, watching now and again the four big bruisers from the building site who were drinking at a table near the door. He felt strange, back in town again, strange sitting here with Loo, and the kids yelling outside, and his father and old Laffey. He kept seeing the hard earth of the exercise yard and not even the beer chased away resentment. The kids kept rushing in, rushing out, their yelps cutting through even the rain hammer.

After a while one of the concreters got up and lunged towards the door, roaring at the kids to shut up. The older boy stopped dead with fright, rolled his eyes, giggled nervously and went scooting up the path to the other entrance. But in a moment he'd forgotten and was back, wriggling and shrieking at the one spot where he could see his dad's and mum's comforting backsides. The concreter hoisted himself again from his chair and boomed, 'I said give it a rest, willya?' He reached behind him for his beer. 'You bloody deaf, kid?' Then he swung his arm forward in a vicious arc and launched his beer right into the boy's goggling face.

For a moment the kid simply stared, then his face, running with snot and beer, crumpled up and he yowled his head off. Loo squeezed her way out and began cuddling the boy while Billy pushed his chair back and slammed across to the other table.

'Watcher do that for, eh? Watcher do that for?'

The concreter eyed Billy insolently for a few seconds and then shoved past him with his empty glass, pausing to lean over Will. He breathed hard. 'Mate of yours?'

'Hey lissen! You lissen!' Billy was elbowing and pushing to get at the man, stumbling over legs, knocking chairs. 'You don't throw no drink on my kid, see? You don't do that to my kid.'

The Block pulled himself up and looked down on the runty little black bugger.

'You talking to me?'

'Yeah. You don't throw no drink on my kid.'

'Who're you saying "don't" to, mate?'

To cries of 'Shove it, Block! Siddown, mate!' he took a step forward, looming above Billy, his sun-spoiled mug, with its untidy collection of features, clouded. He gave Billy a contemptuous shove and the crowd stiffened, waiting for the fight. At the end of the room four Murris playing snooker stopped their game. Will found his protesting hand shaken like a fly off Block's arm. The whole room went quiet, leaving space to rain and television riot, and the pub owner, who hated blacks, but loved their welfare cheques, watched from behind the bar with horrible interest.

Billy went down with the table at his back. Drinkers cursed and grabbed at their glasses but Billy unknitted his feet, scrambled up and swung a punch that caught the surprised Block on the gristle of his nose.

'Why, you little shit! You lousy little black shit!'

He began to rave and hurled his drunkenness forward, lashing out brutally with clubbing fists. Billy ducked. One of the watching Murris slipped quickly through the stilled room and as Block, carried by his own air-punishing weight, lurched forward out of control, he shoved out a skinny leg and sent the concreter thudding over it to crash messily between the tables.

The pub roared: concreters, timber workers, blacks, even the barman, all hauled high on the relief of laughter. Billy began to strut a little as Block heaved himself up, fingering a pulped and bloody mouth. He strutted right out the door after Loo, heading for the safety of the train now with the kids, not hearing the screaming threats. Three drinking mates were holding Block back, dabbing at the ruined face, pouring another beer into him, drowning the rantings, the threats of payback, of punching the stupid black bastard out of his brain.

Old Charley Mumbler wished for invisibility.

Two days after Christmas a cyclone crossed the coast at Port, tore roofs off like wrapping paper, uprooted trees, flung boats about like driftwood and swung out to sea again. The Wet settled in. Mango's streets ran like drains. The shacks at the settlement leaked, dripped with damp and the timbers swelled. All that week the river, fed by creeks higher up the tablelands, kept rising, and just before the new year Billy Mumbler trudged back into Mango with his cousin Clive to relive his victory at the pub.

In the main street leftover bursts of wind were still socking water into doorways and against shop-window fronts. The little town had emptied of tourists. The cafes were closed, the outdoor tables stacked inside for the next season. Inside the pub there was a kind of animal cheer, the false and resonant babble of beery goodwill. Billy felt comfortable. He knew the faces. There was Eldon playing snooker with that Garfield. His old man was drinking out the back with Niggy Pawpaw. That Mister Laffey was reading the paper down one end. No kids. No Loo. No worries. He was walled by voices.

He wriggled his muddy feet and giggled at something Clive said and tossed his beer down fast and went back to the bar to buy two more.

'Set 'em up, Perce,' he said cheekily to the barman, and stood surveying the room while he waited. He even hummed a little tune. Then, in the angle of the front veranda of the pub, he thought he saw a familiar shape. He stepped away from the bar to see better, and, 'Christ,' he whispered, 'oh Christ.' Block. Grabbing the glasses, he slopped his way back to Clive. Bloody hell. 'Think we ought to push off after this, man,' he said. 'Them. They're back. Great load of 'em.'

'Oh bull!' Clive said. He was a husky young man, half islander. He lived for the day. 'I didn't walk all that way for nothing. Drink up an stop lookin, eh? You don't mean no trouble, they won't.'

'There's a mob,' Billy insisted. 'Fuckin great mob.'

'Okay,' Clive said. 'Well okay.' He pushed his glass aside and got up and went down the room and looked at the crowd of men drinking in the angle. There was a speculative and waiting tension about the massed force of blue singlet and belly-stretched shorts.

There was a lot of muscle exposure. Clive couldn't help grinning at his own thoughts as he went back to Billy. 'Pretty big, eh, some of 'em! Them blokes soon gunna have piccaninny!' He rolled about at his own joke.

'Shut up,' Billy hissed. 'Don't draw attention. Them blokes has come to get me, I bet.'

Just along from them was a group of hippies, all hair and beads and the confidence that comes from paid worklessness. They were packed into the space between old Will Laffey and the bar and Billy could hear some of them talking earnestly among themselves about a—what was it? A raid? Payback? He edged his chair back and listened, picking up rumour and part rumour of a hit pack organised in Reeftown now on its way up the range despite rain and rockfalls, to beat hell out of the boongs. He sneaked a look at the speakers and found faces that registered a lot of soft horrified expectation.

Billy fancied the room began to sizzle.

'You hear that?' he asked Clive. 'You hear that, eh?'

'Sit still,' Clive ordered. 'You bloody imagine.'

Billy felt as if he were stuck to his stool. He wanted to pee. His inside heaved.

But nothing happened. That was what was so terrible. Nothing happened.

The clock hands swung through the hours to closing time.

Billy was too drunk now to care or notice much but he saw one of the hippies go up to the barman and start talking hard, and when the kid returned he heard someone else say, 'Police. We need the police.'

Nothing happened.

Then another one plunged into the rainy dark and came back full of outrage. *The point-head*, he reported, meaning the copper, *had shoved his minimal skull round his minimal door and said it was his night off, for God's sake, and gone back to his video.*

They were all waiting for a move.

No move. Not yet.

When? How?

Billy felt his slaughtered forebears shiver through his bones.

Why didn't he leave?

The pub was not cosy, not anymore, but it had the props of cosy—light glinting on scores of bottles as if this earthly supply of liquor would never diminish; the unbroken roar of voices that told, even if they didn't communicate; the thud from a dartboard; the crack of snooker balls; the shudder of the television screen. The whole prism was a fortress against the darkness and rain.

It was a watering-hole and the animals were all there, playing Happy Arks, a cheer-spot on the map where people met and thought they loved people. Don't count the ones who'd left to stagger their drunken disappointment up Main Street or lurchers on the way to vomit their realised loneliness in washroom cubicles or just-reached doorways. Don't count any of that. Just look at these moving mouths, those grinning gawpers. It's cosy. You know it's cosy. But just wait, cobber, just hang in there till the barman calls time.

That old phrase came honeyed with malt. This evening it had an edge to it.

At a minute off the hour, the barman's smoky voice cracked out a couple of times and the wall of din split down its centre like dust-stiffened curtains as drinkers swilled recklessly, lousily frightened to leave a drop. There was general movement to the doors and isolated sounds surfaced as the telly was snapped off, the bar cloth slapped along the counter, the snooker balls and cues slotted away.

'Please,' the barman roared. He said 'Gentlemen.' He said 'Please.'

Billy smacked down his emptied glass and wobbled away without waiting for Clive. Will Laffey folded his paper and saw Billy Mumbler hesitate in the light on the sidewalk. In three minutes the room was almost empty except for two old blacks sitting deafly at the bar angle.

Charley Mumbler and Niggy Pawpaw were stranded by their bones.

'Okay you two,' the barman said. 'Speed it up.'

Billy was suddenly worried for his dad. He loitered out of the light nervously aware of a knotted mob on the footpath, men who watched the door, watched the night, noted the streaked yellow of departing car lights.

'What about your ole man?' Clive asked softly. 'You better wait, eh?'

The men at the doorway looked at them both, winkled them out in the shadows, then looked back into the lighted pub room just as Charley Mumbler and his tottering mate made their stumbling way to the door behind Will Laffey.

Suddenly, chaos.

Block headed the pack. He sprang from nowhere under the knowing eye of the barman, and, grabbing a stool, slung it whistling straight over Laffey's head at old Charley. A leg caught an eye and a scream, bounced off and crashed into the bar rail. The other men raced behind him mashing the air with sticks and fists. Billy saw his father fall beneath the surge of bodies, saw Will Laffey run at the mob protesting until a fist gummed his mouth shut, and saw Niggy Pawpaw drummed backwards under a table.

Sobbing, Billy ran back in to the flattened shapes and was felled by Block, who had been winding up another stool like a spring. He was a madman, screaming as he flailed. There were four bodies on the floor now and the kicking had begun.

Where was the barman?

Where were the police?

Clive had slunk off under the mango trees.

Billy kept coughing out bits of teeth and blood. Next to him a leg was doing fancy bootwork on Niggy Pawpaw's head. He could hear the slobbery whimpers of his father who sat up in the middle of the massacre, one wrinkled black paw to a gushing socket. His own fingers had been chopped across the knuckles and through smears of blood he saw bone glistening white through red. Nearby Will Laffey crawled along the floor out of the scrum, still clutching his paper and trying to pull himself up by one of the tables. Fists beat him back.

For five minutes it was a slaughterhouse. No one could stop the frightful impulse that seemed to have its own momentum. No one tried. Billy, his face mopping up dust and sputum and beer slop on the floor, played dead. There was still the contempt of boots.

Outside in the street came the sound of running, of feet slapping wet bitumen. Had someone tried for help again? At the thought of the law Billy Mumbler smiled savagely through blood.

By the time the sergeant arrived, uniform dragged on over pyjamas for this late-night show, the pack had pulled out, revving their trucks defiantly and blasting their horns before vanishing down the range road. The barman crept out from his bolt-hole in Gents and became busy with the evidence, lugging the flattened victims outside to prop them on the street wall of the pub. Billy Mumbler wrestled with him and was tipped in the gutter.

He looked up from all this slush and saw old Mister Laffey holding a hanky to his father's jellied eye. Their blood mingled and ran into mud. Niggy Pawpaw fell sideways from the wall and was beyond words.

Will Laffey broke off his dabbing and tried to tell the sergeant what had happened, stuttering and coughing.

'I'll do the talking,' Sergeant Purdy said crisply.

He straddled the path, feet wide apart. Carlights slid away behind the triangle of his legs. From inside the pub came the clatter of broken glass being swept into piles. The hippies from up the river near the settlement hung under the mango dark waiting for justice. Ignoring their protests Purdy ordered them on, and ignoring his order they stepped back a few paces until the darkness shielded them, then moved quietly back. The sergeant surveyed the scene, knowing he must be careful. He'd been warned this would happen a week before. When he spoke his voice was full of long-suffering at the trouble caused, full of the realisation of his own irony and unfairness. He saw the doctor paddle in from the rain, a thin young man new to the district and stuffed with stupid ideals. Already he was bending over Charley Mumbler's eye with an expression of disgusted compassion.

'Just a minute, you,' the sergeant said. 'I want to get the facts right.'

'This can't wait,' the young man said without looking up. 'He'll lose his eye.'

'I said hold it,' the sergeant ordered.

Billy raised his head from the gutter and saw the two men staring each other out, faces full of distrust.

'They near killed my ole man,' he squawked through broken teeth. 'Them bastards near killed him.'

The sergeant's self-hate reached out to settle on this mud-covered shape at the edge of the picture.

He looked from him to the men lying against the wall, at the doctor bending over them, and back to this mashed face struggling to stand by the side of the road, and he felt it had all got beyond him.

'All right, Billy,' he decided at last. 'All right.'

He wanted out of this quickly.

Pin a culprit, that was it. Pin one.

It was in order to blame a black skin. The easy way out.

'Can't keep out of trouble, can you? Lousing up everyone's new year. I'm taking you in for disturbing the peace and inciting to riot.'

There was a lot of windy laughter from the trees behind him. The darkness began scoffing as he went over to Billy and jerked him roughly to his feet. The handcuffs rattled.

Billy stood dumbly while the links clasped him. He looked over at the three against the wall.

The mauled faces, the pulped eye, the battered ribs.

The doctor's hands were moving gently from one man to the other.

He heard his father moan and saw old Laffey's face twist as he swallowed words. And even as the sergeant began to haul him off to the wagon, the dark under the mango trees came alive with movement as kinder shapes moved in from the rain.

The Woman at the Window

Sharon takes out another cigarette and reaches for the lighter. Today, before she catches sight of Mickey again, she is letting herself use the lighter; after that it's matches. It's one of her good luck things. She's standing by the kitchen window but she can't take anything in yet because she's still shaking. Thank God people in the other flats wouldn't have heard, they'd have left for work. When Mickey nags it's not a soft mosquito's whine like little Trace but a piercing shriek, as though she's belting the life out of him when she's never so much as laid a finger!

'*Stop* it, Mickey!' she hisses as the sound goes on echoing in her head. She touches her shin. It's going to come up like one of those purple and green eggfruits where the little devil's heel caught her. She grabbed his arms and pushed them into his jacket, the one he ripped but it's got his name and address pinned on to it, then she dragged him, roaring and flailing, out to the landing and gave him a push towards the stairs. 'Get lost, Mickey!'

She jabs out her cigarette in a dirty cup. It's matches now— she can see Mickey's bobbing blond head. He's fine, he's just fine. Arms spread like wings, he's scattering dozens of magpies as he runs across the grassed area between the flats and the church centre. His sneakers will be soaked again. There's a perfectly good path but he never remembers. Sometimes a man comes on a toy tractor and mows the grass. Squawk park, Sharon calls it, because of all the magpies flapping and clamouring and poking their beaks down one another's throats. Now Mickey's stalking one of the parent birds. Walking just ahead of him, the magpie keeps one eye on him and one on the grass. A young bird flies clumsily towards it, overshooting the spot and landing yards away. You often see them dead on the ring-road. Mickey watches the parent run to feed the squawking baby, then himself continues to run, arms outspread, towards the flats.

The magpies nest in the trees overhanging the flats and some of the residents feed them. It stops them swooping, the woman in the adjacent flat tells Sharon. She corners Sharon one morning on the landing, just as Sharon is about to close her door on Mickey and the woman is coming out of hers, all rugged up against the sharp August morning and clutching a plastic bag full of something soft and oozing. Chopped up rump, she tells Sharon. I feed them every morning on my way to work, she says. Sharon ducks her head; the memory of her voice is as sharp as a beak. They don't like mince, the woman says, even though Sharon's door is three-quarters shut by this time and Sharon is staring over her head at a patch of blue sky through the landing window. I told the butcher, I said That says something about the quality of mincemeat, doesn't it, when the magpies refuse to eat it!

Maybe if they swooped a bit more the ranger would come and shoot a few! Sharon says, or thinks about saying. After that morning she's careful never to open her door at the time the woman will be leaving for work, not even if Mickey's teasing baby Tracey or demanding more Cocopops or screaming till Sharon's head bursts.

I would ring the ranger myself, Sharon thinks, hurrying from the kitchen to the living room where the window looks on to the ring-road. There's a phone box below her, next to the pedestrian crossing. She sees herself going down the landing stairs and around the corner, pushing the phone box door inwards so that it folds up on itself like a trick door and dropping in the coin and then the ranger coming with his gun bang! bang! He's wearing his smart ranger uniform and Mickey's off playing somewhere—standing by the pedestrian crossing actually, with his hand on the button. In the palm of her hand Sharon feels the button beating like a slow loud heartbeat. *This time, this time, this time*. The baby's still asleep in Sharon's bed—no, Mickey's cot, it would have to be Mickey's cot—and she says I have always admired that uniform would you care for a sherry . . . only she drank the last of it yesterday, the empty bottle is lying in the middle of the living room. Would you care for cocoa?—cocoa because she's run out of tea and coffee, milk too she remembers, Mickey had that on his Weetbix. Sure would! says the ranger. I have always admired—

But, Sharon interrupts herself, how can I make that call, is it still twenty cents or has that box been changed over to thirty? Is it twenty or thirty? And she twists her hands in her nightdress until it tears a bit more at the shoulder.

Mickey is still standing by the crossing. He's swinging his foot at a dead baby magpie squashed on the ring-road. Every time a car rushes past, its feathery wings blow as though it is trying to fly. Traffic is heavy at this time of day. A stream of cars is pouring into the car park. The signal on the crossing changes from red to green, then back to flashing red. As people from the flats hurry across towards the shops and offices of the city centre, Sharon feels a surge of excitement. The drunks on the seat under the elms at the corner have been shopping already. This time the big man is carrying the paper bag. He places it carefully between his feet, opens a bottle, drinks and passes it to the next man. One of them starts to laugh, bending over then flinging back against the seat until the others join in, rocking backwards and forwards and slapping one another's shoulders. The big man grabs the bottle and, putting it to his mouth, holds it high like a trumpet.

Stragglers on the crossing scurry as the light turns red. Mickey isn't with them. He is pushing between the road edge and the low hedge in front of the flats. Sharon can see his bright curly head through gaps where the hedge has died. His hair curls on to his shoulders. It's like Rob's, soft and fair, whereas Tracey's is straight and dark like Peter's. It was Peter who helped her get this flat. You're in luck, he said. Most people have to wait months. Peter doesn't know about Tracey. He's working in Sydney now.

Sydney, Sharon says, and feels a wave of nostalgia, bitter as morning sickness. Sydney is sand and tanning oil, and your thoughts melting like ice-cream. Sydney is your sisters chatting up that lifesaver with gold crucifix while you whined Come *on*,

Mum'll get mad! Sydney is voices creeping out from broken tiles,
Come on Shar, come and have fun!

That's how she met Rob.

It was at a party. There was this guy down from Canberra. He
kept looking at Sharon. His eyes felt like hands on all the secret
parts of her body. Sharon's friend shouted Who wants a ride on
Rob's Harley Davidson? When it was Sharon's turn she heard herself saying Why don't we keep going till we get to Canberra? And
that made Rob laugh. You'd like Canberra, he said. Sharon pic-
tured a big white Parliament House surrounded by enormous
houses with curving drives and huge green lawns where no one
had to fight over whose turn it was in the bathroom. They
arranged to meet the next day. It was Rob's last day in Sydney. She
rode on the back of the Harley to a quiet beach where Rob had to
see some people. Sharon thought she would go mad if Rob didn't
keep touching her. She thought Rob's friends looked at her funny;
didn't talk much in front of her. Try this, Rob said, passing her a
thin, damp cigarette. They lolled around on the sand while the sun
roared over them like gigantic surf.

When she returned home her mother, who thought she had
gone into town for the day to look for a job, took one look at her
and screamed 'Don't start telling me a pack of lies, I don't want to
hear it!' The next morning, while her parents were still sleeping,
she stuffed what clothes she could into her old school haversack,
stole her mother's collection of Charles and Di fifty cents and
climbed out the bedroom window. She could have walked out the
front door but the window seemed right. At Central Station she
bought a ticket to Canberra and she hasn't been back home since,
not once, nor written, nor telephoned.

'God, this place!' Sharon exclaims, turning her back to the
window. There's a new stain on the sofa, and Mickey must have
been at the horsehair again; it looks like a little animal trying to
hide. Panic washes into Sharon's throat like a scummy tide. There
are dirty cups on the TV and the floor and the window ledge; how
long is it since she washed up? She seizes the empty sherry bottle;
rushes cups, plates, baby's bottles and cutlery into the sink and

pours cold water on to them; snatches up all the clothes she can find on the floor, over chairs, under the bed, never mind if they're dirty or not, she doesn't waste time looking—out, out they go, into the laundry basket. If they all go in, she thinks, if they all go in and nothing falls on the floor, *it will mean good luck*. Sometimes she starts off the day like that: if a bird flies past the window . . . if Mickey wakes up before Tracey . . . or it might be the other way round, if Tracey wakes up before Mickey. The last thing, Mickey's bottom sheet that he's wet again, catches over the edge of the basket and hangs there, touching the floor but not falling either. Sharon's hands are shaking. She needs another cigarette. She's using the lighter again; that's allowed now.

She's down to her last cigarette. There are plenty in the shops of course, milk too, cigarettes and milk and the other things she has run out of. The shops are on the other side of the car park and the car park is on the other side of the ring-road and the ring-road is on the other side of the window.

She has to look away quickly.

She looks away to the seat under the elms where the drunks sit all day, even on days as nippy as this. She has a little fantasy that Rob is one of the men on the seat. Any minute now he'll look up and wave and she'll lock the kids in the flat and go down and they'll share the bottle or maybe a joint. It couldn't be any colder under the elms than it was in midwinter in the garage where she lived with him when she first came to Canberra.

Canberra was ace! Rob took her to parties and gigs or they stayed in the garage smoking hash or cuddled inside two sleeping bags zipped together, or they went over to the house where people were always coming and going. She never got to like the people in the house as much as Rob did; they talked to him more than they talked to her, and they'd bang hard on the bathroom door when she was daydreaming under the shower. Also they never cleaned up the kitchen, no one did except herself. Annie, the other girl who lived there, said 'I don't know why you do it.' But then Annie ate out; she could afford to, she had a job. She was a very bossy sort of girl, *woman* she insisted on, she hated *girl*. Sharon took to going over to the house only when Rob did, even if she was bursting, or she'd hang on till night time and squat behind the fig tree.

At first she thought it was just her body playing a trick. Rob said 'Shit! You'd better do something, Shar!' and gave her six brand-new fifty dollar notes but she kept on putting it off, she got scared, she kept hoping her mother would write or just turn up on the doorstep.

And after a while it was too late.

Rob left Canberra soon after that. He said it was what they'd been talking about all winter, him and her zipping north on the Harley. He's back again now; he does the lighting for a new theatre group just up the road at Gilmore House. He stopped her one day when she was taking the two kids for a walk. 'Sharon! How's things?' He's even been around once with a huge Mickey Mouse for Mickey, but when Sharon said 'What about some regular maintenance, Rob?' he laughed. He said 'You must be joking, Shar. I'm on the dole.'

It was Annie who put her up to saying that to Rob. Annie's at Gilmore House, too—she's part of a women's video group—and she drops in at the flat sometimes for coffee. She drinks dandelion coffee so she brings her own. When Annie's talking, Sharon nods and says Yes Annie, yes, I should do that. Get your name on the waiting list for a three-bedroom house, Annie tells her. You're eligible, Sharon. When Rob cleared out, Annie persuaded her to move into a group house with Annie and two other women. They brought Sharon cups of herbal tea to stop the retching. They massaged her temples. They showed her articles about the effects of smoking on the developing foetus. They said You'll have no trouble getting family day care, Sharon, that's one of the good things about Canberra. They wanted her to have the baby in the house, with everyone helping. They began to talk about 'our baby'. One afternoon, while someone was practising on the drum kit in the living room, Sharon got dressed, climbed out her bedroom window and caught a bus into the city. In the city she did two things: she booked herself in at the hospital, and put her name down for a government flat.

The baby Tracey totters into the living room. She is crying, slow tears washing down her face like July rain. She's wearing an old pyjama coat of Mickey's, so shrunken her arms stick out to the elbows. Her napkin and plastic pants have fallen around her knees. Sharon pulls the napkin right off, then, sliding down to the floor, takes Tracey on to her lap and puts her to her breast. Tracey is going on two but if Sharon tries to wean her she cries, not a full-blooded roar like Mickey but *NnnnNnnn* like an insect trapped against glass.

When Mickey was starting to walk Sharon tried to get a job, a cash-paying job so as not to lose her pension. Cleaning, she thought. Annie wrote her a reference. Every Saturday she bought the paper and went through the Sit. Vac. The first lady she cleaned for asked her not to bring Mickey again, 'little sticky fingers', so Sharon left him locked in the flat until one of the neighbours said that he cried and Sharon got scared of losing her lease. The second lady worked during the day so there were no worries there about taking Mickey. Sharon had the run of the house, she could dream out the windows, gaze all she wanted to at the pool and the green lawns, the mountains so sharply blue they made her throat wobbly, the fledgling new Parliament House with its seven cranes bending down to it. Two days after starting work for this lady she received a letter: 'Dear Sharon, Here is the money I owe you. I shall not be requiring you again. I wonder my dear if you have ever cleaned a house before? . . .' Sharon cried. She thought Tracey wasn't show-ing yet but the third lady said 'You wouldn't be able to continue for long, would you dear? I'm very sorry but I really want somebody permanent.'

'It isn't fair!' exclaims Sharon, putting Tracey aside and jump-ing to her feet. 'It's all right for you!' she declares, staring at some-one invisible across the room. Tracey tugs at her nightdress. Sharon snatches her up and thrusts her back at the breast, but the baby twists her head away. 'Go down on the floor then, Tracey.'

Sharon sighs. She can't get over how different girls are from boys, even kids this age; when Mickey's inside he's at her all the time for Weetbix, fizzy drinks, biscuits. 'What *is it*? Stop it, Trace. You want more titty? Trace?' She bends to lift her once again, but the child slips out of her grasp and, going into the centre of the room, falls to the floor and cries, *NnnnNnnnNnnnNnnn*.

Sharon goes into the bedroom and closes the door. Stumbling over Mickey's broken tip-truck she discovers her purse on the floor, so she sits on her bed and empties it into her lap. She puts the five dollar notes on one side of her, the two on the other; with the coins she makes a little tower that keeps falling over. After a while she peeps into the living room. Tracey has fallen asleep on the floor. Sharon picks her up and puts her into Mickey's unmade cot and pulls the side up. Heaving at it, she feels sick again, and remembers that she hasn't eaten anything since yesterday lunchtime when she finished off Tracey's tin of chicken dinner.

At the back of the refrigerator she finds a slice of bread in its plastic wrap. As she eats it at the kitchen window she watches the magpies in squawk park. The parent birds jab at wriggling things underground, run to the nearest begging baby, run run run on legs like twigs to find more food. The baby birds never stop pestering. Sometimes one of the parents gets really bossy, standing over a young one until it shuts up and pretends dead. Suddenly they all fly up into the trees. Two women and two children are coming along the path. One of the women is much older than the others; she is the mother, Sharon decides. The other woman is younger than herself, a girl really. She is swinging a man's purse by its wrist strap, and she isn't wearing a parka and beanie and scarf like the others, but a coat patterned with great zigzags of colour, red, green, purple, gold.

The mother and the girl in the coat stop to study a map. Visitors to Canberra, Sharon thinks, just as she once was. A tiny bubble of excitement surfaces. The visitors disappear around the corner of the flats and she runs to the living room window to see them reappear by the road. While they are waiting for the green light she tiptoes into the bedroom and pulls on her Indian cotton dress and the thick woollen cardigan that Annie gave her. She stuffs her money into her purse and hurries back to the living room window. There they are; the light has turned green but they are not crossing. *They are waiting for her.*

Mickey is still there between the hedge and the road, jumping on the spot as the cars fly past. Maybe he's said something cheeky to the family because as Sharon watches, the mother pushes past the hedge and speaks to him. He's not listening to her at all, jump jump jump, Sharon can feel those little pounding feet in the back of her head. She'll give him such a belting if he's been swearing again! The mother edges back to the others and speaks to the younger woman, the girl. The two kids giggle. The girl looks up at the flats, shrugs, then, although the light is angry red, turns her back on her mother and stalks across the road. Sharon feels a hot wave of excitement. When the light is green again the others cross too. Now the mother and the girl seem to be having a row. They stand under a pine tree in the car park, the woman pointing back at the flats and waving her arm and the girl staring down at the ground, sulky, Sharon decides, a bad girl, a runaway. Finally the woman and the two kids return to the lights and cross back towards the flats, but whether the girl follows Sharon doesn't wait to see. She didn't want the family to fight. She goes into the kitchen and puts the kettle on. There's a used teabag on the sink. Maybe she can squeeze another cup out of that.

The doorbell rings. That little shit Mickey! She's told him once this morning that there aren't any biscuits. He must have found a chair somewhere to stand on to reach the bell, must have dragged it all the way up the stairs. RRRing! RRRing! If she doesn't answer, if she holds her breath and pretends he's not there, he'll give up and go away again. She hears him ring the bell of the flat next door. The cheek of him! Pity the magpie woman's not home to give him what for.

She lights her last cigarette and goes back to the living room window. The family is still there, all four of them. They're standing by the phone box with their heads together. The mother goes into the box and after a moment comes out. The girl fiddles about in her purse and hands her something, a coin, Sharon supposes, then moves off a short distance, not quite part of the family and not separate either. The mother goes back into the box, leaving the door open. The two kids poke their heads in and listen.

Mickey's down there with them. He's holding on to his doodle and if she's told him not to do that once she's told him a dozen times. Before she has time to think she hurries downstairs and around the corner.

'Get upstairs, Mickey.'

The mother is out of the phone box by now, the two kids at her elbows.

'Excuse me,' says the mother. 'Is this your little boy?'

The girl in the bright coat comes a bit closer at this.

It takes Sharon a few moments to register that the woman is speaking to her. 'Yes?' she says, abrupt and questioning at the same time. The girl and the mother exchange glances. The two kids are staring. Sharon pulls Annie's cardigan closer.

'He was standing—jumping—right on the edge of the road,' the mother begins, as though she wants someone, the girl, Sharon, to take over.

'Yes?' Sharon repeats.

'The traffic's pretty heavy,' the girl tosses in, then stares over everyone's heads as though it's all nothing to do with her.

'And that pretty fair hair,' the mother adds eagerly, so that Sharon thinks Bet you wish yours was still the same! 'He's so pretty,' the mother is saying, 'I mean I didn't realise he *was* a boy until I saw his name pinned on his jacket.'

'And his address,' puts in one of the kids importantly. 'That's how we knew . . .'

Sharon says slowly, 'Well what business is it of mine?'

Their faces crumble with doubt. 'But he *is* your little boy?' the girls asks, while the mother echoes 'This is your mummy, darling?'

'Of course he is!' Sharon snaps. She adds 'He knows about going out on the road. I've told him. He knows.'

'But playing right on the edge——!' says the girl, while the mother cries 'Such a pretty child! Someone might snatch him away!'

'Then it'll be his own fault, won't it?' retorts Sharon. 'If he goes out on the road it'll be his own fault. He knows!' cries Sharon. 'I've told him! You get along upstairs, Mickey!'

On the stairs she keeps saying 'Hurry up, hurry *up*, Mickey!' She adds, 'You heard what those two said—if you're not a good boy someone will try to steal you!'

'*They* did!' wails Mickey. 'That old lady tried to steal me! She told the other one she would give me to a policeman. She said Come on, Mickey, you come with me. And the other one said—'

But what the runaway girl said Sharon doesn't hear, because at that moment the door bell rings again. This time, since it can't be Mickey, she opens it at once. On her doorstep, sharp as a mountain peak in his trim blue uniform, stands a policeman.

He says to Sharon, 'Good morning, madam. Madam, we have just had a phone call . . .'

Sharon stands at the window. Through a dead patch in the hedge she can see Mickey clearly. As his mouth opens she stuffs her fingers in her ears but she can't shut out the bellow. Her hand is still smarting. As though he can't bear to stand still Mickey jumps up and down, up and down, jump jump jump jump, he jumps out into the road and as a car whizzes by he jumps back against the hedge, out and back, out and back—

This time! shrieks a voice in Sharon's head. *This time, Mickey, this time, this time!*

Butterfly

I used to get hysterical about not having a penis. They had a penis and I didn't. I didn't have anything—I was a nothing. I had nothing and they had something. My brother stood up and peed in the bath.

Dad had a giant's penis. Dad got cross because I worried that I didn't have a penis. Dad told me how he'd been a little girl and somehow he became a man, but he didn't explain it very well. Mum said when she'd wanted a baby she'd found me in a strawberry patch. There were strawberries down the bottom of our backyard and I couldn't stop eating them. There was a strawberry on the end of Dad's penis. I had a dream that I sat in the strawberry patch and stuffed strawberries up my butterfly so I'd grow a penis. Mine was a butterfly because it had pink wings that opened—a butterfly with that pink bit down the middle.

Sometimes I'd go off with some girls and we'd get other kids' little brothers. They were so little they had to do everything we said. We'd pull their pants down and have a good look.

My cousin Henry made me look at his penis and it had a pinker strawberry than Dad's. He showed me how to make it stand up. He held his penis and rubbed it up and down and then it got really stiff and stood poking at me like somebody's finger telling you off. Henry's mother had died, and he lived with Grandma. She had a floral carpet and he'd stand there peeing all over it, saying he was watering the flowers. Grandma's carpet stank of pee. Grandma said Henry's mother, Aunt Ruth, had hated her big mammary glands so she went on to slimming pills and got addicted and starved herself to death.

When my brother played with his penis, Mum said she'd take him to the hospital to have it cut off. I thought I could have his penis stitched on to me. Because I wanted to have a penis, Mum said she'd take me to England. There was a special hospital in England where they turned girls into boys.

I got hysterical because they wouldn't let me play football or sell newspapers. There were a lot of things they wouldn't let me do because I wasn't a boy. When I had a dress on, I couldn't climb trees, because I'd show my pants. When I went hysterical, I'd bang my head against the wall. Then I'd be so tired I'd just lie on the bed and pick at the wall, and all the little marks became like birds in the sky.

It was all right to see Dad and my brother without clothes on, but you weren't allowed to be curious. My brother and I used to have a bath together. He'd have the good end and I'd have the plug end with the taps in my back. Once my brother made me sit on the lavatory, and then he peed between my legs.

When Grandpa lay on the beach in his pyjama kind of shorts I looked up the leg and saw a big slug hanging out: Grandpa had a sort of big white slug glued to the side of his leg.

I'd look at men's pants to see if their penis hung on the left or the right side. If they were left-handed their penis was usually on the right side; if they were right-handed they put it away on the left. If you had a penis, you had to flick it to knock the drops off after you'd peed. Dad told my brother to do that.

Once I was in Dad's shed watching him working on the car. And I wanted to go to the lavatory, but I wanted to watch him, and I waited one more minute, and then it came out in my pants. It was hanging there like a sling, and Dad had to take me inside and empty it out.

I was always making lavatories. I'd dig a hole by the strawberry patch and put grass in it. Then I'd pull my pants down and sit in the hole. I liked the soft feeling of the grass.

They started building houses in the paddocks behind our backyard. I'd hold myself in all day, and when the builders went home I'd take some lavatory paper into a house and do it in the big pipe where the lavatory was going to be. But Mum caught me and hit me. She said I was dirty-minded. She was always cleaning me out with Laxettes and worm pills and Velvet soap—Mum would cut off a bit of soap and grab me and jam it up my bottom.

Melva Button lived next door. She had a false tooth and was sort of rabbit looking. And she had a turned-up nose, like it was pushed against a window. The Buttons were Church of Christ and Mr Button used Tally-Ho cigarette papers, but Dad didn't smoke. Melva had Rock Hudson pinned on her bedroom wall, and the Buttons had lots of Pat Boone records. Mr Button had a new FJ Holden and a motorbike with a sidecar and a leather jacket he'd got in the war. He could whistle in perfect tune and kept *Man* magazines in the kitchen drawer next to the knives and forks. When you looked at a *Man* magazine, a feeling came in your butterfly, but if you heard Mr Button coming you'd slam it back in the drawer. Melva said the ones that looked naked weren't, because they wore flesh-coloured tights. Melva and I put our mothers' brassieres on and then filled them up with socks to see whose were the biggest. Mrs Button worked at Mylady's Dainties, so Melva had pants with lace and satin bows, but Mum made mine from old flannel sheets. When Mum gave me a gold locket with a bluebird on it, Melva's mother gave her a bigger one with a photo of Melva inside.

Sometimes I went to the beach with the Buttons, but Melva always saw sharks where I was swimming; and we'd go into the ladies' changing rooms to look at their bottoms when they were undressing and their fronts when they came out of the showers. When it was the caterpillar plague, Melva squashed them and collected their green insides in jars. Melva liked to shut me in rooms and pretend she'd turned the gas on so I'd die, and I'd lie there dying. Melva showed me how filmstars did tongue kissing, but I didn't like the taste of her spit. Melva would fill up a lemonade bottle with water and drink it, then see if she could pee as much as she'd drunk. Melva said how when you were grown up blood came out of your butterfly. I didn't believe it, and when I asked Mum she hit me with the electric jug cord.

Melva made me play Dirty Doctors. Usually we played Dirty Doctors in Melva's playhouse, but sometimes we played it inside Melva's wardrobe with a torch. I was always the patient and Melva would say I looked dreadfully sick and give me injections with Mrs Button's sewing needles and then I'd have to take my pants off.

Melva was Church of Christ and I was Methodist, but Jesus was treated better in the Catholic church round the corner, where they had pictures and statues of Him everywhere. I'd try to make friends with Catholic girls so I could go into their bedrooms to see their statues, and I'd stare at Jesus so hard He'd talk to me. One girl had a crucifix with a hole you looked through to read the Lord's Prayer. I'd lie in the strawberry patch and see the angels coming through the clouds.

The date palms in the park were like big pineapples stuck in the ground. On Palm Sunday we cut palm fronds off and took them to Sunday School. Somebody was Jesus and somebody was the donkey and He rode under our arch of palm fronds. On the way home from Sunday School we danced round and pretended our palm fronds were grass skirts.

Once after Palm Sunday, Melva and I were in the playhouse playing Dirty Doctors. Melva made me lie down and started giving me injections with a palm-frond needle to make me go to sleep. Then she got lots of little stones and put them in my butterfly.

I called it my butterfly, but Mum called it your private. Sometimes I'd see PRIVATE on a door.

ROBIN SHEINER

My Sister's Funeral

The grapes arrived on the day of the funeral. We loaded them onto the back of the truck with the beer then everyone climbed on afterwards. My Japanese friend had to be helped up, Billy on one side of him, and Rosa on the other. He is a very old man now but still he doesn't speak English. He was pleased about the grapes, though. I could tell by the way he smiled. Since he had his teeth pulled out he doesn't smile very much because he can't enjoy a good feed of meat. He always liked a feed of meat but now he has only five teeth at the top and three at the bottom. I think he'll like the grapes.

He came here in 1920 to dive for pearls. They all came then, the Japanese, because they wanted the pearls, and knew how to get them. No-one else did. They liked the coloured girls and were nicer to them than white men were. They made the girls dive but didn't beat them or make them lie down with them afterwards.

I didn't know my old Japanese friend then, even though I lived in this town. Well, not really in the town. My husband and I lived in one of the old boat sheds, with all our kids, out across the mangrove swamp. At night we could hear the swamp gurgling beneath us and sometimes the big mangrove crabs climbed in and walked across us sideways. Our kids had a lot of fun chasing them around the shed. It was all right until the hot came and then the mozzies, ouch, you should have seen them, as big as dragonflies. At least we had shelter, not even the mozzies could drive us out to join other coloured people who slept along the gutters.

There are black and white and yellow people in the town, there are others half and half, and there are others all mixed up so they came out cream. My father was a very important white man. He owned a big station and had three black wives and one Malayan wife. My mother was one of his black wives. He loved her and he loved us, his kids. When they came in a car and took all of us kids away to the mission he wasn't there because he had gone down to the big city to visit his relations who are the people who grow grapes. They have lots of land in the city with grapes like you've never seen—red and glittering like rubies, black like opals, white and shiny like pearls with no seeds. I know this because some of my cousins' kids went down there once. They went all the way. Don't ask me how they got there but they did, and they went to work on the vineyard picking grapes but they weren't treated so good. I told them they should have told the owners they were their relations. Nobody makes their relations live in kerosene tins that let in the sun so bad, and the flies. Some people say black people like the flies. I tell you now, while my sister Rosa writes, we don't like the flies. They get in our eyes and make us go blind. Even now I don't see so good and I am telling this story to my sister Rosa to write down.

Rosa is married to a Malayan, his name is Kim Bin, and she has electric fans in the ceiling of her house to keep her cool. There are only two of us sisters left now because of the funeral. It was three days ago. The beer flowed for two days and Rosa and I were the only ones who didn't drink. Now we are home again and tired and I am asking my sister Rosa to write down how our sister Marcellus is gone. The nuns gave Marcellus her name but our father gave us ours—Clara and Rosa—pretty names to show he cared for us. I have found out from Billy's uncle, who knows everything, that our father died on the other side of the country, a lonely old white man. Where he lived they used to call him the captain and he would walk along the beach with pockets full of lollies for the kids who followed him everywhere. I think he was wondering all the time about us, his own kids who were took away young to be brought up at the mission.

Our sister Marcellus who died never left the mission, she stayed on as a helper in the kitchen to the nuns for forty years. For her funeral everyone, all of us, except the white relations from the city, came. We all went up from here and you should have seen us on the back of the truck. I wouldn't let anyone sit on top of the grapes. It was funny that we didn't ever ask who'd sent them or how they'd known that Marcellus was gone. We were so sure they'd been sent for Marcellus' funeral that we didn't bother to ask. We have learned not to ask questions, especially my old Japanese friend. He could learn English easily if he wanted to but he doesn't try. They tried to make him talk when he was sent away from here to be kept wired-in during the war. They tried to get him to say that he knew who was bombing us. Still he didn't talk. They thought he might be dumb. Big bombs came. We were lucky in the boat shed over the mangrove swamp because they didn't hit us. My husband was sick during the war. Too many mozzies. I couldn't do anything except wring out his singlet in the cool swamp water and lie beside him. There were no Japanese around then, they were wired in, so the pearl luggers were sitting empty not far from our shed. There were lots of sea planes on the water, too, funny looking things like giant birds, and when the bombs tried to hit them they hit some of the luggers instead. I don't think, if it was the Japanese dropping the bombs on us, they would have bombed their own Japanese boats that only wanted to look for pearls.

I was pleased my Japanese friend came for Marcellus' funeral. She would have been pleased, too, because she loved everyone like the nuns had taught her, even Japanese, because Jesus would have done, she said spitting on her hands and rolling out the pastry for the nun's steak and kidney. I didn't care much for Jesus when I was at the mission even though the nuns crammed him down my throat. Our mother would come to the mission gate every day and cry for us to come back to her and cry and cry when the nuns wouldn't let her take us out. So much for Jesus. I could see her crying behind the fence that kept us in and I know what my Japanese friend must have felt like, all wired-in but no-one cried for him to get out. People were glad. So, when he had his teeth out I sat with him and made him warm cloths to put across his cheek because I can guess what it feels like, when all your teeth are gone.

He looked comfortable in the truck, squatting on his heels near the beer crates. We hid the beer when we got to the mission.

Some had been drinking on the way and fell over at the mission and couldn't walk straight. It didn't worry us. We were used to it but the nuns didn't like it, especially at a funeral. They let Rosa and me look at Marcellus when she was lying in the coffin, open, and they had done her up nice and put a flower in her hand and dressed her in her best white dress that she wore for Holy Mass. Rosa started to cry so I stood up very straight and was glad for her sake, and for Marcellus', that I had worn my hat and white gloves. Some people in our town say what does a coloured woman want with hats and white gloves but it doesn't worry me if I am dressed up. Let them worry. My father who owned a station would have been proud of us: Rosa who married a Malayan and Marcellus who worked her life to the bone for the nuns, and I who wear a hat and gloves because they don't think I'd dare. I looked down at Marcellus and she was still the blackest of us three sisters.

Some of the others outside the room with the coffin in it were starting to make a lot of noise, especially the drunk ones who had started wailing and the nuns couldn't quieten them, even when the priest said the holy dedication. The nuns are not happy because the mission is going to close now that there are no more half black children they can bring. No-one these days will let kids be snatched. They used to bring all the ones who had white fathers and black mothers. There weren't any who had black fathers and white mothers because the black men didn't go near the white women. They didn't like them smelling of soap and stiff with corsets, and they would have been hanged if they did. My father's brother, my uncle, hanged lots of people. He was the magistrate in our town and lived in a big house and had black people fan him with banana leaves. Lots of them would run fast past his house because they thought he was the devil, and the nuns had scared them of the devil.

My Japanese friend is not scared of anything, even when he dived for pearls and saw crocodiles as big as boats and great big sea snakes with yellow stripes like lightning. He was not wailing like the others when Marcellus' coffin was wrapped up in the ground but was sitting down on a little stool I had brought for him and he

was smiling because in his hand he had a bunch of grapes and it
didn't matter with grapes that he had no teeth. Soon someone
brought out the whole box of grapes because they were too
scared, even the drunk ones, to bring out the beer in front of the
nuns who could be very fierce if they wanted, especially now their
mission was closing. Next thing, all the grapes were gone, the juice
of them dribbling from our mouths as we stood there and the sun
opening up the sky to let in all the light across Marcellus' grave.
My Japanese friend lay a bunch of grapes next to the flowers my
sister Rosa had brought, across the sun on the grave. The flowers
were withered because we had come such a long way in the truck
and it was a hot day but the grapes were firm and shiny. My
Japanese friend said the gods would like them and they would be
kind to Marcellus but I didn't think Marcellus would be happy
about it, so when he wasn't looking I picked them up from the
grave and gave them to the twins, my grandchildren who are
growing tall and fat. The priest gave a talk about how nice it was
that all of us who had been half-caste children at the mission, and
looked after so well, had come back to see one of our own buried
with the grace of God. Then he said, much louder, that drink was
the temptation of the devil, and we should cast it from us. But I
knew from what Marcellus had told me that the priest drank the
altar wine when he could and that she had seen him without his
cassock and with his fly undone, and had been so frightened she
had said ten holy Mary's, then burnt the cup cakes that she was
going to cut up to make angels' wings. When she went to confession and told what she had seen the priest said she was very wicked
and must scrub the big black pots every night until she washed
away her sins. Marcellus was obedient, not like Rosa and me. We
were proud and did not let anyone put us down or call us half-caste
good for nothings. Rosa learned to swear at them in Malayan if
they did, and I would walk on past, knowing how much it annoyed
them to see me in my hat and gloves.

'Why do you think our father let them take us?' Rosa asked
when we were trying to get everyone back into the truck. I
couldn't answer her because I knew he could have got us back if he

wanted to, an important man like that who had relations who almost owned the city, so my cousins' kids, who went to work for them down there, said. 'It broke our mother's heart,' Rosa told me as we hugged each other.

The sun was going down and everyone was tired. It was good the grapes were gone because it made more room in the truck. As we went along we saw something very funny. There were a lot of emus trying to get through a wire fence, getting very mad and tangling themselves up. We all giggled so much we rolled about the truck and one fell off and we had to stop but he wasn't hurt, so we lifted him back on. It was my cousin's son and his name is Billy. He has seen the city, picked grapes for our relations and come back, drinking worse and worse, sometimes beating his wife who is the daughter of my second cousin Mary.

My Japanese friend squatted on his heels in the middle of us all like that, so quiet with his eyes squinting. He is a good man and never minds being with us half and halfers, neither one thing nor the other but in the strip between. His wife was a mixture, cream coloured. He had married her in a Japanese ceremony, that was when there were lots of Japanese here because there were so many pearls. They had their own temple, even their own graveyard. It's still there with Japanese writing on the headstones. His wife had been a beauty, like all the cream coloureds, and she had run off with a white man, down to the city in a ute. They didn't have no kids. Just as well. He lives with me now in the house the government sold cheap when they were trying to do something about us, tidy us up. In the drawer of the cupboard he made for me he has two big pearls and sometimes he takes them out to look at them. I think he's keeping them for if his wife comes back.

He has given me some pearl shells and I wanted to send one to our white relations when I thought they were kind enough to send us grapes for Marcellus' funeral. I only found out about the grapes when I went down to the big store to buy some powder so my nose wouldn't be red if I cried. 'You,' the shop man said. 'Them there are for you.'

'How do you know?' I asked.

'Ask no questions and you get told no lies,' he said. He is a white man who has been hit on the head with a black man's bottle and he sometimes acts up stupid. But there it was blurred across the side. Even with my eyes blinded from flies I could see it, Clara my name. I held myself proud. 'From my relations in the city for my sister's funeral,' I told him. 'I'll call my cousin's son to carry them. Hoy there Billy, come over and carry this box of grapes for your aunty.' He came across from the hotel where he had been playing snooker with some white friends, just to carry it for me, back home so it could be loaded on to the truck. He's the one who fell off the truck and I'm glad he wasn't hurt through laughing so much at the emus. We have a lot of fun. It's the black side of us. I don't miss out on much. My father laughed a lot but he wasn't like other white men, having all us black kids made him different, and anyway I don't think he could have laughed too much after we were gone. Blacks can laugh at anything, birds dropping shit from the sky, bungarras racing up white ladies' skirts looking for the trees.

It was a long trip home from the funeral and very dusty so we stopped a lot even after Billy fell off and soon all the beer was gone and half the men were snoring on the back of the truck. I was glad my cousin Paddy was driving because he can drive straight even when he is drunk. When it got dark we stopped and all curled up warm together there on the back and my Japanese friend rested his head on my knees. It was nice there looking up at the stars and all together, though I felt sad about Marcellus who had never got away from the mission and was so small, smaller than Rosa and me, when she was taken that she couldn't remember where she had come from.

In the morning we washed ourselves in a pool left by the dried-out river. My cousin Paddy always follows the river road, when it's not flooding in the rainy season, because his truck over-heats all the time and needs water for the radiator. There aren't any garages on the way to the mission and if there were there are lots of whites who wouldn't even give water away to blacks. It was nice to be clean. My Japanese friend washed his feet and slicked down his hair. I put my hat and gloves back on so I would be ready when we arrived back at the town to see anyone and look them in the eye. That's my white side. It doesn't bother me if a white man puts his evil eye on me because I give it to him straight back again. Except I wasn't ready for the policeman who met us at the door of the house the government sold to me, and I wish they hadn't, it's damper than the boat shed in the rainy season.

'Which one here stole the box of grapes?' he asked, and we were all struck dumb.

I climbed down from the truck first. 'They were my grapes,' I said, 'sent to me from my relations who grow grapes in the city.'

'Garn. Tell us another,' the policeman said, 'they were addressed to Mrs Clare, the station owner's wife and she gets them sent up regular. Seen you before, haven't I? Hanging about with whites in the hotel?' He moved across to Billy. We knew what that meant. Billy melted into us and we closed up tight around him. Everyone had climbed down from the truck, even those with hangovers so bad they couldn't make any sense of day or night; the children, glad to be home, had run off whooping.

'You pay for the grapes, or else.' The policeman addressed us all.

It wasn't pension day but that didn't worry me. It was that my relations hadn't known about Marcellus' funeral after all. They hadn't cared that she'd died there like that in the mission, that she'd never got out not for forty years and now she was there forever, buried in the ground. So the grapes hadn't been for her, they had been for the white lady who ordered them regular. A mistake had been made.

I took off my hat and crumpled my gloves up small inside it.

My Japanese friend knows what it's like to be wired-in, and I know for certain he didn't scream when the dentist pulled out his teeth. He stood forward, separating himself from us half and halfers, and he spoke his first words in English. If I hadn't heard it with my own ears I wouldn't have believed it. 'Fuck your grapes,' he said.

The Hair and the Teeth

People broke into the house one time when we were out at the supermarket. I suppose we were gone for about an hour and a half. The older children were at school, but I had the two little ones with me. They were only three and two when this happened, and so whatever we did, we did it fairly slowly.

You drive to the shopping centre and park the car in the basement. Then you take the children out of their car seats and get to the lift that takes you up to the level where the supermarket is. You have to get the children past the toyshop with the Humphrey Bear that will sing and dance if you put money in the slot, past the pink elephant ride, past the Coke machine. If you put the children in the trolley at the supermarket there won't be enough room for the stuff you have to get, but if you don't put them in the trolley you have to be prepared to move very, very slowly. So you move slowly. You get the music, the lights, the smell of disinfectant, and all the colours. Everything shimmers in the supermarket.

(I find the music and the lights and so on very tiring and I am inclined to be irritable.)

You fill up the trolley and stand in the queue. The queue moves very slowly. Every trolley in front of you has things in it that need to have their prices checked. The music shifts from the Ascot Gavotte to the Easter Parade, and you cannot be soothed. You want to just grab the children and leave the full trolley where it is. But you wait and you pay and you wheel the trolley to the lift, to the car. You pack the car, strap the children in, park the trolley, drive to the exit, pay to get out, drive home. It is dusk now. When you get home you put your key in the back door but the door won't open because the burglars (what is the correct word here? Is it robber, intruder, thief, crook, bugger?) the burglars have bolted it from the inside.

As soon as the door would not open, I knew pretty well what had happened. I left the children and the shopping in the car and went round to the front of the house. The window was wide open and the curtain was flapping, in fact billowing out, like a miserable bride or a cheerful ghost. One of the children in the car had started to cry. I went back to the car, took two packets of biscuits from the shopping and gave a packet to each child.

'You can eat these,' I said, tearing open the packets and handing them to the children. The crying stopped and both children looked a bit surprised but they obeyed. I locked them in the car and went round to the front door. This door has no bolt. I opened it, put my hand in to turn on the light, and stood for a few moments listening and looking into the hallway. On the floor at the foot of the stairs was an earring, and halfway between the stairs and the front door was the lid of a jewellery box. The phone is on a table near the front door. I rang the police.

People tell me it takes a long time for the police to come to a break-in, break-ins being so common and policemen so rare, but these police seemed to be there by the time I had put down the phone. Possibly, because of the shock of the whole business, my sense of time was distorted. Anyway, the huge (it seemed to be huge) white car with blue writing and blue lights zoomed up the street and slid (really) in beside the kerb and two police, a man and a woman, jumped (true) out and were suddenly standing beside me. The first thing I thought about was how healthy they looked. They looked just very, very healthy. He was big and young and smiling and sweet. And she was little and young and smiling and sweet. They had hats. They looked very clean—in blue, sky blue and navy. They both smelt of nice soap.

They searched the house for hidden people while I got first the shopping then the children from the car. The children had finished the biscuits. I gave them some chips. By this time the ice-cream was beginning to melt and blood was dripping out of a plastic bag in which there was a chicken.

'Can you leave the kids with a neighbour while we get on with things?' asked the policeman. So I took them in next door. Luckily someone was home and the children were quite happy to stay there watching television.

We went all over the house, the police and I, finding evidence of what they said was the 'work of a real professional'. We sat at the kitchen table and made a list of what was missing.

I used to keep jewellery in the top left-hand drawer of a chest of drawers. They must have emptied the drawer onto the bedspread and then rolled up the bedspread and used it as a sack. I imagine two rat-like little men, real professionals, wearing masks, tiptoeing swiftly down the stairs, one with the sack over his shoulder, the other with an armful of leather coats. I start giving the policeman a list of things that have been taken: coral necklace, princess ring. He writes it all down carefully. The kitchen light seems to be too harsh, the paper the man is writing on too white. The clean strong police faces seem sympathetic but as helpless as the babies we have sent next door. I offer them biscuits and coffee but they say no. Jade ring, silver bracelet with lapis lazuli. They have stolen a basket of firewood. The police cannot explain this. Suddenly I remember that among the sentimental treasures in the drawer were the locks of hair and the baby teeth of the older children. Then my voice starts to waver and I think I am going to cry.

(I had wrapped the teeth in a piece of silk and put them in a tin from a machine in the Paris Metro. Snow was falling. The Metro was warm. I put the money in the machine and got an oval tin of lollies with a wreath of violets on the lid. The lollies inside the tin rattled. They were dusted with sugar.)

Will I tell the police about the teeth and hair? Will I say in my litany:

'Two tortoise-shell combs (Spanish), four ivory bangles (African), nine deciduous teeth (human), and two locks of human hair (golden)'?

They look at me kindly as I sit weeping at the kitchen table. I drink coffee and whisky. They keep writing. Periwinkle necklace, gipsy keeper (garnet).

I ask whether they think I will get any of the things back and they say that, in a case of this nature, it is unlikely we will recover any of the missing items.

I put in the insurance claim and a woman from the insurance company came to interview me. She had a briefcase under her arm and a shrewd look in her eye. She was a bit fat but graceful with a black dress and a fur jacket and beauty parlour make-up, hairdo and fingernails. She was wearing Chanel, and her shoes were Italian. She stood on the doormat with the blue sky behind her and she could have been an advertisement for something, probably wine or, now I come to think of it, insurance. Or funerals.

'Mrs Halliwell from Phoenix. I rang,' she said, and I took her into the sitting room. You couldn't discuss the basket of firewood and the jewellery in the bedspread with Mrs Halliwell in the kitchen. I offered her coffee but she didn't want it. The ordinary rules of hospitality do not apply to the police or to women from the insurance company. She had a typed list of all the things that were stolen. As she sat down, the sofa suddenly looked very shabby. A plastic fire-engine lay just near Mrs Halliwell's left foot.

'I will need more detailed descriptions of some of the items reported missing,' she said, looking up at me over her glasses. 'You will have to be more specific. A princess ring means nothing to me. What is a princess ring?' We came to the coral necklace which I said was made from round beads of coral, pale pink and smooth.

'Polished?' said Mrs Halliwell.

I said I supposed they were polished. 'Angel skin,' she wrote without speaking. Then she asked how long the necklace was, and when I told her she wrote, 'Opera length.' Satisfied, she then said aloud, 'Opera length polished angel skin,' and she almost smiled. 'Is there any other item you have omitted to report missing? This is your final opportunity to claim.' I tried to think of something, as if I needed to please her. Then I thought of saying half the things

I had just told her were lies. Then I remembered the hair and the teeth, and all I said at last was no. She said we would have to put in an alarm system, arrange for security patrol, get security doors and windows, or else get a reliable watchdog. I asked her for the name of somebody who puts in security doors and windows, but she said I would have to look in the *Yellow Pages.* Then she said 'reliable watchdog' again as she tucked her briefcase under her arm. I showed her out.

'And a peephole and a security phone on the door,' she said as she walked away.

The next day a man came to measure the doors and windows for bars. He handed me his card at the door. On the card was a picture of a shark behind wire mesh.

'Jack McClaren,' he said, 'from Shark.' He looked around the garden and said, 'Nice large block you've got here. Surprising in this postal district.'

When he had finished measuring, and when we had discussed the quality of the optional one-way mesh and the need for the tri-safe locking system with the three-point deadlocking and anti-pick lock, he had a cup of coffee in the kitchen. We had some short-bread and a cigarette and I told him about the robbery. He said I was lucky and told me about people who had been completely cleaned out. 'Nothing left standing except the electric light. Lucky you weren't here when they came. Then they'd have done it with violence. It's on the increase. I see all the statistics, of course.'

So then I told him about the hair and the teeth, and he said that was the worst.

'And the mongrels would just chuck those things away, you know. They'd just chuck the babies' curls into the gutter. I went to a lady's place where they'd taken nearly everything. And all these photos of her son that was killed in the war. You know they just let the photos blow away in the street, in the rain. And weeks later the lady was still finding the remains of her photos in the weeds by the side of the road. She never got over it.'

As he talked I remembered something else that must have been in the drawer with the jewellery. Something else that had been stolen. It was a small wax doll. I first saw her one night in the lighted window of a shop. She was a naked little girl with blue glass eye and a wig made from real hair. The next day I went back to the shop when it was open. I thought the doll was very expensive, but I bought her.

BEVERLEY FARMER

The Harem

When Bell was nine the SEC transferred her father from Melbourne to Wangalla for nine months. In no time he was sick and tired of living in a room at Doolan's pub. He sent Bell and her mother scrawled postcards full of loneliness. For the school holidays he found them a cheap house near the station, and they could have the run of it but for Mr Grey's own front room where he kept himself to himself. Bell sneaked in for a look. His double bed was a smelly bundle of grey sheets and blankets. Morning sunshine burned in fluff all over his oiled floor and the dusty mirror over his dressing table.

Mr Grey owned the house opposite too, where the Harem lived. He owned the woodyard next door, its stacks of red-furred wood guarded by a savage dog. It said so on the gate. He owned half of Grey Bros iceworks; sometimes they met him on hot afternoons, chipping out shimmering blocks and carrying them wrapped in sacking on his shoulder into the shaded houses, while his brown horse stamped. Mr Grey was a widower and childless, and ought to have been well off but for his drinking problem. Bell thought he was old, but her mother said no, but he'd let himself go. Mr Grey was affable in the evenings and surly before noon. His little wrinkled eyes were red, and when he yawned he showed yellow pegs of teeth. He spent most afternoons in the pub and even ate there. He shambled in about seven, banging doors, and sometimes crashed and swore, and sometimes sang snatches of *Knees up, Mother Brown* or *Oh, you beautiful doll.*

The yard at Mr Grey's was shaded by a red-leafed tree dripping with little red plums sweet and yellow inside and warm when the sun was in them. A tame bird lived behind the tree. A curlew, Mr Grey said. It squatted in the dust or minced around and cocked its gold eyes. Once Mr Grey caught Bell throwing plums at it to make it hop and bridle.

'Know what happens to kids ut do that, do yer?' he growled. 'Bird gets in at night. Pecks their eyes out and swallers um.'

All night in the dark it hovered. A weird cry, a scimitar beak. Her mother insisted on fresh air. Every night once her light was off Bell leapt up and latched her windows.

Down the lane from the house there was a long footbridge over the railway lines, and the *Spirit of Progress* surged under it gushing white clouds and hooting. The wheels pumped, grinding, glittering. The long blue engine whooped. Every morning Bell rushed to the bridge for the *Spirit* to wrap her in hot white billows.

Once as she tore out she saw that the woodshed gate was open, the red dog bounding up, barking, slavering. She propped, but he only wanted to prance and bow and lick her hands. The *Spirit* shrieked. Bell and the dog took off and reached the bridge in good time. When the train had slid away they sauntered back together.

'If yer take Rover out,' Mr Grey warned, 'watch out yer bring um back. Worth a packet, that dorg is.'

After that whenever the red dog saw Bell he bowed and whined, a slobbery wood-chip in his teeth for her to throw. At *Spirit* time he jumped at the gate with his tail whipping. She called him Red, not Rover. Red was covered in such tight red curls he looked as if June had permed him with her lotions and pins.

June lived with Mr and Mrs Peterson and their daughter Kate in the Harem. Mr Malone the grocer called it that. Met the Harem yet? He winked at Bell's mother but she seemed not to notice.

'Mum, what's a harem?'

'Oh, a sort of Arab family.'

June was tall and heavy, with curly red hair—hennaed, Bell's mother said—as glossy as plum-skins. Advertisements in shop windows said that Miss June Smith did hairdressing in your own home by appointment. Bell's mother said June looked fast, and she was, pedalling along from head to head on a glittering bicycle with netted wheels. Women waited for her with their hair lank and wet in kitchens soaked in the waxen light of hot sun behind holland blinds. Often three or four women would wait in the kitchen of one of them, who laid on tea with buns, or scones, or fruitcake. The teapots wore their best knitted cosies. June's bicycle was parked on all the best Wangalla verandahs. Sometimes it was leaning on the hot brick wall of Doolan's for all the world to see.

When Bell's mother first had her hair done, she hadn't met the other SEC wives, so no-one else was there until Mr Grey slouched in. June laughed and smoked and told long jokes, and ate more than her share of the buttered Boston bun at afternoon tea time. When she had gone, Mr Grey wiped crumbs off his whiskers, sighed, and muttered, 'Fine figure of a woman. They say she's got a temper, but. Stands to reason, eh? Hair like that.'

Bell's mother sniffed.

'I reckon it's a blasted waste,' Mr Grey droned on.

Bell and her mother met Mrs Peterson at the grocer's. She had a toothy grin and long hair coiled in a dun roll on the bone of her nape. She was so homesick for the Old Country. Here the neighbours were so standoffish, weren't they? Do call me Mary, she said. Bell's mother said to call her Judith. Well now, how would Judith's little girl like to come over and play with her Kate? Kate wasn't much older really, only eleven, and so awfully lonely, poor child.

Sullenly dressed up in frills and strap shoes Bell was sent over to play.

Kate was tall and slim with a white face and straight black hair. Bell was tubby and pink, her hair butter-coloured. Kate was allowed to be barefoot, and dressed all in black. She had bitten her scarlet nails. Her eyes when they met Bell's were long and scowling, unsmiling. With her light on in bright daylight she showed Bell her treasures, her jewels, her greasepaints. She was going to be an actress. She let Bell try on in the dressing table mirror her Arabian brass bangles—so they *were* Arabs—and the string of green and gold glass beads she spent her time threading. She showed Bell fuzzy photos of her relatives back home, then they sat on her bed to read her Enid Blyton books, stealing glances at each other in the yellow glare of the lamp.

When Kate said 'grass' it rhymed with 'mass'. She said 'some-think' and 'anythink', and called lemonade 'pop'. Later Bell's mother was annoyed when she said things Kate's way: don't copy poor speech, Annabel, please.

Bell was asked to stay to dinner, and ran across to ask her mother, who said yes. With the door open, the Petersons' kitchen table only just fitted in between the stove and the ice chest. Mr Peterson squeezed in on one side between Mrs Peterson and June, and Bell and Kate sat opposite. The light bulb was on a cord and swilled shadows over them with every gust of the northerly. The table cloth of pages from *The Age* lifted, flapped. They had a sweet-ish red stew with lumps of meat and soft potatoes, and drank 'shandies' of beer and lemonade mixed. They all called the lemon-ade 'pop'. A rare treat for Bell, it was spoilt by the beer. The grown-ups had just beer. Their breaths smelled like the hot buffets of air when the bar doors opened at Doolan's. Bell's parents never touched liquor.

'Coom on, Mary. Drink oop, loov.' Mr Peterson cuddled Mrs Peterson, winking at Bell. But Mrs Peterson only shook her drooping head.

After the stew Bell thought she should say thank you for the lovely dinner and go home, but Mrs Peterson gave them all peaches and spotty apples from the ice chest. They peeled them on to their dinner plates. June, showing Bell how to cut her apple through its equator to make a star-apple, dropped it and splashed stew on Bell's dress. June peeled her own apple all in one piece and tossed the peel over her shoulder to see who she would marry. Mrs Peterson's bony nose turned red. You couldn't make out any letters in the yellow coils of peel. June and Mr Peterson lit ciga-rettes and blew smoke.

'Cheer oop, Mary, for the loov of Mike,' Mr Peterson boomed. 'Ah'll open anoother bottle. Put a bit of life into the blooming proceedings.'

'I'm making coffee, Bob,' was all Mrs Peterson said, putting the jug on. Their coffee wasn't boiled in a saucepan with grounds on top, but mixed with syrup from a long black bottle with a picture on the label of a turbaned Arab. At home Bell was only allowed a drop of tea or coffee in her milk. She and Kate filled their coffee with sugar. Not even Kate was taking any notice of Bell. They were all shiny with sweat.

After the coffee Mr Peterson and June left the table hand in hand and shut themselves in a bedroom. Mrs Peterson sighed and boiled the jug again for the dishes. Bell helped scrape plates. Footsteps shambling down the back path startled them all. 'The boogie man,' breathed Kate in Bell's ear. But with a cough Mr Grey's shabby head was thrust into the lamplight. He said no thanks to coffee. He'd just dropped in to pass the time of day. He'd better be orf home, thanks, Mary.

When Bell asked Kate in her room what her father and June were doing, Kate said that if she didn't know at her age, thut was too bud, wasn't it? She shrugged.

'Bob looves them both. Me moom and June.'

'Oh.'

'He likes me best. He said so.'

'Oh really?' was all Bell's mother had to say to that when she heard.

That was another interesting thing: Kate's father would only answer to 'Bob', not 'Father' or 'Dud'. He wore a bristly brown moustache and once belted Kate with his razor strop, and worked as a foreman at the cannery.

'Mum, can we buy that Arab coffee?'

'No, we can't.'

'But it's lovely!'

'They had no business to give a child coffee. You've got sauce on your dress.'

'June did it. It's stew.'

'Don't answer back.'

'Mum, what's a four man?'

Her parents decided that if she was asked again she was to say thank you, but her tea would be ready, and then come straight home. Because we say so, they said when she asked why. But she could still go over and play. She kept quiet about the shandies.

Kate came over the next morning to see if Bell could go for a swim in the river with them. Mr Grey said he'd be in that: too right he would.

'Well, well, well. Here's K-K-K-Katy,' sang Bell's father jovially, and Kate said, 'My name's Kate.' Bell's mother said definitely not, what with snags and currents and tiger snakes in the river. Bell's mother and father were awful. Kate was, too. They all were.

That was the Sunday the roast leg of lamb got blown as it waited on the table for the vegetables to cook. Her mother said the flies had got to it, but Bell could only see little white threads in rows, like specks of fat. Her mother said she wasn't to tell a soul, did she hear, and ran over to the Harem to borrow some meat. Bell and Dad read the Sydney Sunday papers. The hot darkness by the fire-stove was full of the sweaty smell of the roast. A long time later her mother came back with a tin of Spam, and served it cold with the vegetables. Bell sulked and said it was a blasted waste, but had to eat Spam or starve, while in the woodyard Red tore and gulped the grey leg and lay dreaming afterwards with the bone in his paws. The treacly dripping had to be poured into a hole in the garden, not back into its hole in the waxy speckled dripping-basin.

Bell's mother told Dad that she had found poor Mary alone and in such a state that she had to stay and calm her down. They sent Bell out to play while she told him all about it.

'Oh. But there's nothing to *do*.'

'Go on, sticky-beak,' grinned Dad.

There were some very hot days that week. For hours Bell lay and read in nothing but bathing togs on the cool linoleum in the kitchen. She was allowed to spray herself with the hose in the yard, squinting through rainbows and sheets of wet light, water pounding her. Tawny butterflies shook their wings. She swung ropes of glittering water under the tree, where the dry lawn glowed all over with soft plums. Her mother spent one whole afternoon boiling and bottling jam, some for them and some for Mr Grey. At teatime she sighed, saying how in Melbourne they could have just hopped on a bus and been at the beach in no time. She and Dad quarrelled that night in their hot room beyond the wall. Things were scurrying on top of Bell's ceiling. Her mother was always hoping to high heaven it was nothing worse than possums.

At the window the curlew wailed.

Bell was sent over to the Harem with a jar of plum jam. In her yellow room Kate made her shut her eyes. 'Now open them,' Kate said. She had a solid glass egg. When Bell cupped it in her hands like a chicken it was cold and glowed, a heavy drop of stony water, magnifying her palms. Through it she could see all the bulging golden room. A rainbow light lay deep inside. The egg caught lamplight and sunlight and nursed them like seeds.

'It's crystal,' Kate whispered. 'Bob gave it to me. It's valuable. I can tell fortunes in it. I can read minds.'

Bell peered again.

'No, it only works for me.'

'How does it work?'

'Never you mind.'

She swore Bell to secrecy. Even so, she hid the egg away and wouldn't say where, or even let Bell have another little look, however much she begged and wheedled.

For a week Bell clung to Kate's side. Every afternoon they walked Red along the river banks or behind the ice cart for chips of ice to suck. Kate showed Bell her school with its empty yard of asphalt and yellow tussocks. Bell showed Kate Mr Grey's curlew. Kate threw plums and one hit it. She wouldn't talk about the crystal egg.

At last, alone in Kate's room while Kate went to the WC, Bell gave in to temptation. Evening was falling from a hot sky the colour of apricots. In Kate's golden room Bell dared to kneel and go rummaging. But as she grasped it, hard and icy in a singlet in the bottom drawer of the dressing table, Kate's face appeared. It glared down at her in the lit mirror.

'Put it down, you thief!' Kate hissed.

Bell, sick with shock, turned around to Kate's white face. Had Kate read her mind? They were both shaking, both in pyjamas and slippers, as were the grown-ups, it was so hot.

'I only wanted a look!'

'Oh, did you now? Well, just for thut, you're never going to see it again. I've a good mind to tell Bob on you.'

'No, Kate, please!'

'He'll belt you till you bleed.'

'I wasn't going to take it! Why *can't* I have a look? Aren't I your friend?'

'No. You're not. Go home, Sneak.'

Bell stared and burned.

'Go on. Before I change me mind. Tell your moom you're a thief. Tell her I'm not her babysitter.'

Shaken with sobs, Bell ran home. No-one saw. She latched her windows and got straight into bed to hide in her hot pillow. She pretended to be asleep when her mother looked in, opened a window and switched off the light. Bell latched it again. The slow night passed. Over breakfast the next day she told about the shandies and so was banned from the Harem forever. She brought up her breakfast though, and had to go back to bed. Her mother and father brought her cool drinks, and food that she couldn't face; they read to her, sponged her, took her temperature and worried all day whether to call a doctor. By teatime she felt a lot better. She had scrambled eggs and slept for fourteen hours.

Next morning Kate was out on the footpath with scrawny Cynthia Malone, the grocer's daughter, drawing with chalks, so Bell had to make herself go out for the *Spirit*, with Red for company, prancing. They whispered and giggled behind her back. Afterwards they were still there having snail races, prodding the frothed brown shells and barracking. Cynthia's baby brother that she was supposed to be minding picked one up and ate it.

The gas heater blew up that afternoon. No-one could have a bath. Bell's mother cried. She said it was the last straw. Then she said that the last matinee of the panto at the Tivoli was next Saturday, so they could still see it if Bell wanted to, but only if they went home a week early. Bell was overjoyed. She wanted to go home very badly. Even though it would mean leaving Dad and Red. So that was all settled.

June came over after tea to give Bell's mother's hair a quick trim. She was in a hurry and took puffs of her cigarette as she snipped.

'No time for a coopa, thanks, dear,' she said. 'No rest for the wicked.'

'June?' Bell said. 'Can Kate really read minds with her crystal egg?'

'Not now, Bell, June's busy.'

'What's thut, Bell? Did Kate tell you she had a crystal egg?'

'She *showed* me. It's beautiful.'

'Well, well. And where does she keep it?'

'In her bottom drawer in a singlet. It's valuable.'

'I'm sure it is. I'd like to see it.'

'Oh, she won't show you. It's a secret.'

'Oh, I think she will.'

June's face was dark, her crimson lips thin and tight. Bell kept quiet, then.

Over the road that night the lights were still on late, all the lights, and there were shouts and doors slammed. Bell was up way past her bedtime helping her mother with the ironing that she'd put off till then in the cool of the night. Dad looked up from his cross-word.

'Sounds like the Sheik's got a war on his hands. Might just pop over and help him out. Even up the odds, eh?'

'It's no laughing matter, Alan. It's a disgrace!'

'Who do you back to win? I'll have two bob on June.' He winked. 'Or one? One Bob on June.'

'Oh, Alan, really. That poor little girl, that's all I can say. What hope has she got?'

'Why's Kate a poor little girl?'

'Never you mind. Off you go now, lovey, it's high time you were in bed.'

'Oh, Mu-um.'

Bell lay awake for ages with her door half-open in the dark, listening to squeals and scamperings above; bird cries outside; silence from the Harem. Her parents' light and Mr Grey's were yellow stripes under their doors.

In the morning the Harem was still silent behind its blinds until, just before the *Spirit* was due, the front gate slammed. June was out there alone, holding a suitcase and wheeling her bicycle. Her eyes and hair were hidden by her black-veiled hat, but her plummy lips were tight, her head high for the benefit of starers in the gardens and front windows. As she faltered in the dazing sun, Mr Grey appeared in pyjamas in his doorway, padded to the front door, and opened it. Then June came striding over.

'Well, here I am, Tom Grey,' she said. 'If you still want me.'

'Too right I do,' he said, white under his whiskers. So in she came and snibbed the gate, propped up her bicycle, handed her suitcase to Mr Grey still sagging in the doorway in his fluffed pyjamas, and kissed him. Bell and her mother stood by open-mouthed as Mr Grey and June, hand in hand, shut themselves in his bedroom.

Bell hung round as long as she could, until the *Spirit* hooted: there were only a few mornings left. That was the golden day they had sandwiches and cordial on a bank of the river where ruffled branches hung their shadows looping in brown water. Red capered then snoozed. Her mother let her take snaps with the Box Brownie, and asked if she was sorry to go and if she'd miss Kate. When Bell said she'd never really liked Kate, her mother nodded, and left it at that.

At teatime they went out for a fish-and-chips tea at the Bridge Cafe, for the first time ever, to give the lovebirds a go.

'How's that for calling a bloke's bluff, eh?' Dad couldn't get over it. 'Well, he's bitten off more than *he* can chew. What a woman!'

'Can I ask June for a ride on her bike?'

'No, you can't. Don't talk with your mouth full.'

'Must've really done her block to walk out,' Dad went on. 'What set her off, I wonder? That's redheads for you.'

'It's dyed.'

Dad went on about how the blokes at work would be all agog, especially the ones that drank at Doolan's and had seen it coming. Her mother's answers were in such long words, Bell lost the thread, watching how the white bubbles heaved in a milk shake when you blew down the straw. Her father paid the bill and slipped some pennies in Bell's pocket. They all strolled home arm in arm the long way as the sky turned green and stars showed.

The next few days were a flurry of washing and pegging out wrung sheets and shirts that flapped like yacht sails on the lines; packing suitcases; having goodbye cups of tea in waxy kitchens. Bell and her mother were booked on the *Spirit*, and Dad was moving back to Doolan's pub. The bicycle stayed proudly on the verandah, but June and Mr Grey never seemed to be in. No-one saw Kate or her parents at all, but Mr Grey told Dad that Bob and Kate were moving to Sydney and Mrs Peterson was on her way back to the Old Country. He wrote down Bell's Melbourne address for the wedding invitation.

The day before they went Bell said goodbye to all the house and the yard, the glowing shaggy plum tree stripped of its plums, the ruffled curlew, and poor sad Red who sensed it and whined, thrusting his rough head into her hands. In the house she visited every corner, remembering moments. No-one was home. Her heart was thumping, she pushed open the door of Mr Grey's front room. His bed was flat now. Silver brushes and combs and bottles of green-gold scent stood on lace on his dressing table. The mirror, burning, reflected Bell's joy and amazement. There at last was the crystal egg. It was glowing with inner fire among the ornaments.

HELEN GARNER

What We Say

I was kneeling at the open door, with the cloth in my right hand and the glass shelf balanced on the palm of my left. She came past at a fast clip, wearing my black shoes and pretending I wasn't there. I spoke sharply to her, from my supplicant's posture.

'Death to mother. Death,' she replied, and clapped the gate to behind her.

It had once been a kind of family joke, but I lost the knack of the shelf for a moment and though it didn't break there was quite a bit of blood. After I had cleaned up and put the apron in a bucket to soak, I went to the phone and began to make arrangements.

In Sydney my friend, the old-fashioned sort of friend who works on your visit and wants you to be happy, gave me two tickets to the morning dress rehearsal of *Rigoletto*. I went with Natalie. She knew how to get there and which door to go in. 'At your age, you've never been inside the *Opera* House?' Great things and small forged through the blinding water. We hurried, we ran.

At the first interval we went outside. A man I knew said, 'I like your shirt. What would you call that colour—hyacinth?' At the second interval we stayed in our seats so we could keep up our conversation which is no more I suppose than exalted gossip but which seems, because of her oblique perceptions, a most delicate, hilarious and ephemeral tissue of mind.

At lunchtime we dashed, puffy-eyed and red-cheeked, into the kitchen of my thoughtful friend. He was standing at the stove, looking up at us over his shoulder and smiling: he likes to teach me things, he likes to see me learning.

'How was it?'

'Fabulous! We cried *buckets*!'

Another man was leaning against the window frame with his arms crossed and his hair standing on end. His skin was pale, as if he had crept out from some burrow where he had lain for a long time in a cramped and twisted position.

'You cried?' he said. 'You mean you actually shed tears?'

Look out, I thought; one of these. I was still having to blow my nose, and was ready to ride rough-shod. My friend put the spaghetti on the table and we all sat down.

'I'm starving,' said Natalie.

'What a plot,' I raved. 'So tight you couldn't stick a pin in it.'

'What was your worst moment?' said Natalie.

'Oh, when he bends over the sack to gloat, and then from off-stage comes the Duke's voice, singing his song. The way he freezes, in that bent-over posture, over the sack.'

The sack, in a sack. I had a best friend once, my intellectual companion of ten years, on paper from land to land and then in person: she was the one who first told me the story of *Rigoletto* and I will never forget the way her voice sank to a thread of horror: 'And the murderer gives him his daughter's body on the river bank, *in a sack.*' A river flows: that is its nature. Its sluggish water can work any discarded object loose from the bank and carry it further, lump it lengthwise, nudge it and roll it and shift it, bear it away and along and out of sight.

'Yes, that was bad, all right,' said Natalie, 'but mine was when he realized that his daughter was in the bedchamber with the Duke.'

We picked up our forks and began to eat. The back door opened on to a narrow concrete yard, but light was bouncing down the grey walls and the air was warm, and as I ate I thought, Why don't I live here? In the sun?

'Also,' I said, 'I *love* what it's about. About the impossibility of shielding your children from the evil of the world.'

There was a pause.

'Well, yes, it is about that,' said my tactful friend, 'but it's also about the greatest fear men have. Which is the fear of losing their daughters. Of losing them to younger men. Into the world of sex.'

We sat at the table quietly eating. Words which people use and pretend to understand floated in silence and bumped among our heads: virgin; treasure; perfect; clean; my darling; anima; soul.

Natalie spoke in her light, courteous voice. 'If that's what it's about,' she said, 'what do you think the women in the audience were responding to?'—for in our bags were two sodden handkerchiefs.

The salad went round.

'I don't know,' said my friend. 'You tell me.'

We said nothing. We looked into our plates.

'That fear men have,' said my friend. 'Literature and art are full of it.'

My skin gave a mutinous prickle. *Your* literature.

'*Do* women have a fundamental fear?' said my friend.

Natalie and I glanced at each other and back to the tabletop.

'A fear of violation, maybe?' he said. He got up and filled the kettle. The silence was not a silence but a quietness of thinking. I knew what Natalie was thinking. She was wishing the conversation had not taken this particular turn. I was wishing the same thing. Stumped, struck dumb: failed again, failed to think and talk in that pattern they use. I had nothing to say. Nothing came to my mind that had any bearing on the matter.

Should I say 'But violation is our destiny?' Or should I say '*Nothing can be sole or whole / That has not been rent*'? But before I could open my mouth, a worst moment came to me: the letter arrives from my best friend on the road in a far country: 'He was wearing mirror sun-glasses which he did not take off, I tried to plead but I could not speak his language, he tore out handfuls of my hair, he kicked me and pushed me out of the car, I crawled to the river, I could smell the water, it was dirty but I washed myself, a farm girl found me, her family is looking after me, I think I will be all right, please answer, above all, don't tell my father, love.' I got down on my elbows in the yard and put my face into the dirt, I wept, I groaned. That night I went as usual to the lesson. *All I can do is try to make something perfect for you, for your poor body with my clumsy and ignorant one*: I breathed and moved as the teacher showed us, and she came past me in the class and touched me on the head and said, 'This must mean a lot to you—you are doing it so beautifully.'

'Violation,' said Natalie, as if to gain time.

'It would be necessary,' I said, 'to examine all of women's writing, to see if the fear of violation is the major theme of it.'

'Some feminist theoretician somewhere has probably already done it,' said the stranger who had been surprised that *Rigoletto* could draw tears.

'Barbara Baynton, for instance,' said my friend. 'Have you read that story of hers called *The Chosen Vessel*? The woman knows the man is outside waiting for dark. She puts the brooch on the table. It's the only valuable thing she owns. She puts it there as an offering—to appease him. She wants to buy him off.'

The brooch. The mirror sunglasses. The feeble lock. The weakened wall that gives. What stops these conversations is shame, and grief.

'We don't have a tradition in the way you blokes do,' I said. Everybody laughed, with relief.

'There must be a line of women's writing,' said Natalie, 'running from the beginning till now.'

'It's a shadow tradition,' I said. 'It's there, but nobody knows what it is.'

'We've been trained in *your* tradition,' said Natalie. 'We're honorary men.'

She was not looking at me, nor I at her.

The coffee was ready, and we drank it. Natalie went to pick up her children from school. My friend put in the plug and began to wash the dishes. The stranger tilted his chair back against the wall, and I leaned on the bench.

'What happened to your hand?' he said.

'I cut it on the glass shelf yesterday,' I said, 'when I was defrosting the fridge.'

'There's a packet of Bandaids in the fruit bowl,' said my friend from the sink.

I stripped off the old plaster and took a fresh one from the dish. But before I could yank its little ripcord and pull it out of its wrapper, the stranger got up from his chair, walked all the way round the table and across the room, and stopped in front of me. He took the Bandaid and said,

'Do you want me to put it on for you?'

I drew a breath to say *what we say*: 'Oh, it's all right, thanks— I can do it myself.'

But instead, I don't know why, I let out my independent breath, and took another. I gave him my hand.

'Do you like dressing wounds?' I said, in a smart tone to cover my surprise.

He did not answer this, but spread out my palm and had a good look at the cut. It was deep and precise, like a freshly dug trench, bloody still at the bottom, but with nasty white soggy edges where the plaster had prevented the skin from drying.

'You've made a mess of yourself, haven't you,' he said.

'Oh, it's nothing much,' I said airily. 'It only hurt while it was actually happening.'

He was not listening. He was concentrating on the thing. His fingers were pale, square and clean. He peeled off the two protective flaps and laid the sticky bandage across the cut. He pressed one side of it, and then the other, against my skin, smoothed them flat with his thumbs, and let go.

The Girls Love Each Other

The girls love each other these days. That's what I told Beth last week. She'd just got back from Bali and we were having one of our catch-up sessions: Beth comes into the salon at eight and we talk our heads off while I give her a shampoo and brush-up before work. By half past there's cold coffee and cigarette ash and photos all over the bench. We're always frantic—that's our word—but it's our only time to really talk since Beth moved in with Douglas, and I've got Morveen at home most of the time. With friends.

That's what I was trying to talk about with Beth. That was my news. After she'd shown me her tan (she was worried she was *too* dark), and given me my carving and the batik for Morveen and gone on about all the tourists who'd been after Mardi's body and even hers—I told her that I was sharing my house with *three* unemployed teenage girls.

'Jan, you're too easy-going,' Beth said, for about the thousandth time. Two weeks alone with Mardi (her daughter, Morveen's age) had been enough for her, thank you, though they'd had their good times too, some good talks. I started to say that yes, so had we, it was interesting in a way.

'Actually,' Beth went on, bending her head away from the blower, 'it's not the girls so much I mind, it's all the boyfriends hanging around.'

'There's no boyfriends,' I said. I was standing over Beth, layering up her left side, she's got lovely hair, coarse, blonde, shapes up beautifully. Then I found myself saying it, as if it had been on my mind all the time: 'The girls love each other these days.'

There was just that moment when Beth looked up and caught my eye waiting in the mirror, and looked down again. Ticking back over ten years like I'd been doing.

'First I've heard of it,' she said.

Morveen and Mardi practically share a birthday—they're both Leos—but it took Beth and me quite a time to give up on pretending they were friends. They learned ballet and tap together until Morveen just wouldn't get into the car one day. And in the school holidays Beth and I would take a day off and drag the girls round town to lunch and a matinee. 'Go on your own,' they told us in the end. Then by the time Mardi was fourteen you'd have thought she was twenty: she's working out at Channel 9 now and the trip to Bali was the prize for the Beach Queen heat last year.

Morveen's like me, no show pony, she doesn't even try. But up to now there's always been this little thing between Beth and me, that our girls were in the same race, only Morveen was shy and young for her age.

I suddenly remembered how different Beth and I were. How when we used to work together at Max's she wouldn't talk to any of the clients she thought were 'weirdos', and called old Max 'the poofter' behind his back. And how she just doesn't say anything about Morveen going on the dole when she could have got a place in the Teachers' College. Morveen had said she wanted a break to think things over, and I know what she means. I'd wanted that too once, and then when Johnny my son left, I'd *had* to have it—Morveen's had a lot to handle, one way or another. There are some things Beth doesn't understand.

'You know,' I started, though I didn't know what I was going to say. But Beth jumped up, she had to rush, she was frantic, she had to be in Perth by nine (she's a cosmetic rep these days) and Douglas had asked all these people over for drinks that night.

'Sure you won't come?' she asked, patting her hair in the mirror. 'Bring Bradley? How is he these days?'

'I haven't seen him for a while,' I said, 'since the girls came.'

'Take care,' she said (it's one of Douglas's expressions). We kissed each other at the door.

Friday is our busy day at the salon, but every time I turned on the blower I was taken back to what I'd said to Beth. I thought about the girls. How they just seemed to appear in my life, sitting round the kitchen table. I'd been to a movie with Bradley; we nearly fell over a couple of duffle bags in the hall. Then we saw these three cropped heads turning towards us at the kitchen door. Morveen had a little glittery catch in her eyes that she gets when she's pleased about something.

It turned out that Steph is a sort of cousin by friendship. Lily Carson, her grandmother, was my mother's best friend. I just remember Lily before she moved to Sydney, but something about Steph's neat sharp face and her quick way of talking reminded me of her.

'Yeah, everyone says that,' Steph said. It seemed that Linda, Steph's friend, who's got a soft baby face and smokes a lot, had been having hassles with the Youth Hostel. They'd been telling Morveen about it. They wondered if . . . So I said they could have Johnny's room.

Bradley didn't stay long. It didn't feel right somehow, to go into the lounge with the whisky and close the sliding doors like we usually do. He stood up and straightened his jacket and said: 'Goodnight . . . girls.'

'Night,' they said, hardly looking at him.

At the door he said: 'Be careful Janet. Don't let them take advantage of you.' We didn't make any plans for the next weekend.

It soon became clear that the last thing those girls wanted was to take advantage of a fellow woman. They decided that since I was the worker they would do all the shopping and cooking and washing-up.

'That's how a co-operative works,' Linda explained to me.

'In some circumstances,' I said, 'it's also called marriage.'

'We're not asking you for sexual favours,' Steph said with a little smile.

But it worked out pretty well. In fact shopping and cooking seemed to be all they did do.

'It's such lovely weather,' I said, 'and you've hardly seen anything of Perth.'

'Depends what you're interested in,' Steph said. She smiled at Morveen and me. She's got a lovely smile.

Some nights they borrowed my old Torana and went to hear some music in a pub or see a film in Fremantle. Mostly they sat around talking. On nights that we were all at home I seemed to be expected to join in. I must say there was something about the way Steph gave you all her attention, with big nods at everything you'd say, that really got you going. I'd never heard Morveen talk as much either.

Steph tackled me about my job. How did I feel, she asked, that as a hairdresser, I basically 'exploited the beauty trip' that men laid on women? I said that most of my clients at 'Janette's' were older women coming in for a trim or a perm. 'Nobody wants hair down to their ankles,' I said.

'Come on Jan, I'm talking about fashion.'

'Look at you three, that's a fashion isn't it? Who cuts your hair anyway?'

'It's not fashion, it's anti-fashion. It's cut by a friend in Sydney who's dropped out of the straight hair-dressing scene.'

'And it *feels* good,' put in Linda.

'So does my hair,' I said. 'And I can blow-dry it in a few minutes.'

'Whether you know it or not,' Steph said, 'you wear it like that to attract men.'

'Yeah,' said Morveen.

'Well who are you trying to attract with your hairdos then?' I said. 'Each other?'

They seemed to think this was a huge joke. Linda started to clap and knocked her drink over Steph's record.

'By the way,' Steph said, grabbing the record off Linda and wiping it without looking at her, 'I need a trim. You wouldn't . . .?'

'No, I wouldn't,' I said.

It was good for Morveen and me, having the others there. It was a relief not to come home and find her sleeping with five apple-cores beside her bed. Or hear the fridge door open and close all evening while she ate as if she had to save her life.

When had I last heard her hum like she did when she was cooking the co-operative meals? I guess it was when she was a kid and she'd come in after Johnny had taken her for a ride on his bike. She's never been one for smiling much—all chins and frown as a baby—but when we'd all been talking and it was getting late, she had this sort of sleepy soft look about her, and she'd rest her head on the nearest shoulder. When it was mine I wanted to stop talking, everything, and put my arms around her, but I'm not that silly.

I found out that all this time she'd never liked her name.

'It was your grandmother's name,' I said. 'It's Welsh.'

'So?' she said. 'I don't like it. *Mor—veen.*' She beat her fist on the table in time and glared at me. 'Mor—veen—Jones.' Bang, bang, bang.

'I never thought of it like that,' I said. Lennie had wanted it, and then it had become part of a different sound, 'Johnny and Morveen', the sound that kept me going.

But the next time I came home I heard Steph say quite casually as she put on a record, 'Do you know this one, Veen?' From then on it was 'Veen this' and 'Veen that'. No one said a word about it.

The story of my marriage went down very well. They sat there shaking their heads through the saga of Lennie and his disappearing act. Linda jumped up and started massaging my neck. Not that their own family histories sounded much better. Though I must say it surprised me that a son of old Lily Carson would be a 'mental wife-beater' and an 'alcoholic capitalist exploiter'. His wife's only sin seemed to be that she 'freshened up before hubby came home'. I don't suppose I came off any better when I'd gone to work.

Then the last Saturday before they went, I was lying out the back in my bikini, soaking up the lovely late summer sun. Even my face, though Beth's told me off about that often enough. I still get a kick out of my backyard after all those years in the flat. It's just a big square of brown grass sloping down to an old peppermint tree by the fence.

Then I heard the crying. It was coming from Johnny's room on the back verandah. Not just crying, but an awful rising wail that seemed to curl around my stomach. I picked it out, like you do with little children, as Linda's voice. I sat up and everything went blurry. I heard the other two run in to her. She screamed 'You!' There was talking, and the crying dropped away.

It was all over in a minute. I lay down again but my stomach kept on tightening. I could see our washing dancing at me on the line, the girls' big clown clothes flapping against my uniforms and panty-hose and bras. After a while I made my way inside. I just kept thinking, I don't know, I don't know anything.

I took the girls out to the bus station on Saturday afternoon, as soon as I got home from work. The co-operative had been winding down that last week, the girls had gone out a lot more. I was glad, I was tired: even at work I seemed to be hearing their young voices all day, back and forth with mine.

They didn't talk much in the car. Every time I'd say something to Morveen next to me, she'd say 'What?' She kept looking out the window, humming.

At the bus station Steph fished out their tickets from the little purse she wears looped around her waist, and Linda queued with their bags. There seemed to be a rhythm going round between them all. I watched Steph, standing there with her head just nodding and one foot tapping away in its old tennis shoe. I thought, she's so sure. She's dangerous.

They stood waiting for the call then, the three of them, with their arms around one another. When it was time to go there were big serious hugs all round.

'Jan, thank you,' Linda said through tears. I watched them darting off behind the other passengers, like children. When I turned, I found that Morveen had already set off. I saw her striding ahead of me towards the car.

It seemed so quiet at home that afternoon, you could hear the peppermint tree tossing about in the wind. Morveen went straight to her room. I couldn't settle to anything. I put a few things back to their old places in the kitchen. In the end I jumped in the shower. Then Morveen stuck her head round the door and said: 'It's the big B for you on the phone.'

Bradley's voice seemed to come from another world. I stood there watching the mist spread out from my hot toes over the polished boards. He was trying to let me know how busy he'd been these past weeks.

'Are you all right?' he asked.

'I've missed you.'

There was a pause. Then very gruff he said:

'Pick you up at eight then—sweetie.'

Morveen came into the hall.

'Are you going out tonight?' The same old question.

'Yes,' I said. 'Are you?'

'I'm not into socialising, just for the sake of it.'

'Some of us actually enjoy a man's company from time to time. Drinking and talking like you've been doing every night.'

'We had real talk. But Bradley's a shithead. They've all been shitheads, you know that.'

'Don't you think,' I said at last, 'that there's any good men around?'

'Well one thing's for sure,' she said, walking off. 'I don't need them.'

I headed outside then and sat on the front steps, still in my dressing gown. There are no houses in front of us, just a lovely stretch of sky over the railway line. The street lights had come on and the evening traffic was starting up. I watched the cars, joined up by headlights, filing towards the subway.

Saturday nights. The city. Morveen always hated me going out in the old days. She'd scream and scream so Johnny'd have to take her for a ride around the block while Beth and I drove off. 'She's just jealous,' Beth would say, accelerating. 'You deserve a bit of fun.'

Morveen hated me talking on the phone too, those long sessions picking up the pieces after all the fun. Every two minutes one of us would have to break off to hiss and slap and bribe with biscuits, just to stay on that life-line, just to say: 'Do you know what that bastard said to me?'

And now here was Morveen saying she could do without all that. You could hardly blame her. I think her view's lopsided: she thinks mine is. We're opposite each other like a pair of scales. But for a long time my side carried the weights. Maybe Morveen was pushed out of balance, right from the start.

I *had* learnt some things. Not enough for Morveen now, not enough to even up. But I learned to pay my own way. In the beginning, when I married Lennie Jones, I thought that from then on I'd be taken care of. Even afterwards, when I was alone, I had my sheikh dream. I'd be walking to the bus-stop after work (Jan, you get along now, Max'd always say, dead on five, I'd spend all year wondering what I could buy him for Christmas), two buses I needed to get the kids home, and I'd think that if a big fat sheikh pulled up beside me in a limousine, I'd just crawl right in. 'Come on kids,' I'd say. 'We're going to live in a harem. Won't that be fun?'

Beth came along and she taught me: you always pay your own way. Now I didn't ask for much, just my own place, and a chat with Beth, and Bradley turning up from time to time.

Bradley's a shithead. Well I know what she means. You think he's good-looking, so clean and well-cut, till you get up close and there's something missing in his face, he has to practise looking you in the eye. And practise having what he calls his 'R and R': he fits me in between badminton and bushwalks, and then cuts everything short to get a good night's sleep. He can't cope otherwise, he says. Well, that's how he is.

So why do I bother? Just sometimes, out of the blue, driving home late, or having breakfast, once when we were standing in a queue, I start to tease him, I can't stop myself, I'm laughing like nothing matters any more. And he bends his head to me (he's very tall) and calls me a terrible girl, and keeps looking at me sideways in a shy, pleased way . . . So I hang in there, while the weeks build up again between us, work and the telephone, dinner and a show. Waiting for those real times again.

Morveen was sitting beside me in the dark.

'Jan. I'm going to Sydney.'

'When?' The stars seemed tiny above the lights on the road.

'As soon as I can get my act together.'

'What'll you do there?'

'Live with the others. They've got a big place, there's six of them.'

'Six girls,' I said.

'I'll look for work of course. I'm not going to bludge forever.'

'Six girls, in a house. Don't you think that's a bit . . . narrow?'

'People come and go a lot, Steph says. Anyway, what are you trying to say?'

'I dunno love. It's not my way I guess.' *You pay for your choices*, I wanted to say.

Morveen had put her arm around me.

'Mum, why don't you come over when I'm settled and have a holiday? We'd have a good time I know. We could look for Johnny . . . Steph and Linda reckon you should.'

'Thanks love. I'll think about it.'

Morveen jumped up soon and went inside. She couldn't keep still for long that night.

I felt very tired out there. Too tired to get ready for Bradley. It was getting cold.

The phone rang. Beth.

'I know this is an awful time to ring,' she said as usual. 'It's just that I'm feeling so *flat*.'

'That makes two of us.'

Then she was off. Douglas hadn't come home yet, he was on his high horse, he said she drank too much when she was with his friends. Who were so boring anyway . . .

'Honestly Jan, sometimes I miss the old days. When you and I used to hit the town. I think I'm a romantic at heart.'

Also her tan was peeling, and Mardi was off looking for a flat. 'God knows what she'll get up to then,' she said.

In the kitchen Morveen had switched on the light and the radio. I smelt scrambled eggs and I felt like a glass of wine. This was something that seemed to stretch right back to Mum and Lily Carson. A kind of talk. I'd been speaking it for years now at the back of all the heads of those faces in the mirror.

'Hold on a sec Beth,' I said. I whipped into the kitchen and filled up a glass from the cask with a wink at Morveen.

'Anyway, how's things with you?' Beth asked. You always have to remind her that you've got a life ticking away there too. 'How's Morveen and the girls?'

'The girls have gone back to Sydney,' I said, 'and Morveen's going to go over there too.' I took a deep sip while Beth went on about how they all leave us and how we'd probably end up in a Home together.

'Morveen wants me to come over for a holiday.'

'Yeah?' said Beth, listening.

'I dunno, I'd have to get someone in at the salon, and it might put Bradley out a bit, and I'm tired, there doesn't seem much point . . .'

'Well hang it all,' Beth said, out of the silence. 'Hang it all, why don't you go?'

Conrad's Bear

Behind us a voice on the video was announcing that breast feeding is the most natural and fulfilling thing in the world. The voice continued with a description of how the sucking action is healthy for baby. A groan shivered along the queue. An Aboriginal kid began bashing a stick on the only empty chair. Every time his stick hit the red vinyl, it made a plastic *squwach.*

I gave the receptionist the letter from my doctor, and she told me to wait in the line for the Breast Clinic. Two women who knew each other were talking quietly. 'Last night,' the tall one said, moving her bracelets up her arm, 'I dreamt that when they opened up my breast, it was made of wood. Music came out from my insides, from my pipes and tubes. And glands. The doctor couldn't work it out. After a while I regained consciousness, and they'd taken a baby out of my breast. Tiny and coloured, like a Russian doll.'

The queue had moved on and I was at the desk again. The same woman gave me some forms to take down a corridor to the X-ray clinic. A doctor rushed toward me, opening the plastic flap doors against my arm. 'Sorry,' she called, 'emergency.' There was a swell of jittering and shushing noises behind me.

The waiting room for the X-ray clinic had wood panelling like a railway carriage. I sat on a long bench seat, facing cubicles numbered 1, 2, 3.

Three other women were staring at the cubicles already: a small one, who wanted a cigarette; a large one with a handbag upright on her lap; and a European lady surrounded by shopping bags, who was reading a book written in Spanish. The small one couldn't stop talking. She came from Narrabeen, she said. I took out a book also, and that left the large lady with the handbag to respond. She turned sideways and frowned politely.

'Northern beaches,' the small one said. 'When I squeezed my breast this morning, blood came out of the nipple.'

I looked down at the cover of my book; *Para-criticisms: seven speculations of the times*. I opened it in the middle and began to read.

> Beckett, we recall, ends *How It Is* by confessing that it wasn't.
>
> 'Joyce's last novel is not an end but a start.
> The argument for its position in a literature of silence, in a tradition of anti-literature . . .'
>
> Here the Speaker stops, dismayed by intimations from his audience, and before he can resume, a voice interrupts.
> THE VOICE
> Pedantry and peeling plaster. Tradition is a cushion, a chair, a construct.
>
> The issue is still symbolism, i.e., the crisis of forms, i.e., the re-making of human consciousness.

'Blood?' the large lady said, 'you must be very worried.'

'I am, a bit. Do you live in Sydney?'

The large lady laughed, and opened her handbag. She took out a photo and held it out.

'This is where I live. Wee Waa.'

And getting no response, she said, 'Cotton country. That's our farm.'

'Very dry, isn't it?' the other one said.

The large woman laughed again. 'Not now it isn't, it's flooded now,' she said. 'The roads are cut off.'

'Oh dear,' the small woman said. She turned the photo over in her hand, as if she expected to see the flooded cotton appear on the back, and then returned it. The clasp on the handbag snapped shut and the large lady leaned back and closed her eyes.

I began to read again . . .

> There is a curious music in the wood: the dream of the longest night of the year. Joyce says: 'I have put the language to sleep.'

. . . But still Nora frets: 'Why don't you write sensible books that people can understand?'

The small woman is hoping it's a blocked milk duct. Her daughter came in last year for a lump; her daughter is twenty-four. Now the small woman turned sideways to face the large one.

'I get very tender, specially at certain times of the month. I don't get periods but I still get cranky, and I get sore here.'

They both have their hands on their sore breasts, hand on heart. They exchange the following information: the large one has a prolapsed bowel and bladder; the small one a prolapsed womb.

At that moment my eyes were drawn to a sentence at the bottom of the page: something about the prelapsarian world, and I tried to imagine these women in Eden, thirty years ago.

Now the two talkers pass on to how many kids they've reared, and what their husbands do, and where they live. The small one said a six-lane highway had been put in, right outside her bedroom window. She thinks they might sell up, she's had enough.

'Of the rat race,' the other one said.

The small woman had taken off her shoes, and was rearranging them in her stockinged feet. She noticed my silver vinyl sneakers and my black-and-silver striped lame socks, and she nudged the large lady. I kept my head in the book.

The door of Cubicle 3 swung open and the tall woman with bracelets, dressed in a blue surgical gown, leaned out and told us confidentially that the X-ray would hurt. 'The mammogram is so painful,' she said, 'they put a balloon on you and press.' A nurse called her from the room on the other side of the cubicles, the door to our side shut, she disappeared.

The talkers agreed that they were both used to a lot of pain. The small one said her third child took fifty-six hours. 'They should have done a Caesarean, the doctor said after the prolapse. When they took my uterus out, they were amazed. They said it was the smallest thing they'd ever seen.'

The tall woman with bracelets reappeared, dressed in street clothes. 'All that squeezing could *give* me cancer if I haven't already got it.' The Spanish lady looked up from her book and clucked her tongue. As the tall woman left, she called over her shoulder: 'Get out your tissues!'

'My daughter didn't say it hurt,' the small one said. 'I'm sure *she* would have said.'

The voice from the other side of the cubicles called out a foreign name and then a curt, 'Take everything off down to your waist.' The Spanish lady, despite her bulk, leapt up from the seat and made several trips to the cubicle with her things. The three of us remaining stared at the bulge of her shopping bags under the door. She was taking off her shoes.

This reminded the small woman of her own shoes, which she now put back on. 'They say anything worthwhile hurts, don't they.' She smiled at me, and at the large lady. Her neck was full of tiny creases, her face perky and bright as a bird's.

Both women crossed their legs and sat in silence. After a time, they re-crossed their legs, as if by some agreed on symmetry.

'My doctor called it a mammeograph,' the large one said, 'and yours calls it a mammogram. I wonder why.'

'You wonder about doctors,' the small one replied.

My book was now describing how Samuel Beckett came to visit James Joyce in Paris, 1933, and how he courted Joyce's mad daughter, Lucia.

> The room is comfortable, is sordid in the middle-class way. There are chairs everywhere. Two men, tall and lank, sit together, legs crossed, toe of the upper leg under the instep of the lower. They do not speak. Joyce is sad for himself, and Beckett sad for the world.
>
> Lucia is not in the room. Beckett has not really come to see her. Her infatuation with Sam will pass into madness. Jim and Sam continue in silence.

'Cotton country,' the large woman said to a new arrival, 'Wee Waa. So I hope I don't have to come back, it's a long way. We're staying over on the north side. We got all the red lights, coming here.' We have all moved up one place on the bench.

In the machine my breast was flattened by two plates, one from above, a clear perspex one, and another from beneath. I saw my breast flattened to a triangle. Two curved black-dotted lines on the perspex showed against the white flesh, and now my breast looked like a chart in the butcher's shop.

'Come back in two hours,' someone said.

I went to see my mother who had forty minutes between trains at Central. She was on her way to visit my sister, who had had a baby the week before. It was a boy called Conrad. I wanted to give Mum something to take to the baby, but the shops at Central sold only souvenirs, and that didn't seem appropriate.

'I told Dad I was entitled to my own opinion,' she said. The train was leaving in six minutes. 'I told him I thought his behaviour at Christmas was . . . what did I say now?' (she looked around the train for her word).

We had been to the cafeteria and eaten bread rolls with a boiled egg and pickled onions.

'How is your writing?' she asked.

'Difficult.'

I gave her a thermos of coffee and some sandwiches and dried figs for the trip: she was going the long way, taking the train to Yass and then a bus to Canberra. 'Enjoy your adventure,' I said as we kissed goodbye. She put back her head and puffed out her cheeks. It was the first time she had gone on a trip on her own.

When I got back to the hospital the Sister said they would need to take another X-ray, but the clinic didn't open for half an hour.

I sat in the doctor's waiting-room and a woman said to me: 'She's all right, they said. It's just hormonal. Something to do with the change.' I looked up: it was the large Wee Waa cotton farm woman with her handbag still upright like a small dog on her lap.

'You mean the woman from Narrabeen,' I said.

'Yes, she's gone now. All OK.'

I felt I ought to be pleased, but I couldn't form a smile and I couldn't sit through any more difficult births, prolapses, cancer scares. I read in my book that Joyce and Beckett divide language between them, but at that time I couldn't see how they had done it.

I crossed the road to the main section of the hospital and went into a shop which sold aftershave and slippers and teddy bears. I spent fifteen minutes looking at all the bears, one by one. In the end, I chose the one which looked most like a bear, and paid the man on the till $18.95. The man kissed the bear on the nose before he wrapped it: it was his favourite of the lot, too, he said. I asked if he had any Panadol. 'We're not allowed to sell it in the hospital,' he said.

I took the bear to the cafeteria next to the shop. People were standing in the queue and asking themselves, 'What do I want?' There was a choice of products containing sugar, salt, food additives, preservatives, artificial colouring and flavouring, and there was nicotine. No, they didn't sell headache tablets. They weren't allowed. There was a chemist in Newtown, only three or four blocks away. I looked outside at the heat rising off the bitumen.

I sat down with a ginger beer and lit a cigarette. Then the Aboriginal woman noticed my tobacco and came over and asked could she roll one, so I pushed it across the table to her. I looked around for the kid with the stick, but he wasn't there.

All this time I had the teddy bear under my arm, and although it was wrapped in brown paper which crackled, I realized I was holding it to comfort myself. My parcel. I made a note to post it that afternoon. I suppose it was fear. I didn't feel fear, only the headaches.

Back at the waiting-room, two doctors, a woman and a man, wheeled in a huge machine and took it up in the lift. So many machines to find out about the body's diseases. A blue nurse and a white nurse walked past in step, one behind the other. When they came back, still in step, I asked the blue nurse whether she might find me a Panadol. 'I'll get the doctor to write you a script,' she said. 'We have our own pharmacy here.'

At three o'clock I went back to the clinic and the radiologist who must have seen every size and shape and colour of breast which exists in the world, put me in the chair and manoeuvred the machine again. 'Lean right into it. I won't break your ribs, don't worry. Turn your head this way, lean in now.'

The doctor was younger than me. He admired my shoes and socks and told me to take off my blouse and bra. I took off my blouse, which was a three-second operation, and stood there in my trousers and fancy shoes. I tried not to look at him; he had the soft glowing skin of a twenty-year-old. My mother had laughed at my shoes: 'You always liked weird shoes,' she said, 'and gumboots. There was a whole year when you'd only wear gumboots, and I had to buy them for the other five. Do you remember that?' I didn't remember then, but standing in the doctor's office now I remembered a photo of the girls, all in a line wearing gumboots.

I lay on the examination bed and closed my eyes. The doctor felt carefully for lumps. Where the pain was, no lump. An unexplained pain. 'How did you notice it?' he asked.

'The car,' I said, 'this is where the seatbelt crosses me.'

'Yes,' he said, 'a lot of people find it that way. But I can't feel anything.'

He rang the X-ray clinic while I was getting dressed. As the radiologist spoke, the doctor covered the mouthpiece and smiled at me. 'Nothing on the X-rays,' he whispered. Beckett, I thought, 'How it is by confessing that it wasn't.'

My headache thumped against the walls of the corridor *whump*, and came back to me. 'Any luck getting me a Panadol?' I said to the nurse. 'X-rays clear? Yes, we can always tell by your faces. That's good, you're one of the lucky ones.' On my behalf she breathed a sigh of relief. I drove home in the heat, the bear in brown paper on my lap, no sensation of relief, just the mirage on the road, and the seatbelt crossing me.

The Test is, if They Drown

Miss Spear in number forty-two is a witch. From the street we can see her sometimes on her verandah, spreading her hair over a towel on her shoulders to dry in the sun. We gather at a safe distance and whisper across the sunny air—Witch! The hiss fades before it reaches her. She never looks around at us.

Behind her house, up on The Rock, my gang and Mick's gang meet. From high above we can look down into her garden, where the cat stalks among great clumps of vine-smothered rose bushes, and sometimes Miss Spear herself comes out and drags ineffectually at the consuming creepers.

Miss Spear is what happens to you if the orange peel doesn't make a letter when you drop it on the ground. It nearly always makes an S. That means you'll marry Steven or Sam or Stan. Sometimes it makes a C and you take a second look at Carl and Conrad. Miss Spear's what happens to you if you don't step on all the cracks in the footpath between the school gate and Spencer's shop. Miss Spear's what happens to you if the numbers on the bottom of the bus ticket don't add up to an even number. She's what happens when you lose a game of Old Maid.

When she leaves the house to shop, she wears a skirt that reaches her ankles, and sandshoes. She's never been seen without the unravelling straw hat with the feathers stuck in the band. The cat comes to the gate with her and sits with its front paws tidily together and its eyes narrowed waiting for her to come home.

Mum calls her *Poor Miss Spear*, and says there's a sad story there somewhere. Dad says that Miss Spear wasn't ever anything to

write home about. Mum shakes her head and mashes the spuds
with a great rattle, punishing them, her lips gone thin. She thumps
the saucepan down on the table and says that it's a good thing Miss
Spear's got her house and a bit of independence at least. Dad
laughs as he pulls the potatoes towards him and says he reckons
she's got a bob or two stashed away in there.

At the shops she buys fish and milk and according to Mr
Spencer the grocer, more eggs than you'd believe. The butcher
skilfully rolls the corned beef and ties it with string, living proof
that no-one needs more than two fingers on each hand. He tells
Mum that Miss Spear comes in once a month for a piece of best
fillet. He doesn't see hide nor hair, he says, then regular as clock-
work there she is wanting a bit of best fillet. The butcher says he
supposes Old Spear's harmless, and Mum agrees with a sigh as she
puts the corned beef in the basket.

Of course Miss Spear isn't really just an old maid whose dad
left her the house when he died, like they say. She can't really be
just an old stick whose cat gets fish every day while she makes do
with eggs except for a treat once a month. An old lady wearing
funny clothes living in a big house with a cat must be a witch. No
way she can be anything else. A witch a murderer a gobbler of
children a creature from another planet. An alien.

Up on The Rock we watch her cat stalking a butterfly through
the long grass, sliding on its belly, ears flattened to its skull. My
gang has just beaten Mick's gang at spitting. All us girls got it
further than the boys. And in spite of her ladylike pucker, Sonia got
it furthest of all.

Mick shifts round restlessly, looking for a way to impress us.

'Betchas don't know what she did, the Witch,' he says.
'Betchas can't guess.'

I lean back and pick a scab on my knee. I'm not worried, I can
beat him at anything except Indian wrestling and even then I can
usually trick him into losing. I'm better at nearly everything than
the boys. Pam and Sonia are hopeless the way they're always
worried about getting dirty or being home late for tea. But they're
my gang and I'm the only girl that's got one.

Mick hasn't done too well with the suspense so he hurries to the punch line.

'She murdered her mum. Got this carving knife see and chopped her in little bits.'

Stewart and Ross are impressed. Ross wipes a fleck of saliva from the corner of his mouth and says avidly:

'Geez what she done with the bits eh Mick?'

Mick hasn't thought that far.

'That's, um, a secret.'

He purses his lips and pretends to be very interested in the way a bird is flying past above us.

'Aw come on Mick tell us, tell us.'

Pam and Sonia won't let him off the hook.

'Betcha don't know, come on tell us or that means you don't know.'

An impressive pause from Mick. Stewart and Ross lean forward agog.

'She buried the bits in the garden. Right down there.'

He points dramatically down into the tangles below.

'S'that all?'

Pam and Sonia are openly contemptuous and even Ross and Stewart are disappointed. Mick'e eyes dart around as he tries to come up with an embellishment. This is my moment.

''Fraid you've got it all wrong,' I say casually.

They all look at me expectantly. Girl or no girl they know I always deliver the goods.

'It was her dad. She killed her dad.'

Mick is beginning a shrug. Mum or dad, so what?

'With cyanide. One drop in his tea every day for six months. She mixed it with the sugar so when he put sugar in his tea he got the cyanide.'

The awed silence seems to demand some more details.

'And then when he was dead . . . she stuffed him. Like Phar Lap. He's in a glass case in her bedroom. To keep the dust off.'

Stewart's mouth is hanging open and he's breathing loudly through his nose as he always does when concentrating.

'Geez what a weirdo eh.'

Mick jabs him with a sharp elbow and shouts:

'Oh yeah, sez who. You gunna believe a girl, fellas?'

Stewart snaps his mouth shut like carp and nods. But his eyes are still glassy with the idea of such a sweet and unsuspecting death.

Ross glances at Mick and mutters to me furtively:

'What did she stuff him with? She pull his brains out his nose like them Egyptians did? What she done with the guts?'

I've got all the answers. But Mick's tired of having his thunder stolen.

'Shaddup stoopid, she doesn't know nuffin. What ja believe her for?'

He hawks and spits the same way I've seen his father do.

'C'mon, I can't be bothered hanging round these sissy girls any more. C'mon gang, I've had it.'

We sit in silence after they leave. Sonia blows a huge bubble with her gum and watches it cross-eyed before sucking it back in. She chews it and tucks it away in the corner of her mouth.

'That for real, she knocked off her dad? Howja know?'

Leadership means having no fear of the next lie. I say immediately:

'I looked in the window. He's sitting up there in this glass case.'

Pam stops sucking the end of her plait and tosses it back over her shoulder.

'He got clothes on? Or not?'

She's watching me closely.

'Course he's got clothes on. His pyjamas.'

'What colour, Sandy?'

'Blue and white stripes.'

Lies must always be switched truths. The glass case from the skeleton at the Museum. Dad's blue and white pyjamas.

Sonia blows a great flecked bubble and we all watch as it trembles, threatening to burst over her face. She deflates it masterfully and gets up.

'Time for tea.'

Leadership is never being quite sure if they believe you.

'Oooaah Sandy you've got all moss on your shorts, your Mum'll kill you.'

Her smooth pink face expresses satisfaction at this.

Sometimes I hate girls.

I plan my raid carefully, and alone of course. Pam and Sonia would giggle at the wrong moment or get panicky about spiders. And although I almost believe now in the body and the glass case, I want to be alone when I make sure.

I watch from behind the oleander until Miss Spear comes out to go to the shops. She sets off without seeing me, her hair showing through the hole in the top of her hat. The cat slips through the bars of the gate and sits blinking. It yawns once and begins washing its ears.

I watch Miss Spear until she turns the corner, and wonder what she is. Women don't wear hats like that, that you can see hair through. Women don't wear sandshoes and no socks so their ankles show red and sinewy. And women don't chop heads off dandelions with a stick as she's doing now. If Mrs Longman at school with her smooth chignon and her dainty handkerchiefs is a woman, where does that leave Miss Spear?

When she's disappeared I cross the road and pull aside a loose paling in the fence. I glance up and down the street before sliding through the hole and dragging the plank back into place behind me.

Straight away everything becomes terribly quiet. I can still hear the billycarts rattling down Bent Street, and a dog barking across the road, but all these sounds are very far away, and seem to fade as I stand listening, until I can only hear silence ringing in my ears. Miss Spear's garden has locked me into its stillness. Behind the thick bushes and the fence, the street is invisible and belongs to some other world. It may not even exist any more. A leaf gives me a fright, planing down suddenly onto my shoulder, and my gasp seems deafening. The windows of Miss Spear's house stare at me and the verandah gapes open-mouthed. The shadow of one of the tall chimneys lies over my feet and I step aside quickly. It's a few minutes before I can make myself tiptoe down the overgrown path towards the back of the house. Damp hydrangea bushes, as tall as I am, crowd over the path, holding out clammy flowers like brains. The leaves are as smooth as skin as I push through and some are heavy with the weight of snails glued to them. Sonia and Pam would be squealing by now.

In the back garden, the grass has not been cut for a long time, and blows in the breeze like wheat. I creep towards one of the windows on hands and knees, moving twigs out of the way so they won't snap noisily. I'm doing well, being very silent. I am feeling better about all this when a mild voice behind me says hello.

For a few mad seconds I think that if I stay quite still I won't be seen. My green sweater against the green grass, the famous chameleon girl.

'I thought you were a little dog at first.'

Since the earth does not seem about to open and swallow me, I stand up. Miss Spear is holding a carton of eggs and a bottle of milk. I see her teeth as she smiles, and her eyes under the shadow of her hat. I can see freckles across the bridge of her nose and a small dark mole beside her mouth. I've never been so close to her before.

'Exploring?'

I stand numbly, waiting for a miracle. No miracle occurs and she moves closer and says:

'You live down the street don't you? I've seen you around.'

She watches me in a friendly way while I wonder if I could pretend to be deaf and dumb. The cat comes and winds itself around her ankles, smoothing its tail along her shins.

'You want some milk, don't you. This is Augustus,' she explains to me. 'He's greedy but he's good at catching mice. Augustus, say hello to our visitor.'

She pushes her hat further back on her head so that I can see her whole face. It is a perfectly ordinary old face with wrinkles in all the usual places.

'I don't know your name,' she says, and smiles so that the wrinkles deepen.

'Sandy,' I hear myself say, and become hot in the face.

It is too late now to pretend to be deaf and dumb.

'Sandy, that's a boy's name,' she says. 'I've got a boy's name too.'

She looks at my hat.

'Your hat's a bit like mine,' she says. 'And we both collect feathers.'

I pull the hat off my head and crush it between my hands. My hat is nothing like hers.

'I've got something you might like,' she says. 'I never use it, but someone should have it. Won't you come in for a moment?'

Even Mrs Longman would not be able to be more genteel.

'Perhaps you'd like a glass of milk.'

Anyone would think it's quite normal to be a mad spinster in sandshoes. I follow her into a kitchen more or less like most kitchens and watch as she pours some milk into a saucer and gives it to Augustus. She pours a glass for me and I sit down and drink it while she rummages in a drawer. I glance around between sips, feeling congested by this situation. But in this kitchen there's a stove and a lino floor and a broom in the corner. Just the usual things.

'Here we are.'

She hands me a penknife and I open all the blades and look at it. It's a very good one. It even has a tiny pair of scissors. When I've inspected it I become aware of her watching me. I hand it back to her, but she won't take it.

'No,' she says, 'it's for you. It used to be mine when I was a tomboy like you.'

I turn the knife over in my hands, feeling clumsy. My hands seem to be a few sizes too big and I feel that I'm breathing noisily. Here I am, sitting talking to Miss Spear the alien, drinking the milk of Miss Spear the poisoner, accepting a gift from the witch.

She takes the knife and attaches it to my belt.

'Look, you can clip it on here,' she says. 'Then it won't get lost.'

She sits across the table and with both hands carefully lifts her hat off her head. When she sees me watching, she wrinkles up her eyes at me.

'Sometimes I forget I've got it on,' she says.

Augustus jumps into her lap and whisks her cheeks with his tail. She brushes the tail away as if it's tickling her, sneezes, and says:

'He's very affectionate. As you can see.'

She strokes the cat and smiles through the swishing tail at me. I can hear a tap dripping in a sink. The sound is peaceful and I find myself relaxing. I unclip the knife and while I'm having another look at it, I try to frame some impossible question. How come you're so normal? I could ask, or: What's it like being a witch?

'It's great,' I bring out at last. 'Thanks a lot Miss Spear.'

She goes on stroking Augustus and smiling. I can't think of anything else to say. I want to go, yet I like it here. I want to find the others and tell them all about it, and yet I don't want to say anything to anyone about it. Miss Spear puts the cat down and gets up.

'Drop in any time. Next time I'll show you the tree house.'

Out on the street, the proper standards resume their places. Miss Spear is loony. I take the knife off my belt and put it in my pocket. I keep it in my hand, but out of sight. Mick has decided he wants to hear about the brains being pulled down the nostrils, after all. But now I don't want to tell him.

Stewart glows with righteous indignation.

'We oughter tell the cops about her. She outer be locked up I reckon. Them shoes she wears and that old hat like a . . . bunch of weeds.'

Ross nods energetically, and his eyes bulge more than usual as he says:

'She's not normal my mum says. Oughter be locked up in the loony bin.'

Mick says loudly:

'My dad says what she needs is a good fuck.'

We all stare, shocked and admiring. Sonia giggles behind her hand. Mick takes courage from this and calls down into Miss Spear's backyard: What you need is a good fuck. The hydrangea bushes shift in the breeze and I feel the knife in my pocket. Sonia beside me shrills out: Silly old witch, and Pam joins in: Witchy witchy ugly old witchy. Ross takes up the idea: Witchetty grub witchetty grub. Mick stares at me.

'What's up Sandy, you scared or summing?'

I want to push him over the cliff, ram moss into his mouth, stab him to the heart.

'She's just an old bird. Leave her alone.'

Sonia stares at me making her blue eyes very wide and surprised.

'Oh yeah? Since when? You gone potty or summing?'

Pam grabs my hat.

'They'd make a good pair, look at this dirty old thing just like hers.'

She stares, pretending to be frightened.

'She's turning into a witch, quick Sonia, look.'

Sonia stares at me, her mouth in an artificial smile like the one Mrs Longman uses when she explains silkily how girls don't shout like that Sandra dear. Pam is staring at me too. I see them ready to tear me limb from limb. I look at the boys and see them too, waiting to pounce, waiting for me to go further and step out of line. Their eyes are like knives, like packs of snapping dogs, like slow poison, like sharp weapons raised to kill.

Miss Spear comes into her backyard and pulls at a few tendrils creeping over a rose bush. Mick nudges me.

'Go on, say something. I dare you.'

They're all watching me and waiting. Leadership means falling into line. Miss Spear is directly underneath, her hair poking through the hole in her hat, Augustus following a few yards behind as she walks among the roses. I want to stab Mick and Sonia and

Pam and rip the smiles off their faces. Or is it Miss Spear I want to stamp on and destroy? Below us she looks small, weak, hateful. I want to crush her like an ant, to be part of the pack and hunt her down as she runs alone.

'Silly old witch, silly old witch,' I yell.

My voice is carried away on the breeze. She doesn't look up. Behind me the others are chanting:

'Ugly old witch, silly old witch.'

Sonia uses some imagination.

'Red white and blue, the boys love you.'

She laughs so hard she begins to dribble. We take up the chant, laughing at Sonia's dribble and the way Miss Spear can't hear us. Mick yells:

'Come on beautiful, give us a kiss!'

I'm laughing, or something, so hard the tears are running down my face and I can hardly breathe. I hear myself screaming:

'Nasty old witch, nasty old witch, I hate you!'

The last words carry and she looks up at last. We all stare in silence across the air. I seem to be staring straight into her flecked hazel eyes. Mick nudges me.

'I dare you, tell her she needs a good fuck.'

The tears rise in my throat and run down my cheeks and across the silent air I hear myself yell, yell straight into her eyes, see her face on a level with mine and see the freckles across her nose like mine and her smile as she says I was a tomboy like you are, I hear myself yell and see her face change across the distance as I screech, You need a good fuck, fucking witch, until my voice cracks, I see her look down and turn away and walk into the house.

It's very quiet. I look around for the others but they've already turned away. Sonia picks her way down the first part of the rocks and turns back to look up at me.

'You've got all dirt on your face,' she says. 'You look real silly.'

She turns away again and climbs down out of sight. Without looking at me, Pam follows her. Mick and his gang have already gone down the other way.

The hydrangeas, the house, the sky shudder and fracture and I stand with my hands in my pockets holding Miss Spear's knife and whispering, witch, ugly fucking old witch, until at last the tears clear and I see the garden again, and watch Augustus as he darts out from under a bush. He glances up and seems to meet my gaze for an accusing second before he slips across the grass to the verandah. The house closes smoothly behind him like water.

The Serpent's Covenant

A nation chants, *But we know your story already*. The bells peal every-where. Church bells calling the faithful to the tabernacle where the gates of heaven will open, but not for the wicked. Calling inno-cent little black girls from a distant Aboriginal community where the white dove bearing an olive branch never lands. Little girls who come back home after church on Sunday, who look around themselves at the human fallout and announce matter-of-factly, *Armageddon begins here*.

From time immemorial the ancestral serpent, a creature larger than storm clouds, gathered on the horizon, came down from the stars laden with its own enormity of creative pursuits. Perhaps it moved graciously—if you had been watching with the eyes of a bird hovering in the sky far above the ground. Looking down at the serpent's wet body, glistening from an ancient sunlight reflecting off its body, long before man was a creature who could contem-plate the next moment in time. Perhaps it moved those billions of years ago, with a speed unknown to measuring devices, to crawl on its heavy belly all around the wet clay soils in the Gulf of Carpentaria.

Picture the creative serpent, scoring deep into—perhaps scouring down through—the slippery underground of the mud flats, leaving in its wake the thunderous sounds of tunnels collaps-ing behind the tip of its tail, to form deep sunken valleys. Instantaneously, the sea water following in the serpent's wake, swarming in a frenzy of tidal waves, soon changed colour from ocean blue to yellow mud. The water filled the swirling rocks to form the mighty bending rivers spread across the vast plains of the Gulf country. So the serpent travelled over stretches of marine plains, past the mangrove forests, over the salt flats, through the sand ridges and crawled inland. Then it went back to the sea. And it came out at another spot along the coastline and crawled inland and back again.

When it finished creating the many rivers in its wake, it created one last river, no larger or smaller than the others, that offers no apologies for its nature of discontent with people who do not know it. This is where the giant serpent continues to live deep down under the ground in a vast network of limestone aquifers. They say its being is porous, it permeates everything. It is all around in the atmosphere and is attached to the lives of the river people like skin.

It is in this tidal river snake of flowing mud, that its body takes in breaths of a size that is difficult to comprehend to a human mind no longer able to dream. Imagine the serpent's breathing rhythms as the tide flowing inland, edging towards the spring waters nestled deeply in gorges of ancient limestone plateaux, covered with rattling grasses dried yellow from the prevailing winds. Then, with the outward breath, the tide turns and the serpent flows back to its own circulating mass of shallow waters in a giant water basin, in a crook of the mainland geography whose sides separate it from the open sea.

To catch this breath in the river you need the patience of one who can spend days doing nothing. If you wait under the river gum where those up-to-no-good type, Mission-bred kids accidentally hanged *Cry-baby Sally*, the tip of the dead branch points to where the serpent's breath fights its way through a tunnel of wind, creating ripples that shimmer silver, similar to the scales of a small, nocturnal serpent; thrashing in anger whenever the light hits its slippery translucent body, making it writhe and wrench to escape back into its natural environment of darkness.

The inside knowledge about this river and coastal region is the traditional knowledge of Aboriginal law handed down through the ages since time began. Otherwise, how would one know where to look in the hidden underwater courses of the vast flooding mud-plains, full of serpents and fish in the monsoon season of summer? Can someone who did not grow up in a place that is sometimes under water, that is sometimes bone-dry, know when the trade winds blowing off the southern and northern hemispheres will merge in summer? Know the moment of climatic change better than they know themselves? Know who fishes in the yellow-coloured monsoonal runoff from the drainages, with sheets of deep water pouring into the wide rivers swollen over its banks, filling vast plains with flood water? Meanwhile, the cyclones linger and regroup, the rain never stops pouring, but the fat fish are abundant.

It takes a particular kind of knowledge to go with the river, whatever its mood. It is about there being no difference between you and the movement of water. Where you know already in your own mind that you are already moving with the water as it is sea-sonally shifting its tracks according to its own mood. A river that spurns human endeavour in one dramatic gesture of jilting a lover who had never really been known, as it did to the frontier town built on its banks in the hectic heyday of colonial vigour. A town intended to serve as a port for the shipping trade for the hinterland of Northern Australia.

In one moment, during one wet season early in the century, the town lost its harbour waters when the river simply decided to change course, to bypass it by several kilometres. Just like that. The waterless port survives with more-or-less nothing to do. Meanwhile, its citizens continue to engage in dialogue with them-selves passed down the generations, on why the town should con-tinue to exist. They stayed on to safeguard the northern coastline from a locally predicted invasion of the Yellow Peril. A dreadful vision, a long yellow streak marching behind an arrowhead point-ing straight for Port D'Arcy. Eventually the heat subsided over that issue. When the Yellow Peril did not invade, everyone had a good look around and found a more contemporary reason for existence. It meant the town still had to be vigilant. Duty did not fall on one or two; duty was everybody's business. To keep a good eye out for whenever the moment presented itself, to give voice to a testimonial far beyond personal experience—to comment on the state of their local Blacks. It was regarded as an economic contribution to state rights, then, as an afterthought, to the maintenance of the decent society of the whole nation.

Norm Phantom was an old tribal man who lived all of his life in the dense prickle-bush scrub on the edge of town. He lived amidst thickets of closely growing slender plants with barely anything for leaves, that never gave an ant an inch of shelter under a thousand of its thorny branches. This foreign infestation on the edge of Port D'Arcy grew out of the era long before anyone in the Phantom family could remember. They had lived out there in a human dumping-ground next to the smell of the town tip since the day Norm was born. All choked up, living piled up together in trash humpies made of tin, cloth and plastic too, salvaged from the rubbish dump. The descendants of the pioneer families, who claimed ownership of the town, said, *The Aborigines were really not part of the town at all*. Sure, they worked the dunny cart in the old days, carted the rubbish and swept the streets. *Furthermore*, they said, *the Aborigines were dumped here by the pastoralists, because they refused to pay the blackfellas equal wages, even when they came in*. Right on the edge of somebody else's town, didn't they? Dumped the lot of them without any sign of lock, stock or barrel.

No, the prickle-bush was from the time just before the motor car, when goods and chattels came up by camel train, until the old Afghan brothers, Abdullah and Abdul, disappeared along the track called the 'lifeline', connecting north to south. After much time had passed the jokes came about Afghans being *shifty dogs, dodgy dogs, murdering dogs* and—*unreliable*. When the cupboards turned bare, the town talk finally turned into one sensible realisation that very likely the camel men were never coming back—then everyone in town assumed they had died. A few of the Christian-minded, trying to capitalise on the gross lack of decency in town, sniffed, *Well! That ought to teach you now, won't it?* But no-one else thought so, because by then the grog and the tucker were being freighted up by mail truck, which everyone thought was a more convenient method of road transport by any stretch of the imagination.

One cloud-covered night, the camels finally turned up in Port D'Arcy, jingling and a-jangling, their foreign bells swaying around their necks, vespers on such a still night. At once, the residents woke up in childlike fright, sitting straight up in their beds, eyes wide open like zombies seeing dark figures moving in their pitch-black bedroom, same time reckoning it was ghosts with an Afghan smell, true God, just came straight in, levitating, taking over, helping themselves, walking around people's homes with no *mind youse*, not one shred of good manners whatsoever. Couldn't even knock on the door first before coming into someone's house. That was the trouble with New Australians the town claimed: *even dead ones had no manners.* Unnaturalised. Really un-Australian. *You shoulda sent out a search party?* Tongue-eating cats. Hissing in such a horrible night. Neighbours passing the buck in mind-talk. What a relief it was for dawn to come early and everyone could see for themselves it was just poor old Abdullah's and Abdul's camels.

Over the following days no-one thought to capture the animals to retrieve the rotting pack saddles. The townsfolk had a deeply felt aversion to touching the belongings of dark-skinned foreigners—or their animals. So, the camels just wandered around at their own will, all covered with yaws from the rotting packs of foodstuffs: flour, sugar, grain-growing sprouts that had died, still strapped over and hanging off their backs until something had to be done. The poor beasts were officially rounded up. The screaming, uncooperative animals didn't comprehend English, or barbarism either. After being hounded, stoned and whipped for several hours by their pursuers on foot and horseback, the camels were eventually moved out over the claypans and shot. In the archival records, written with a thick nib by a heavy-handed municipal clerk, it is recorded *Camels removed*. The first entry of work completed by the town's Municipal Council.

In the old camel-drivers' camps the seeds of Mimosa became embedded in camel dung and sprouted their hard little shoots in the wet season. Thousands of seeds spread along every track and gully, flooding with sheet water from the rain to regenerate in shallow mud pools. The shoots sent down their fat roots to take a steely grip on the clay pans, holding the land together in a permanent mirage that looked like it might last forever without water. In this mirage the cattle properties prospered on traditional lands taken but never ceded. Today, herds of Brahman cattle leave their tracks crisscrossing the landscape in the dry season, as they search for stubbly patches of blue grass and grind the top layers of poor soil to powdered bulldust.

The prickle-bush mob say that Norm could grab hold of the river in his mind and live with it as his father's fathers had done before him. His ancestors were the river people who were living with the river from before time began. Norm was like ebbing water, he came and went on the flowing waters of the river right out to the sea. He stayed away on the water as long as he pleased. So it seemed to everyone who talked about him. He knew fish and he was on friendly terms with gropers, the giant cod fish of the Gulf sea, that swam in schools of fifty or more; on the move right up the river following his boat in for company. The old people say that the groper lives for hundreds of years and maybe Norm would too. When he talked about the stars, they said he knew as much about the sky as he did about water. The prickle-bush mob said he had always chased the constellations: *We watched him as a little boy running off into the night trying to catch stars.* They were certain he knew the secret of getting there. They thought he would go right up to the stars in the company of groper fish when it stormed at sea, when the sea and the sky became one, because, otherwise, how could he have come back?

'How do you do that?' was the question everyone asked.

'The water doesn't worry me,' Norm answered simply, although he knew that when his mind went for a walk, his body followed.

Everyone at Port D'Arcy was used to the sight of Norm's jeep driving north to meet up with the river's edge. It was the only vehicle Norm ever owned. Always, the small tinnie boat, full of dints, a stray bullet hole or two, strapped onto the roof. A vessel purchased with cross-country road transport in mind, much more than water safety.

They say he knew these deep muddy waters better than the big salties: crocs that got tangled up in the nets in the middle of the night. Glassy-eyed monsters that came over the side of his tiny craft looking for action with the big river man. Angry jaws charging for a 'winner-takes-all' kind of fight in the swamping boat, snapping in full flight, water splashing up into a storm with the swishing, thrash, thrash, thrashing of an angry tail against the side of the boat. People like to remember Norm saying, in melancholic fashion (faking a thoroughly modern Americanised impersonation of a presidential Captain Hook) that those snapping jaws meant diddly-squat to him. Must have remembered seeing it on TV.

Meanwhile, he moved like a hopping hare, fumbling for what seemed like ages to find the gun. Norm ended hundreds of lives of prehistoric living fossils this way with his gun pointing all over the place in a turmoil of water and thick leather crankiness, until he made a direct hit between the eyes of the reptile caught in an instant of moonlight. The rifle he claimed to have won in a fight, albeit, according to more local gossip, taken while screaming for *the Lord to buy him a Mercedes Benz*, shaking the loaded weapon around like a mad dog, in an ugly gesture of conquest in one of many episodes of pub brawling.

Even so, in this otherwise quietly living population of about 300 people, no living soul remembered what the port looked like. No picture could be put on display in a showcase at the museum of scarce memorabilia, because no-one at the time of the heyday thought it was worthwhile to take a photo. But it was clear that everybody knew that this was Norm's river.

One day, someone in town was languishing around in a laconic stupor following several months of heatwave in the wet season buildup, waiting for the rain to come. Lying flat-out like a corpse on the bare linoleum floor in the hall-way of a house exactly like the one next door. Capturing in a long sigh of appreciation the northern sea-breeze that came waltzing straight over twenty-five kilometres of mud flats, whistling their arrival through the front door while, on the way out, slamming the back door open and shut. All of a sudden this someone thought of changing the name of the river to *Norm*. And, in a town where change never came easy, it came to be.

There was a celebration by the local Shire Council. The occasion was the anniversary of the port's first one hundred years. It coincided with a spate of unusual happenings that occurred under a short-lived era of Aboriginal domination of the Council. *Harmless coercing of the natives*, the social planners hummed, anxious to make deals happen for the impending mining boom. Meaningful coexistence could now accommodate almost any request whatsoever, including changing a river's name to Norm. On the other hand, during this 'honeymoon' period, those Aboriginal people who took the plunge to be councillors wisely used their time in public office to pursue scraps of personal gain for their own families living amidst the muck of third world poverty.

All this was part and parcel of the excitement of Port D'Arcy when the first multinational mining company came into the region. Numerous short-lived profiteering schemes were concocted for the locals, in order to serve the big company's own predetermined interests as it set about to pillage the region's treasure trove. A publicly touted curve of an underground range embedded with rich mineralisation.

The elaborate, white linen ceremony attracted southern politicians from the state government, who flew in for the day. Most of them were known by the local dignitaries as a bunch of fly-by-nighters. And what's more, as they rolled out the welcome smile, some locals whispered unmentionable insults behind the backs of their very important visitors. Other locals, who liked the sound of their own voices, attacked the politicians straight out with insults. Yelling out, the crowd picked up bits wafting in the wind gusts: *Youse are always cowering down on the ground! . . . Are youse the runt of the Australian political litter or something? . . . Yah! Falling*

*over yaselves to any foreign investor flocking up the steps of State
Parliament, knocking on the big door, and kind-of smelling like money . . .*

The politicians and mining executives who sponsored the
event with more-or-less an open cheque-book, mingled uncomfortably with the crowd, and pushed themselves up against old
Norm for a photo opportunity. They got snapped by members of
the media circus who had jockeyed for any free rides on the official
executive jets to attend the event.

Except, the proceedings had to be rushed through by the
compère, a popular radio personality from the Mother of all
Mining Cities in the neighbouring Shire. This was because everything got ruined by a normal sort of dust-storm thundering in
from the south. A thick wall of red dust mingled with all manner
of crunched vegetation and plastic shopping bags that it gathered
up in its path, damaged all of the cut sandwiches when it came
through. All of the fingers, toes, eyes, ears, noses, lips, fidget-
prone adults panicked, running for cover along with their red and
green cordial-stained, screaming children.

Then came a violent electrical storm where the rain ruined
the day anyway—as the town's sceptics said it would. A taut
occasion, despite these dramatic interventions; nevertheless,
enough time had transpired for the now-disposed-of State Premier
to complete the ceremony of officially changing the name of the
river, from that of a long-deceased Imperial Queen, to 'Norm's
River'. Traditional people gathered up for the event mumbled,
Ngabarn, Ngabarn, Mandagi, and so did Norm in a very loud and
sour-sounding voice over the loud-speaker in his extremely short
thank you address, although those who knew a fruit salad full of
abuse in the local languages, knew he was not saying *Thank you!
Thank you!* and belly-laughed themselves silly because the river
only had one name from the beginning of time. It was called
Wangala.

It was a funny thing about the river. Everybody wanted to
have a part of it, perhaps hoping to be a little bit like Norm.
Anybody and everybody thought they might ride this river like
some legendary buckjumping, wild horse called Diesel or Gidgee

or Mulga. Lots of people were always travelling up to the northern coastline over the rough roads of the Gulf on long weekends. They'd haul up and launch straight over the side into the yellow river: flash fishing boats called sixties C&W names like *Donna, Stella* and *Trixie*. Bright-coloured boats, powered by engines of many horsepower, bought with top dollar gained from doing stretch-shifts two kilometres down underground, hauling up rich ores scraped from the motherlode embedded in sequences of rock that looked like the growth rings of a powerful, ancient being.

And on the water they would cast a line here, a line there, over the sides with state-of-the-art fishing tackle, but no know-ledge of the way of the river. Nothing was thought about it. What mattered was that a considerable number of people lived in the region now, with the great influx of mine workers who had nothing to do on their days off. Their little *boom and die* towns were fast and modern, even if they just barely represented a country-and-western style, commercial frontierism. Meanwhile, more new mines became established in the region with little regard for what was anyone's say-so.

When the mining stopped, neither Norm Phantom and his family, his family's relations, past or present, rated a mention in the official version of the region's history. There was no tangible evidence of their existence. Even in Uncle Micky's collection of bullet cartridges.

Micky had lived with a metal detector for God knows how long. He said he had a fever which drove him on because he would never know when he picked up the last piece of evidence—all of those forty-fours, thirty-thirtys, three-o-threes, twelve gauges—all kinds of cartridges used in the massacre of the local tribes. He had maps, names of witnesses, details, the lot. A walk-ing encyclopaedia. Now his voice lives on in the great archive of cassettes which he left for the war trials he predicted would happen one day.

But no tourists go to Micky's museum. Maybe because it was built in the wrong spot. But that's fighting for you. Fighting, fighting all the time for a bit of land and a little bit of recognition.

Then all the old mines, old mining equipment, old miners, old miner's huts, skeletons of miners in the cupboard, anything to do with mining was packaged in a mishmash of nothing and marketed on gloss as the ultimate of local tourist attractions. The shiny covers of these tourist brochures celebrating selected historical sites and museums ought to grab you from across the room at airports, hotels and motels, or from the rack of any tourist or travel centre selling the highlights of mining. You can't even hide the stuff because of its iridescence.

But this was not vaudeville. Wars were fought here. If you had your patch destroyed you'd be screaming too. The serpent's covenant permeated everything, even the little black girls with hair combed back off their face and bobby-pinned neatly for church, listening quietly to the nation that claims to know everything except the exact dates its world will end. Then, almost whispering, they shyly ask, has the weather been forecast correctly today?

If you are someone who visits old cemeteries, wait awhile if you visit the water people. The old Gulf country men and women who took our besieged memories to the grave might just climb out of the mud and tell you the real story of what happened here.

Other Places

I

The intersecting other place of this recollection is the island of Timor. On maps it appears as a tiny oblong, hanging at the end of the Indonesian archipelago, floating inconspicuously to the north of Australia. It is small but precise, a material place, with a politics, a currency, poor roads, monsoons, mountains, wild deer. There have been books written about it; it is certified, real. One can point on the map with a confident finger and say: here it is, you see, this is where I journeyed.

But as I recollect now—in this most facile of transportations, this space-negating shift, this cartographical defiance, the island begins to quiver and become deliquescent; it melts suddenly away into the sapphire-blue sea, subsides as easily and tremulously as any fiction.

How to substantiate? How to refabricate the unfashionable 'real'?

Let me begin—distrusting as I do the general and sempiternal—with a central spot and a specific time. The spot is the market place in the city of Dili, the capital of East Timor. Nothing about this market is fixed or permanent; there are no stalls or trestles, shelters or plastic signs, such as one sees elsewhere in commercial Asia. Nor is there anything of the pleasures of exchange, the colour of commodities, the lurid ornaments of display, the bustle of buyers. This is a place which is crude and rudimentary; it is a place of poverty.

Vendors leave their villages in the inhospitable dark, walk jungle miles with straw baskets and slings, and come, eventually and in centripetal procession, to a large rectangle of stone foundations, the only remains of a once grand civic building bombed by the Japanese and never reconstructed. In this vacant site, this blank of a building, they assemble in an imperfect geometry of rows, lay their goods on the stones, squat on their haunches, and wait for light.

When sunrise comes there is a second, more casual convergence of pedestrians. Other poor people enter the place of stones, move about slowly between the human rows, gaze down upon bananas, rice and fish, and begin to establish the equations of transaction. Tiny silver coins of minute denominations preciously travel from palm to palm. There is a certain polite haggling over paltry sums governed by the scrupulous justice of scarcity. Then finally the coins are deposited in laps, in concaves of fabric sumptuously patterned over by triangles, spheres, zig-zags and diamonds, intermingled with hibiscus, oleander and plume shaped leaves.

The fabrics these people wear invert the substance of their lives; they carry in representation the proclivities of decoration and embellishment they do not otherwise enjoy. The fabrics are dirty and faded, but this does not at all distract from the quality of anomaly.

As the sun moves higher the vendors will place shallow baskets on their heads to serve as hats. Men stand up from time to time to air their hot genitals by flapping the splendid cloth of their lap-making sarongs.

Women employ fans at beautiful, bronze, emaciated faces— faces a Eurocentric artist might wish to construe in the Exotic Island genre, might render, in consequence, more fleshly and more erotic. But the women at this moment evade the sublime. Their thinness is unpainterly, their poses unconventional; moreover, like the men they chew the oblivion-giving betel nut. Their open mouths appear as cavernous pools of blood; their lips are red-ringed. Jets of scarlet spittle are expertly ejected in long narrow arcs. The betel nut chewing is culturally enclosing; in this way the market women remain narcotic and aloof.

The heat becomes visible in a series of verticals and begins at this stage to corrupt the produce on display: mounds of carmine chillies shrivel untidily inwards; fish begin to stink and turn at the edges; bananas gain spots and exaggerate their curves. By noon most of the sunstruck food is removed. The disappointed people in their anomalous fabrics disassemble the rows and walk away into the sunlight, by now overhead and incandescently severe.

The time of this market is the month of December in 1974. At this world-historical juncture East Timor is ruled over by the remote but not disinterested nation of Portugal.

In the 1520s Portuguese merchants usurped the island, hoping for spices, slaves, minerals, sandalwood; longing, perhaps for the piratical exercise of illicit lusts, the adventure of governance, the amenities of power, the excesses of the imperial. On the Belunese and Atoni, the main indigenous clans, they imposed ineffectually a language and a religion; more effectually they wrought a system of economic deprivation.

Apart from a few ostentatious stone buildings, a church here and there, a makeshift airport, there is little physical evidence of over four hundred years of colonial rule. The people still live in their ancient thatched huts (which come in rectangles, ovals and attractive beehives), still farm in a laborious and primitive fashion (the Asiatic mode-of-production intact, with no gifts of machinery from the mechanised West), still suffer the misery of decimating famines (with the saying 'hunger as usual' as their most famous slogan) and still honour the complex, devoluted authority of tribal chiefs, local allegiances, and matrilinearity (despite the Western exercise of larger and apparently more salient powers).

When, in the august year of 1904, the Luso-Hollandesa treaty finally settled the vexed issue of Dutch contestation of Timor—by granting the West to Holland and the East to Portugal—the people of the island did not appear to celebrate. Maps were redrawn in lavish offices by uniformed men, but life nearer the equator continued unmapped. Rebellions arose and were efficiently crushed; certain uniformed men gained swift promotion. The Imperial mode, with all its cannibal appetites, was, in the language of the smiling victors, 'firmly reconsolidated'.

This tiny half-island is about to be granted independence and nationhood. In the month of October voices in Lisbon announced the future: East Timor would be liberated in 1976. Thus around the stone market, burdened by boredom and watching the leaving women with lazy appraisal, move conscripted soldiers from a regime made recently more redundant, more vicarious and more risible than usual.

The soldiers wait out their thankless historical allocation, their—let us say—devious misplacement. They slump with their rifles in the immoderate heat, or drive in failing jeeps over treacherous roads. At night they will gather to share subsidised wine which bears on its labels the names of their home towns and then, as if in this far colony mere names were enough, they will drink and drink until the name enjoins fluidly with the cascade of alcohol so that they are flushed nostalgically, rushed away, sent buoyantly backwards on bargain basement currents to the places of reference. Noise will ensue, prostitutes will be found, and the men will eventually return, sodden and saddened, by way of all flesh.

The soldiers are already anticipating the wine; you can see it in the focusless vacancy of gaze that follows only vaguely the women's dispersal.

II

Into this scene and this time steps an inexperienced young traveller in search of lunch. She steps over hot stones which bloom, like a garish carpet of disordered poppies, with a thousand spat blossoms of dried betel juice. Most of the food is already removed; she settled for a hand of pink-coloured bananas from a man slow in leaving.

A group of soldiers nearby start to whistle and raise their voices, noting, apparently, the familiar vulnerability of the single female. She becomes self-conscious and is suddenly tentative. She retreats uneasily, lassoed by looks and knowing she has supplied some extra code of exploitation in the ease of her capture.

Over to the left—past the official white-washed buildings and the modest Hotel Turisto, past a cluster of shabby Chinese owned shops, from which men invite, with blackmarket obsequiousness, the exchange of Escudos for dollars, past a barracks storehouse, a tawdry bar, a pearly monument of the Virgin hovering unnuminous at a street corner—a commotion occurs to intercept our little drama. A speeding truck, upon which chanting men are crowded, swings into view.

In the traveller's sunglasses the truck is reduplicated; and its miniatures enlarge as it speeds towards her. She forgets the soldiers and the soldiers forget her. They have lifted their rifles. The young woman leaps back against a stucco wall pockmarked by bullet holes from the last world war and smells in the same instant the scent of squashed banana.

The men on the truck, some in Western dress, chant 'FRETILIN, FRETILIN, FRETILIN'.

Their arms are upraised in a revolutionary salute. They are weaponless and smiling. The truck begins blurring past, speed-transfigured, but then it skids unexpectedly to a jerking stop. The soldiers tense up, hoping, trigger-happy, for trouble-to-write-home-about, for significant danger, perhaps a glimpse of atrocity, but to their disappointment are hailed in the friendliest of fashions by a civilian white man who has climbed down from the back of the vehicle. He is apparently enjoying his anti-climactic arrival; he laughs with the others before he signals with a wave for the driver to move on. The chants resume their noisy barrage of fricatives: 'FRETILIN, FRETILIN, FRETILIN', and the miniatures diminish even faster than they arrived, and no less animate.

Our traveller is stuck in a tight clasp of time: the heat is arresting, the sunshine vertiginous. She will later reprimand herself for so public a fear, but now she looks up and her sunglasses receive, in both smooth screens, the approaching white man.

He ambles towards her, halts within inches, smiles politely, and bends to his knees. Then without yet speaking a single word of hallo, he removes a handkerchief from his pocket and sets about wiping a smear of banana from the cloth of her skirt. The traveller keenly watches the top of his head; there is a definite circle of premature baldness which, with its simple ordinariness and rather more complex invitation of caress, unfastens the clasp and replaces the instability of the moment. There is also the cleansing gesture which, mediaevally supplicant, modest, deftly intimate, compels above all her act of attention.

III

Shall I lapse sentimental? Connive with the expectation of traveller's tales confessions? Lust and indiscretion in foreign lands? The suppliant embrace of a sultry stranger beneath silhouetted palms and a crescent moon?

No commodious clichés embrace these memories: I cast about, circumlocutory, for forms of expression, and find myself recentred on the candour of the specific, on the fallible face, on the miserable inexactitude of what one believes to have been actual.

I met Patrick Donelly when he bent to wipe banana from the cloth of my skirt. At that time he was working as a doctor in the Dili hospital, the only foreign volunteer, I was later to discover, among a population of medicos conscripted from Portugal. I looked down upon his head, and thought his simple action a signifier of romance: I thought him gallant and prepossessing, assumed, by his confidence, a certain dynamics of physical attraction.

As it happened this was mistaken: Patrick had stopped because he thought me a visiting Australian journalist (rumoured to be arriving any day that week) and wished to enlist aid in publicising the country's shortage of food and medical supplies. His motive was political, his disappointment evident, and I, in response, felt awkwardly apologetic. When we later lunched

together—over tiny buffalo steaks and large mugs of red wine—
we reconciled our mis-meeting through slight inebriation and the
easy camaraderie of dislocated persons.

Dr Patrick Donelly was garrulous and comic, but one of those
men who one knows must carry an undisclosed gravity tucked
somewhere within. I recall that even from the beginning I watched
his face with a lover's interest, noticed the flaws of his skin, an
uneven shave, a slight asymmetry of features. With the elapse of
time this face is now posthumous, yet I remember it with all the
precision of originary presence, as though Patrick is still alive
somewhere to claim and confirm his own memory-dispersed
image.

And this—let me be candid—is the burden of other
places: that they are contiguous in recollection with one's lost
affections, that no matter-of-fact, sensible, or contrivedly
objective description, nor, I might add, no sentimental style,
no encircling banality, manages quite to dispel the aspect of
personalised elegy.

So there is Patrick Donelly with his mug of cheap wine, sitting
beneath a neat dome of pink and mauve oleander, sitting in the
shade of his modest thatched hut—at once singular, humorous,
erratically handsome, unaware of the fast approaching cruelties of
history, and thus assuming, as we all do, a disposition and an aura
of fortunate permanence.

IV

Into the highlands, rude as conquistadors. The car imperious, the
subjugation of space, the tourist-whizz of lives caught snap-shot
emblematic. Voluptuous green. Animals in flight. The thrill of
collapsing and transitory images.

The ostensible reason for our trip was vaccination. We loaded an
army jeep with medical paraphernalia, and drove off in the company of one Afonso Vieira, a soldier of high rank whom Patrick had

greeted, to my jealous dismay, with a prolonged and passionate kiss upon the lips.

We three sped into the hills, left the coastal plain and rose into the emerald and abundant forest, into dominions and repetitions of tidy padi field, past high hills prodigious with Arabica coffee, through scatterings of village life (chickens leaping directionless in a flap of feathers, children racing alongside, workers pausing to register the shape of our invasion), along serpentine roads only speculatively in existence.

Afonso, not I, was the lover of Patrick; in our several weeks together we noted in each other the same kind of longing. There was the same conjunction of attention, forms of copycat behaviour. Our desire enjoined our gazes and led us secretly to a respectful and affectionate collusion. But my rival clearly carried the poise of the chosen: he drove determinatively, smiled, laughed.

In these highlands, said Patrick, there exists a tribe of elusive cleft-palated and red-haired people whom I have never vaccinated. Such seclusion is both admirable and medically inefficacious.

In these highlands, said Patrick, fifty per cent of babies die in their first year of life. Yet the mourning is never attenuated or any the less impassioned.

In these highlands, said Patrick, there are whole villages of people who through dietary deficiency develop goitres of their necks. Some carry formations the size of rockmelons, like marine encrustations.

In these highlands, said Patrick, the population is among the most deprived in the world: you will notice some children disturbingly skeletal. Their bones are as fragile as sticks of chalk.

In these highlands, said Patrick, Fretilin forces are gathering. They are a nationalist group whose philosophy, *mauberismo*, is the liberation of these people, the poorest of the poor.

When Patrick was not talking he sang, in his beautiful bass, the blues of Leadbelly and Robert Johnson. It was a peculiar distraction. We careened round mountains, passing through canopies of dark shadow into oleaginous yellow light, shadow, light, shadow, light, and backwards, windblown, flew negro melancholia. Afonso hummed along; I played the records in parallel in my head, and glimpsed through the window disturbingly skeletal children (entirely unmitigated by Patrick's prediction) pivot to our engine sounds, leap up and weakly chase. (Later the goitres would also shock; there were women so deformed that they appeared almost to possess a second head at their necks.)

The place of our arrival, the base from which we worked, was the district governor's house in the southern region of foothills. We camped with our gear on the open verandah, and set off each day on medical excursions. I remember that Patrick and I dressed in the sarongs of the country, both mock-indigenous and also appropriating, as it were, that consolation of decoration in such grim surrounds. Afonso, I must add, retained his military uniform, and thus commanded servility in every village he entered.

Together we became acquainted with the rigmarole of suffering. We performed doctorly deeds in situations of distress. We were utterly insufficient.

At this point my recollections condense and centre. After goitres, hypodermics, and anxious faces (the melodrama of the true, as Patrick called it), after mad buffalo and gentle deer, after cliffs and rivers, after the denudations of labour and the exhaustion of pity, there is a single special night I remarkably retain.

We had retired rather early to our hard straw mats, and entered, for some reason, on a contract of confession. As children on a school camp—lulled by the expedient communality of darkness, intimate by virtue of the treat of proximity—might choose, in the small hours, to offer up long kept secrets, so we each agreed that night honestly to disclose. Firstly we agreed to talk of some other place, to refuse where we were and to transfer elsewhere. We agreed also to speak of something risky and private, something never before revealed, something that, in the morning, we would hold secret inside us.

By a kind of desperate ventriloquism—since their voices elude me, since I have a tongue and a body and they are mute and incorporeal—I now break open our contract and record these confessions.

It was a moonless night. There were poinciana aroused by breeze, spiralling mosquito coils, oppressive heat.

Afonso: When I was a child we lived in Sintra eleven kilometres from the coast. Do you know Portugal? Well Sintra is not far to the north-west of Lisbon. It lies at the foot of very jagged mountains, so that the scenery all around is green and spectacular. There are two famous castles, set apart and aloof, on a single peak, and these castles appear and reappear through the town, and especially in the capital, on the faces of postcards. So you say the word 'Sintra' and visitors who have been there will think not of villas and apartments of stucco and tile, ancient pastels and orange roofs crowded too close together, communal washing, in the poor quarters, flapping gaily above the streets; nor of the more private wealthier houses that are walled and secretive, sprouting lush gardens, also pastelly and old; they will think instead of the famous castles. One castle, I should have mentioned, is merely fancy ruins: it is Moorish, eighth century. But the other, the magnificent Castelo da Pena, is exactly as a world famous castle should be, fulfilling, as they say, the requirements of imagination. It is of pale grey stone and is a complex arrangement of towers, cupolas and battlemented walls. It is a fairytale vision; it is solid but fabulous, and it is utterly unconnected to the reality that is Sintra.

Children in the town liked to make up little stories about the Castelo da Pena: we lived, you see, almost directly beneath it; it hovered over our heads like a persistent dream and on cloudy days it appeared suddenly more dreamlike than ever, remote, vague, apparently floating. It was like something transported from the realm of picture books; it didn't look as if it ought to exist there in the mountains, which we knew as ordinary, the territory of our picnics and Sunday outings.

The place I return to when I think of my childhood, when I think of Sintra, is not the famous castles—which, incidentally, I never actually visited—it is my grandmother's room. We lived in a grand villa behind a huge wall so that the house I grew up in was engulfed by shadows. But my grandmother's room was built like an attic: that is to say it projected above the roof and above the wall, so that it was wonderfully sunlit and looked out onto the world. From one window you could actually glimpse the Castelo da Pena: it was as though she possessed her own private picture postcard, enlarged and extra clear, framed upon the wall. It was one of many pictures because my grandmother—Nina, her name was, and that was how I addressed her—Nina was a collector of religious icons; and all around the room, on the same level as the castle, were the faces of saints, madonnas, pathetic looking Jesuses, and blue-winged angels. She was very devout and was never seen without her black lace mantilla, so that you would always think she was dressed up and ready to go to church. When she was inside, inside her own room, she still wore the mantilla, and I used to place my little-boy fingers in the eyelets and loops and flower-holes of the lace as she cradled me in her arms.

Nina's room was special not only for its light—which covered its spaces in a variety of yellows and always distinguished it beautifully from the submarine gloom of the rest of the house—but because of her eccentricity. I was not allowed to enter without bidding good day to each face on the wall and then, for some reason, saluting the castle with a kind of parodic militarism. This done Nina would spread her capacious body on an old chintz lounge that lay beneath the window, and I would run and leap onto her, collapsing with giggles into her pillowy breasts, the drapery of her clothes, her womanly, musty, mysterious scents. Then—and it always happened exactly like this, time and again!—I would position myself against her so that I could pull the end of the mantilla across my eyes and look around the room through its complex fine tracery of black flowers and holes. This simple transformation always enchanted me: what was gold became suddenly shaded and dark stencilled; what was known became strange and obscurely dimensioned. Overlays, underlays. New configurations. Faces redesigned. As I fiddled with the lace Nina would start to chatter away in a slow, low monologue: she addressed the faces on the wall in friendly tones, prayed, sometimes, or reminisced, told libellous tales of the people of the town. I lay back against her in that state of greedy physical luxuriance only children can properly practise, with the castle above my head and the gallery of larger-than-lifes on equal and intimate terms, believing my grandmother to be a woman of truly mythic proportions.

This room of my memory contained, apart from icons, many very lovely and enchanting objects. First of all there was an abundance of expensive lace— on the backs of chairs, spread over the bed and the table, hung in corners of the room, even dangling from the lampshade—this compensated, Nina claimed, for a laceless childhood. It gave the room an appearance of frippery which always seemed to me rather at odds with the more serious and tasteful pictures on the wall. There was also a collection of hand-blown glass flower bases—perhaps twenty or more—arranged around the room. These usually stood empty, as exquisite ornaments, some carefully placed to catch light from the window. But on religious high days the flowers would arrive and the room became a kind of florist's dream; the vases bloomed bouquets of every conceivable type and shade. I remember now that there were also ornate candelabras, paperweights and jewels, and of course, a Catholic saint or two crassly reincarnated as plaster monstrosities. At the end of the bed, on a small antique chest of burnished rosewood, lay a stack of my comic books. Nina was illiterate but shared my fanatical pleasure in illustrations and super-heroes. We spent many happy hours reclined on her couch enjoined in the adventures of the Portuguese Spiderman.

Now let me tell you what happened. Nina, to put it frankly, was not of our class. She had been a 'varina', what in English you call a fishwife. My grandfather married her against custom because of her beauty and my father, a proud man, was very ashamed of his mother. Nina liked to embarrass him in company by displaying her fishing knowledge, by speaking in the language of the harbour, and sometimes by pulling me between her gigantic breasts in a way her son thought unseemly and rather vulgar. They always argued loudly and on one occasion he stormed into her room to pick a fight over something, and swung into a fury, sending two glass vases to glittering smithereens and decapitating a little statue of St Anthony of Padua. (St Anthony, needless to say, was Nina's favourite saint, being both Portuguese born and alleged to have preached to a school of fish.) Nina threw me from her, leaped up from the couch, and began shouting obscenities. She was so filled up with noisy anger that I thought the very haloes of the Holy would be set atrembling, that the Madonna would turn her pretty shocked face, that Christ himself would fearfully flinch.

But none of the pictures changed disposition; the outcome of the argument—it was so very sudden, and even now it upsets me—was that Nina disappeared. Father said she had gone mad and was recovering in hospital, but I never saw her again after the drama of that day. I waited and I waited, waited even as the objects in her room were gradually sold or taken away, refusing the evidence of my own sad eyes. Without Nina's presence, or rather with her absence, the room became intolerable. After a while I didn't even bother to climb the stairs; I stayed down in the shadows and tried to forget she had ever existed.

About a year later we moved to live in Lisbon, a move I have always attributed to my father's guilt. New school chums would say, 'Ah, Sintra, the castles!', and I would respond with bravado fantasies about ghosts and warriors and screams from the windows. I would describe with accuracy the Castelo da Pena at the peak of the mountain, and then fill it to the brim with furious kings, headless saints, demented mistresses, spider-limbed heroes. I was extremely popular, as you can imagine. But all the while I was thinking of Nina's room, of its pictures and vases and extravagant lace.

And then there came a moment—I recall it exactly—when I remembered a particular, unusual word Nina had one day used to describe the light in her room. 'Ardentia,' she said, lifting back the curtain, standing, expansive, in a broad ray of silver twilight. Ardentia is a certain strange phosphorescence on the bodies of fish that fishermen learn to see on moonless nights. Her own grandfather, she told me, had taken her on a night cruise when she was very, very small just to see this legendary marine phenomenon. 'Ardentia.' At that moment of recollection I suddenly wept, since it replaced me on the spot, in her arms, beneath the mantilla—this state I had believed irrevocable—with the breath of her speaking, ever so soft and airy, down the back of my neck.

Patrick: The place I am thinking of is a small, out-of-the-way beach resort which I visited as a child for thirteen consecutive summers.

We lived in Melbourne where my father worked as an accounting clerk in an office in the city. We were quite a large family——I had four older brothers——so that we were, as my mother insisted, 'decently poor', living in the inner city in a 'decently shabby' semi-detached house. Our neighbours, as it happened, were a family of five daughters, similarly aged; this coincidence produced a childhood full of cinematically confected expectations of romance, tales of secret dalliances, crossings and criss-crossings of affection and regard, relentless flirtation, impossible desire. The whole neighbourhood seemed to delight in our statistically unlikely symmetry: matches were forecast by amused old ladies; scurrilous jokes were told by adolescents; visitors invariably remarked.

My brothers, I know, took great pride in these circumstances; indeed it later became the basis for their inflated reputations as local casanovas. But I found the entanglement——which was, in any case, mostly based on lies—— very troubling and confining. I felt as if my life were threaded in and knotted to the family of girls, that somehow certain decisions had already been made without my agreement, that I had been caught in a design not of my own making. I watched my mother nightly embroider her industrious way over faint brown-inked lines and believed this was how it was: that I was sewn, bound, and predisposed. This belief somehow included the idea that I would never ever escape our tiny house, that I would be stuck forever sharing a cramped room with others and longing always for little moments of peace and quiet.

I should not overstate. Most of the time I was approximately happy, and was even, as predicted, an especial and close friend of the youngest neighbour. (Her name was Maria and we shared a keen interest in collecting postage stamps.) But it was the conditions of our home life that made our annual visit to the beach so very important.

Since the year of his marriage my father had rented the same beach house for the same two weeks each and every January. This beach house was old, brilliantly whitewashed, and comprehensively comfortable. It had three small bedrooms, and also a wide-latticed, dog-rose entwined, part falling-to-pieces verandah where, in the domestic economy of redistributed bodies (and to my great pleasure), I was allotted a space. Here against the lattice I slept on a stretcher bed under a hanging mosquito net. Entering the net—— this is how I always thought of it——was like creeping indecently under the skirts of some movie star dancer, so flimsy and cosseting and feminine were its folds. But it was a place of encompassing privacy and inertia. In the bleach-bright net I was singular, alone, removed from my brothers who fought in noisy pairs for the upper bunk in each bedroom, removed, more importantly, from the dim house in the city in which, apart from physical discomfort and sibling contestations, there were always high-pitched girl voices issuing in annoying streamers through the too-thin walls.

At night, I remember, I lay awake in the dark for as long as possible. Sleeping half outside was something of an adventure. The sky was very loud with the sound of the sea. Frisky possums skittered in rascal-packs across the roof. And through the superimposition of net and lattice I could see black bobbing rose-heads, trees wind-stirred into hideous shapes, and further, beyond that, a luminous ceiling of nameable stars. When I finally slept it was with these several dark dimensions rising and capsizing, depending on focus, through the layers of the night.

From the very moment I arrived at the summer beach house I began to feel released from my sewn up life. In the first place the pattern of our daily living changed. My mother, her appearance altered by a sun hat she wore only in our January fortnight, no longer prepared meals by the rigorous clock, but became gastronomically inconsistent and explorative. Meals were at all hours and likely to come labelled as 'Monday Surprise' or 'Wednesday Magic'. And she no longer sewed—stitches for pennies—but stretched relaxed on a wicker chair engrossed in magazines which bore smiling women's faces. My father, too, was markedly changed. A man of reticence and regularity, he would stay up late, sleep in, consume alcohol, enlargen, become talkative, friendly, almost accessible; he would dispatch, in short, his city-office self. We were all thus emancipated; our bodies returned to us more definitely sensual, as though we had been shades or Melbourne-embalmed; we remembered how to swim, how to run, how to shout; I tumbled with my brothers on warm subsiding sand, placed my body beside others in the full canary sunlight, slept long and dream-full and wholly languorous.

Yet the most profound change—for me, in any case—occurred in the sea, in the particular little bay at which we daily swam. As I sank my body in, *watching goosebumps arise on flesh becoming blue, gasping from the cold of it—for which, after so many summers, I was still never quite prepared— feeling the inundation of every skin surface, both public and private, I imagined a state of physical dissolution. I imagined that the invisible threads by which I was bound unravelled through the water and were taken by currents, that filaments or skeins trailed away from my body—not, I should say, as if I were some sea-going creature, such as this sounds, but as a mystical being, spool-fashioned and exhilarated. I imagined that I was cleansed and wonderfully renewed. This belief was such that my daily run from the beach house to the sea, through teatree and paperbarks, past rocks to the sand, was filled with a more delicious sense of anticipation than I have ever since experienced. The submersion that followed was slow and solemn, up till the point, that is, when fraternal splashing and horeseplay would invade my imagining.*

So there was the house with its verandah and the sea with its renewal. Year after year we regularly returned; I came to think of the holiday as a kind of incorruptible, bright, cellophane-shiny space in which were distilled only those qualities that countered the city. My life, I thought, subtended always to that point, those two weeks elsewhere, those unencumbered, sea-washed, net-embraced two weeks.

The twelfth summer, however, was different from the rest. Our first week was as usual—I was still on the verandah, still swam, still played. But in the second week there were bushfires somewhere to the west, so that for three whole days the sky was dense with suspended ash. Ash fell in fine sprinkles on the roses over the verandah, it coated the furniture and we could taste it on our tongues. The air became brownish and the sun recoloured an ugly rust red. But worse than this, far worse to my child-mind, was that ash also fell pervasively upon the sea. Waves were dark fringed and ash was deposited in scallop shaped tidal lines all along the beach. I remember that my brothers ran around the bay, scooping up handfuls of the filthy stuff and flinging it at each other, while I stood and stared, utterly dumbfounded, at the sullied sea water. Yet—and this is the strange thing—I still thought it important, vitally important, to swim. To miss even a day would be to destroy the ritual repetition upon which my holiday was founded.

So eventually I walked into the impure sea, I, alone among my brothers, and duly submerged. I did not unravel. I did not transform into unwinding glory. I did not cast off my parents, or the girls next door, or my stupid-seeming brothers. I stayed tight and wound up and when I arose my skin was stained and explicitly polluted. Around me the sun had broken into scarlet fragments that rocked against my body. Particles of ash swam up to adhere to me. The water stank. My brothers called from the shore in mocking voices and I could see my mother in her sun hat move to the middle distance beside the rocks to see what was going on. So it was, that day, that I did not actually cry—since I could not at all bear the thought of witness—but swam into shore pretending to be wholly unaffected and untouched. Yet the swill of ash would later recur in nightmares, terribly multiplied, as a drowning sludge, viscid, suffocating and final.

The thirteenth summer was entirely clean. I thoughtlessly enjoyed myself, not knowing that the visit to the beach house would be my last, that the owner would sell it in the following spring.

My fourteenth summer was thus spent at our house in the city, miserable in exile, bisected in spirit, and dreaming of a seaside which returned contradictorily both in consoling memories and awful nightmares, a seaside which had once, just once, been horribly contaminated, but which was before and ever after absolutely pure.

Narrator: The place which I will tell you about is really my sister's place, for it was she who discovered it, she who boldly claimed it as personal and private, she who appointed it with lavish, fantastic, invisible decorations, spun from the munificence of her own daredevilish mind. No introverted soul, she flung out whimsy and visions as other children do chatter; she was larger-than-life, astonishing, an addict of novelties. I loved her, of course, as she commanded to be loved, with exceeding passion.

The place Anna discovered was a cave at the very edge, the very boundary, of our property. My parents owned a dairy farm in the south-west of Western Australia; it was small and unprofitable, and stood precariously on ancient limestone that reached deep below the earth in a series of caverns and chambers. My father told stories of how, in the past, cattle had been *swallowed whole and in one hungry gulp by the treacherous, disguised hollows of his patch of land, but always added—with due parental regard for the not-too-frightening—that all was now safer and much more stable. Nevertheless he warned us never to investigate new depressions or unfamiliar, unusual chinks or cavities: these, my father announced (tapping his pipe in a gesture of emphasis), were the swallowing kind, the mouth to look out for.*

I trod the soil twice daily with my older sister as we brought in the cows for milking at dawn and at dusk. My feet were unsure. I lived for many years—until, in fact, the discovery of the cave—with the belief that I might one day precipitously be claimed by an instant hole, that I might suddenly fall away into an awful, oral darkness, and never be recovered. (Anna was not bothered by such terrestrial threats; in fact she was a child of apparently no fears at all, convinced of her own invincible tangibility.)

Yet I enjoyed the farm. Our house was set low in a slight valley or declension so that around us rose paddocks unfolding in a vista of mounts and undulations, creek channels and gullies, all of which were spotted with immobile looking cows and over-hung and over-seen by drifting hawks. The paddocks were green and pungent with dung, the cows black and white, the hawks an indefinite aerial brown. Red gums and sheoaks stood in isolated native patches: fences perspectively trailed. There was a glistening dam, and a few large rocky outcrops. A wooden milking shed quaintly showed dilapidation; another, newer and of corrugated iron, housed a hire-purchase tractor.

So lovely and specific in re-creation, this farmscape existed then as the unobtrusive circumstance, the mere daily condition, of my childhood life. (Like many rural born I know my home more exactly with excommunication.) I moved through its features barely aware, charmed, perhaps, but also largely indifferent, and with only the risk of a plunge disturbing my habitual unreflection.

Anna, I believe, was more observant than I. It was she, that day, who pointed with an ah ha! at the rocks near the boundary. We were upon our horses, inspecting the fences, but finding fencelines too strict and boringly imperative, Anna had trotted off southwards on some slight deviation into an area of wild scrub. When she called me to join her I was confronted with the history book posture of white explorers: Anna, still mounted, sat stiff on her horse with her arm extended and a finger firmly pointed in expeditionary certainty. This image I retain of her—humorous, bold, replete with instinctive satire; more particularly a ring of light just so on her yellow hair, a face unable to suppress its grin, spatters of shadow on the theatrical arm, and the horse, the necessary addition to so many of her games, heaving its sides slightly but otherwise obediently still.

The hole in the rocks I knew at once to be terrible. It was the precise apparition my father had described, not a walk-in room but a sneaky dark aperture, a going nowhere tunnel, a body-sized orifice. To my great alarm Anna hastily dismounted, threw herself headfirst into the rocky hole and wriggled quickly away, her feet following immediately like scrabbling little animals. I burst into tears—as I was wont to do—and begged and begged and begged her to return. I screamed into the hole and reached in my arms, hoping to snatch at a retreating toe. Whereupon, after apparently interminable distress, Anna duly returned, again headfirst, her dirty face smiling at my shameful display.

It was weeks before Anna persuaded me underground. Each time she took torches, books, candles and food, and I waited, excluded, on the lonely surface. Bound to absolute secrecy—by an exchange of blood squeezed from pinpricks to the thumbs on the stroke of midnight—I was privately miserable, sequestered away in my foolish and untellable fear. And when I finally descended it was with a rope around my waist so that I would not fall away forever to the centre of the earth, but be caught by a tree-hold and able to climb out.

    After a slanting, constricted, knee-scraping belly crawl the cave itself was unexpectedly spacious. It rose to a vault from which young stalactites and sinuous plant roots depended. The walls were partly of earth and partly of rock, so that the sense of containment was not, as I had imagined, tight and sculptured, but rather pleasantly burrowish, with a sweet scent of vegetable life moderating the musk of mineral lime. It was also vaguely lit—Anna's candles and torches had implied to me pitch blackness—by a space in the ceiling through which a lucent spot of sky was clearly visible, a spot which, for its tiny size, conveyed a disproportionate quantity of fluctuating blue light.

Into this special enclosure we emptied ourselves. In this secret cave, this secret receptacle, so far from the tap of our father's pipe, we fashioned playtimes and stories with exuberant skill and preternatural pleasure. Anna was a genius of nonsense and invention. She was a performing chatter-box, silly, burlesque, endlessly entertaining. I sat in the half dark and watched, captivated, as my sister danced and revolved around me, a human cinema, a cluster of characters, a congregation of worlds all completely compelling. Anna's voices were louder tied in by convexity, her body much larger rescaled by compartment. She achieved in our cave that gift of multiplicity, that high pitch of largesse, for which actors of all kinds persistently strive.

The farm became changed with the advent of the secret—a secret which, by the way, Anna called Our Den of Iniquity. I was no longer afraid of the swallowing earth; rather I imagined that we trod over dozens of perfect hollows, a honeycomb of dwellings which were the residences of creatures ebullient as children, but in other ways indescribable. And the shape of the farm seemed also to change. I looked out of my window up the slopes of the paddocks, past the static cows and the lazy wooded creek, and imposed upon the land, from a hawk's eye view, a neat triangulation to the point of the cave. This private geography I nightly rehearsed; before I lay beside my sister I would gaze into the dark, reconstruct swift diagonals and a pointy apex, and bid the hidden cave a succinct goodnight.

Anna was just twelve, and I only nine, when she died. She overturned a tractor and was instantly broken. My parents buried their daughter beside the house, fulfilling both the stringencies of poverty and their own fervent atheism.

All the long, lonely, Anna-less years of my adolescence I continued to visit Our Den of Iniquity. Anna's hieroglyphics remained chalked upon the wall, still indecipherably Egyptian. Her dress-ups and books stayed unmoved on the floor. Her feathers, her marbles, her magnifying glass, her sketches, these tokens of solidarity with the world of substance, all remained crudely and

disloyally in existence. Her fantastic life gone, the cave forfeited, in response,
its most congenial aspects—of the rambunctious and the ridiculous, of
the higgledy-piggledy, the hugger-mugger, the harum-scarum. And when I
lay in the half dark, with the little spot of light directly above my head,
I did not dare replace Anna there in the secret cave, now so sad, so dismal,
so sister-deprived, but instead reversed my imagining so that the vectors
of my mind-map extended back in converging lines to the grave beside
the house, her new underground, her body-sized cave, back where, thinking
very hard with my eyes tightly closed, I sought and sought her skedaddled
soul.

When we finished our stories we lay back in the dark. Night
insects could be heard. The breeze had increased and seemed to
bring with it a visible increase in blackness. Later, when they
thought me safely and soundly asleep, I heard Patrick and Afonso
move close enough to embrace.

And in my lonely singularity I contemplated the connection
between us all, the connection of space, the connection of narrative. As I heard Patrick's lips upon Afonso's body (or was it vice
versa?), I tried to imagine the ways in which the individual kiss and
all its individualising implications might be installed and respected
in the larger occurrences of a country's history. And simply could
not.

V

Do you know this history? Let me be brief. From August to
December 1975 East Timor was governed defacto by the popu-
larly supported Fretilin movement.

East Timor declared itself independent on the twenty-eighth of
November: nine days later Indonesia unexpectedly invaded,
engaged war with the local people and took control.

In the next eighteen months of conflict one hundred thousand
people, or one-sixth of the population, were killed.

Portugal was preoccupied with internal affairs. Its army and its people were riven in revolutionary and counter-revolutionary contestation.

Requests for diplomatic help from Australia against unprovoked aggression and the denial of national self-determination were met with dithering disengagement. East Timor was unimaginable and therefore considered inconsequential.

Fretilin fighters were driven to the vaccinated highlands where they engaged (knowing the cliffs and rivers, the serpentine roads) in guerrilla warfare. They lost.

Patrick Donelly, my friend, was with a group of five Australian journalists who, seeking frontline dispatches in that miserable territory, were confronted in a surprised moment by Indonesian machine-guns only to discover, pathetically, that no protestations of nationality deflected bullets. His brutalised body was burned in a pit. He was reduced to ash with dozens of others, who, though still remaining nameless to outside intelligence, were no less loved, no less specific, and no less precious than he.

Afonso Vieira, hearing the news from the safety of his Portuguese villa, sent me a letter of grief smudged over by apparently unrestrainable tears. A year later a note arrived from the city of Sintra, the city of the castles. It was from an old friend of Afonso and stated, with rather too strict a tone of impersonality, that he had committed suicide.

VI

Sometimes in the summer I wear my Timorese sarong and think of the women in the stone market place who through some intrinsic dignity and the extra aid of narcotics resisted the misappropriating gaze of the soldiers. This continues to preoccupy me, the evidence of resistance, this imperturbable solidity.

I remember that, as a tourist, I wore a pair of reflecting sunglasses by which I carried, with bland incomprehension, doubled images of the country in little screens upon my face. Doubled highlands. Doubled soldiers. Doubled peasants or *mauberes*.

I remember too that there were masses of purple bougainvillea in severely bright light. There were pockmarked buildings on the verge of disintegration, jungles, wild deer, Fretilin supporters on trucks, a statue of the Virgin colonially dislocated, a certain doctor's face.

And there is another small detail which I irresistibly recall, but pause to include since it seems too obscurely symbolic for this fact-seeking prose. Yet it is a detail of precisely that clarity of punctilious emplacement that I long to record.

There is a bridge in the centre of the eastern half of Timor which is incomplete. This is not to say that the builders did not finish their work, nor that it collapsed in some area or other. Rather, there are two concrete arcs—designed in Portugal by map-consulting engineers—which begin on each bank of a broad brown river, stretch forward to meet, both in their strong bows, but then, through some stupid or unfortunate miscalculation of space, fail entirely to join. In the dry season this monumental mistake is ignored, since the riverbed is empty, and one may walk safely across the absent water. But when the wet season comes flimsy ferries are employed, and each year people drown, are swept swiftly seawards under the concrete arms, cursing as they go.

A Tour Guide in Utopia

I often start my day in a fug of unreality, but this was ridiculous. One minute, I was market shopping, next I witnessed an apparition: the thin, polluted air swirled and out stepped a girl my age. She looked like a Pre-Raphaelite pin-up—impossibly pallid and ethereal, her hair like a halo in the early morning sun—but with *intelligence*. As I watched, she blinked, focusing; then joyous surprise filled her face.

I glanced around, but the shoppers had taken no notice of this visitor. Someone else had—but Weasel the beggar, who lived in her own peculiar reality, had merely noted an easy mark. Instantly she insinuated herself through the crowd and into the stranger's company.

'Spare you two dollars?' the girl exclaimed. 'But that's American currency! Have we been invaded?'

Weasel was momentarily thrown by that rejoinder, just long enough for me to intervene. As I did, a heavy bag in the arms of a man coming out of the fishmonger's split, and we were suddenly ankle-deep in whitebait. The girl took a step in her buttoned boots, but skidded; as if I were a romance hero, I offered her my arm. She accepted it, and I led her out of the fishy crush.

'Thank you, Sir,' she said, releasing me.

I nodded in reply, wondering how to say I was a Ms—despite my cropped hair, jeans and Docs. Moreover, I was acutely aware that her touch had felt glassy, unreal. She was corporeal, but somehow not quite there. The situation seemed uncannily familiar, as if I had read it in one of the musty, foxed, incredible books that were the subjects of my thesis. And then I knew that I had.

My life was currently dominated by Catherine Helen Spence, Henrietta Dugdale and many minor others, nineteenth-century women writers of a future perfect society, an Australian utopia. I had read, until anybody else would have revolted, of Victorian women transported by laudanum dreams, or on angel-back, or in time machines, into their future, an idealized era bearing minimal resemblance to my own imperfect twentieth century. For me to encounter, as if sprung from the page, a fellow-traveller of theirs, seemed perfectly natural.

The visitor was watching Weasel milk the people exiting from the delicatessen. 'I perceive that some things haven't changed,' she commented sadly. 'Yet I've never been asked for more than ha'pennies before. Sir, I must know—are we now part of an American Empire?'

I paused, eyeing the nearby MacDonald's. 'Not *formally*. And I'm not a man either.'

She regarded me admiringly. 'How splendid that the teachings of the Rational Dress Association should prevail! There were so few at our picnics, where we felt very daring in knickerbockers.'

Luckily she had her back to the girl in hotpants and platform boots.

I hesitated, then, since it had to be asked, did so: 'Are you, like Henrietta Dugdale, spending *A Few Hours in a Far-off Age?*'

'A great work,' she said, smiling. 'I longed to do the same, but differently . . .'

'And you have,' I said. 'In reality. Shall we talk further, in a quieter place perhaps?'

As we crossed the road a tram passed and she stopped in not only her tracks, but those of the tram coming from the opposite direction until I dragged her to safety. 'Exquisite, your modern transport!' she enthused as I led her into the café I thought least likely to give her future shock.

She declined refreshment, but I ordered strong coffee, feeling in need of it, for she was now in an alarming state of excitement, squirming as if she had ants under her long skirt. The businessman at the next table took one look then hid behind his newspaper. I was suddenly transfixed by its date: 4 December 1993.

'You're Futura,' I said.

She looked at me evenly. 'My name is Ida Pemberton. Futura is a pseudonym, used for my little poems in *The Worker*.'

I knew I had to tread carefully here. 'Futura' had written the minor but intriguing 'A Century From To-Day', a short story published in *The Worker*. It had been several chapters back since I had discussed the tale, and it had receded in my memory. Yet I could remember the specific date of Futura's day in Utopia.

As if she could read my mind, she also glanced at the paper. 'Fancy! Exactly 100 years since Mr Radvansky suggested an evening of mesmerism.'

It was slowly coming back to me that the narrator of 'A Century' had been hypnotized . . .

'After he had waved his pendulum at me, I felt a sleepiness, from which I opened my eyes to find myself coiled around the gasalier, looking down at my pale, still form. I had a great sense of freedom—that I could go wherever I wanted, unfettered by the constraints of an earthly, girlish body. So I decided to visit the future.'

My coffee arrived and she eyed it uninterestedly. 'If I ate,' she remarked, 'would I be a Persephone, unable to return?'

I was wishing I could recall more of 'A Century', which I now knew to be not fiction, but reportage, so that I had some inkling of what this unpredictable prophetess would do next. 'You do return to 1893, I assure you,' I replied.

'And to renown, I assume,' she said happily. 'Else how would you know my pseudonym?'

I hesitated, not wanting to say that only a specialist would have read Futura's solitary story. But she had become distracted by the passing marketeers: 'O brave new world that has such people in it!' she said, tears in her eyes. 'We hoped so much for a better world, my friends and I . . .'

A world, I thought, where women voted, where no child lived in poverty (hum!), where the rich did not oppress the poor (hum again!), where education was a right and not a privilege (triple hum!). I knew the dreams of the utopianists all too well. But, before I could become emotional myself, she had taken hold of my hand, entreating: 'Please show me your wonderful time.'

Vaguely I remembered that Futura had in her story, like many writers of the future, a native guide. Yet never could I have imagined that this useful person was muggins me.

'Delighted!' I lied. My quiet day of thesis-writing would just have to be postponed.

The short walk back to my car was murder, for everything was new to her and she dawdled like a two-year-old. Her first ride in an 'automobile' left her awestruck and silent all the way back to my flatlet. After I stowed my shopping, we did a guided tour, of which the highlight, unexpectedly, was the toilet. Once I had demonstrated the flush, she had to do it herself—repeatedly. Giggles and rushing water resounded through the flat as I took the opportunity to dash into the study for my photocopy of 'A Century'. It eluded me and I was about to re-read my critique of it in the thesis when she reappeared.

'A future treasure!' she said brightly. 'Unlike your maid, who's scamped the bathtub.'

I forbore to mention that the slattern in question was myself and switched off my 'typewriter run by electrickery', as she called the computer. Without guidance from the story, I would have to create my own tour itinerary for Futura, traveller from that foreign country, the past. Without thinking, I turned on the radio for the weather report.

'Well I never!' she said. 'A newspaper read aloud by an invisible spirit.'

Words failed me at the prospect of explaining telecommunications, but she did not question me, listening intently to the bulletin. 'Such strange placenames!' she said. 'I thought I knew my geography, being a postmistress, but I am an ignoramus here.'

It was an oddly benign bulletin, no bad news, except near the end, when I switched off at the mention of Bosnia. There were no wars in Utopia, I recalled. What there were though, invariably, were institutes of learning . . .

'Our next stop,' I said, 'will be the University!'

It had existed in Futura's time and as we parked in sight of the familiar Gothic towers she nodded in recognition, rather curtly. When we entered the grounds she began to laugh uncontrollably.

'Oh, how delightful! To turn it into a Ladies' Seminary.'

The fashion of the male students around us tending towards *faux* hippie, the mistake was understandable; and she soon noticed enough conventional lads to correct it slightly. But her glee remained. 'I never came here,' she confided. 'My dunce of a brother did because he was the only son.'

We toured the library and the computer centre, where the sight of a girl at an open access terminal, busy typing a creative writing exercise (Futura sneaked a peek) made my companion sigh. 'I had to hide my poems from Mamma. She tore them up lest brainwork rot my womb.'

'A phallusy,' I said. To prove it, I made our next stop a Feminist Bookshop, filled wall to wall with women's brainwork. She stroked the spines and their myriad Ursulas, Germaines and Susans, then shyly asked the saleswoman, 'Do you have any Futura?'

Oh no, I thought, but the bookseller, not wanting to admit ignorance, saved the day. 'Not at the moment,' she boomed. 'But any Wimmin's book you want, we can order in.'

'Thank you,' said Futura.

And so our day passed, Futura's visit entirely in keeping with the utopias we had both read, texts edifying rather than thrilling, for perfection precludes adventure. I drove out to the airport, where a 747's take-off made Futura dance on the spot with delight; transported her on trains and trams; narrowly prevented her walking, all unawares, into a Sex Shop; and even showed her the most up-to-date gadgets of her time displayed as museum pieces.

All my thesis texts were from the viewpoint of the visitant, never from that of the visited, so I had never known that it was bloody hard work being a tour guide in Utopia. Trying to stave off exhaustion, I overreached myself. 'How about Parliament?' I said, as we left the Museum; she nodded, still enthusiastic.

Short-cutting, I took her through Chinatown, where she goggled in dismay: 'The Yellow Peril!'

'Ssh!'

'There's so many of them,' she said, bewildered. I sped up, trying to get into a more Caucasian area of town before we got into trouble. She trotted behind me, protesting: 'Australia doesn't need their disease and opium.'

Out of the frying pan into the fire, I thought, as I espied, unmistakable in their Mabo T-shirts and red-black-yellow head-bands, a group of—

'Darkies!' she exclaimed. 'They shouldn't be here. Inferior races can't face Progress, everyone knows that. All we can do is smooth the dying pillow . . .'

The nearest Koori raised his eyes heavenward.

'Well, they are here, in your future, my present, so you can just put up with it!' In the general direction of these original inhabitants of Australia, I yelled: 'I apologize for my friend.' There was no response and I continued on, too angry to speak, although I had read far worse examples of nineteenth-century racism.

Futura lagged behind me, still arguing: 'You didn't need to apologize, they don't have feelings like we do.'

'Another word and I won't take you to see female Parliamentarians!'

She shut up, looking annoyed, an expression slowly super-seded by joyous anticipation. 'To think of women here!' she said as we walked up the carpeted stairs to the Visitors' Gallery. At the sight of the House in session, I suddenly realized my mistake: rows of sombre suits confronted us, relieved only intermittently by the brighter plumage of the female MPs.

'Why so few?' she asked.

I looked away, ashamed, then brightened as a figure in red took the parliamentary floor. 'Look, a woman minister!'

'Never!' her voice rose in anger. She had, I could tell, addressed a few public meetings in her time. 'No respectable woman dyes her hair!' It was rather a lurid gold. 'And her face! She's a painted harlot!'

The minister had been called many things, from fake man to Thatcher clone, but this remark, clearly audible across the chamber, made the Opposition males snigger, and her dulcet tones faltered. What happened next I don't know, for we were unceremoniously hustled out of Parliament by the security staff.

On the steps of Parliament House we sat, Futura weeping softly into her skirt. I watched the day wane and the stream of lights from the rush-hour traffic, wondering when to interrupt her grief. But she did it herself, suddenly sitting up straight, one last tear falling onto the granite where it slid away like mercury.

'They're beginning to revive me from the trance,' she said. She stood, composing herself. 'Forgive me. Your world is stranger than I can comprehend.'

The air around her began to eddy. 'Goodbye,' she said. 'I thank you, gracious guide.'

I felt embarrassed. 'Aw, it was nothing.' She smiled, her widest grin yet, and then—vanished.

I reached out and touched only air. 'Don't go,' I murmured, too late. I had wanted to thank her, too, for my edifying, tiring, marvellous day with a nineteenth-century feminist. I couldn't use a skerrick of it in my thesis, but now I knew exactly what my subjects had been like.

Back home I finally located my copy of 'A Century' and read it ravenously. The narrative stopped after the Museum visit with the coy phrase: 'And there was much more, which I cannot tell, lest I fatigue *The Worker*'s readers.' Or shock them, I thought cynically, as Futura had been shocked by multiculturalism and painted lady MPs. Otherwise it was all there—Futura's ever-helpful guide, the University, the airport—but seen through a rosy, distorting mirror. My present, as coloured by 1890s idealism, the limits of Futura's perceptions, and my inept explanations, was recognizable, but impossibly benevolent.

Yet Futura told her tale well and I wondered, as I had on first reading the 'story', why she hadn't been published more. Now, though, I had more than a pseudonym. I had the author's real name. A nasty suspicion nagged at me; I recalled how unhealthy the Pre-Raphaelite lasses had been. Might Futura's otherworldly appearance have been due to more than mesmeric projection? A trip to the genealogy archives confirmed it: looking at the Register of Deaths, 1894, under P for Pemberton, I found Ida May, dead of tuberculosis at 26.

Poor Futura, I thought on the way home, never to have a brilliant career, never to see women's suffrage. But then it occurred to me that she had not lived to have her optimism destroyed by Stalin, or Hitler, or the A-bomb. I glanced up, startled at this thought, to see a news-stand with its tidings of overpopulation, ozone depletion, ecological disaster, our future Dystopia.

'Oh lucky Ida,' I cried, 'to have the dream of a hopeful future!'

Cousins

All the long evening, he tells me things. His baby is like an aston-ished creature of the night: big, black, nocturnal eyes. He says they're the eyes of his mother and looks beyond me, his own eyes full of the past and flecked like a cat's. Outside, the sun illuminates the jacaranda flowers. Deep purple so my heart aches. Across the valley the hills are veined. The river is far below and barely a glint through the trees.

The baby whimpers in this early summer heat and falls asleep against his chest. Tufts of hair curl and sweat on the small neck and he twills them in his fingers like a spinner. Some memories are so sharp I have to bend my head away. Below the veranda, the swimming pool is deathly still. The red airbed is dead centre and doesn't move. I can see circles of hot spiralling weeds and the lawn-mower abandoned. Earlier, I'd been mowing. The weeds had poisoned red flowers the shape of small crooked hearts. They were tough and stalky. The juice spurting out stung the skin of my legs. *Weeping Wanderers*, he called them as he handed me an iced drink. We sat together on freshly mown lawn. I melted ice cubes on the hot varicose vein that winds down the front of my thigh and wondered about middle-aged seductions.

The mower is tied together with string and bits of rag that could once have been his favourite nightshirt. Even from this dis-tance I can imagine the familiar patterns. Not impossible that it should have survived this long. The last two decades? Perhaps? For like all his mother's gifts, the nightshirt had been thick, soft, expensive.

One night in 1969, he fucked me standing up in that night-shirt. There were men on the moon. There were stars and cres-cents and zodiac signs on his nightshirt and he fucked me quietly, with expertise, in the corridor of his mother's house. She was in the sitting room, watching the impossible. *Come and see! Come and see! Alex! Rhys!* She was calling out. *The moon men.The moon men*, like she'd found some sort of answer. The walls of the hallway were ice-cold. It was July. It was a frosty far north coast winter and he had to rip my pyjamas just a little to find a way in. *My dear. Ma chère*, he whispered fiercely or in French. A child in France, he could summon a seductive accent and always seemed petit and supple. I used to wonder how he managed after I became so suddenly tall with big bones jutting in every direction. The wall against my back grew hot. I thought I could hear the deathwatch beetles his mother worried about, gnawing away at the foundations. But maybe they were the noises inside us. My feet sweated grey marks into new wool slippers. His teeth left scars. For days they slowly turned the colour of old nails. His sucking lips made blue bruises in the creases of my body and my heart strained with the forbidden, ice-blue lust.

His mother came looking and nearly caught her apple-cheeked son with his prick inside her favourite niece. Just in time we heard her stumble. *Those astonishing astronauts.* She was drinking cream sherry and had lipsticked her mouth slightly to the left. It gave her a crazier look. Beatles songs on the record player saved the night from too much talking. *Don't let me down.* But we did. She embarrassed and loved us too much. Later, we all stood under the sputnik-shaped fairy lights, a special mail order from a Sydney department store, toasting the astronauts with French champagne. She tugged at her elbow-length white evening gloves and mentioned the mole on her chin was moving towards her ear.

Sitting on the veranda, not exactly facing me, he tells a story about his mother and still—after such a time—seems to find something enticing about his memory of her madness.

One day, when he was eleven years old, his mother walked him home from his riding lesson. They walked through his favourite big park and he kicked up a fine, white dust with his leather boots—specially made to measure for one so small and precious. And he carried a tiny, hand-plaited, tan whip. The miniature jodhpurs puffed and billowed. His mother stroked his thick black curls and said there was something she must say. He strutted and swung his whip to touch the marble brightness of his favourite equestrian statue. The whip made a lovely swish in the autumn air. Autumn was just tingeing the lines of chestnuts dead-gold but by the fountains, summer lingered on. He says he remembers the brightness, the watching, the silent hot seductions going on all around—the hot tight breasts of women who smiled as he sauntered by. His mother said she wanted to tell him something and grabbed his hand and *No, he couldn't sail a boat today*. Her hat was crooked and he wanted to tell her to straighten it up.

He looked back and could have cried because now he thought he saw the pretty women laughing at him. Into the cool avenue of trees, she walked. Too fast. She went too fast for his small legs and she had the funny look on under her hat. What she had to say was a strange story to tell an eleven-year-old son on his way home from a riding lesson where his teacher had been full of congratulations and flattery. Dark in the trees. Dark after the light. Momentarily blinded, he sucked in his breath and hoped against hope for a treat. A salty liquorice lollipop, a knob of pink nougat. But she gripped his hand and told how in 1942, soldiers had watched her sighing and touching herself. In a hotel room on the Rue Saint Victoire, she said, which was why his father had been swapped with a spy, a stranger, somebody who looked like, but wasn't, her dear husband Paul. In the thick golden shade, he tried to shake his little-boy hand from his mother's. It was slipping with her sweat but she held on tight and looked at him with the big, queer, black lights in her eyes. Her nostrils were huge and flaring with emotion. *You're hurting, Mumma*, he could have cried. He wanted to sail the fountain ships and tell how he'd learnt to grip with his knees when his pony trotted. She squeezed tighter and spoke shrilly of breasts, soldiers, spies, kisses and the mole on her chin moving at night. Swish, swish, went his ever so special whip, meant only to tap his fat-bellied pony with. Swish. He slashed her and struggled. Her hat fell off and he spun out of her grip running. Running so his leather soled boots made the pale gravel fly. Eyes to the ground so as not to trip on the splitting conkers. Running, suddenly saved, in the direction of his tall, fat father—who was coming to meet them. Airily, his father came closer. He had two pink ices and said, *whoa whoa, steady old fellow*, when his little son came crashing out of the trees, into his body.

The baby against his grown-up chest sleeps on. Over the pool, there is a smokiness, a dimness. It comes floating towards us. Sometime during the story, the baby has flooded its nappy. I offer to change it but he says it's best to let them sleep when they're asleep. He curves the baby to a comfortable position and smiles disarmingly, proudly. He is forty-three this year, with the face of a sad child. His gentleness nearly makes me weep with some kind of lost desire. I feel weak with it and say it's time for a swim. I walk down the wood-slat steps, hobble across the bindies and dive in without my bikini top on. I have no children so my breasts are fairly firm even if the rest of me no longer is. The neck he used to kiss is old and collapsing. *Too much sun, Alexandra*, he fingered it lightly today, fondly, as a friend—and offered me the use of some of his young wife's moisturisers. It is unfair that my first and best and only cousin had hardly aged at all. In fact, he seems more at ease with his good looks. Or maybe just more skilful these days at flaunting his light, thin hips? There is a poised enthusiasm in his voice. His apple-red cheeks have not fallen in. Only when we kissed hello, cheek kisses, proper cousin kisses, did a certain softness betray itself. Like sinking my lips against a very ripe, though still enticing, piece of fruit.

The water is warm. Mosquitoes moan in swarms above my flat belly. I let them land on my wet floating breasts before turning a slow, ungraceful somersault. Warm water goes up my nose. Noises—of his snuffling baby, of the uncertain past, of hot wind blowing the jacaranda bells—drift above and around me. He calls something and disappears from the veranda. He brings out the baby and various baby paraphernalia and after setting everything up to his satisfaction, joins me in the pool.

The cock I used to suck in secret is small and hidden in his baggy board shorts. Somehow he has kept the creaminess of his olive skin that I lost to middle age a few years ago. His legs are spindly still and I dive under to see from below his thin, brown stomach. It coils with more black hair than I remember. His nipples are tight and sharp. My eyes sting with chlorine but I keep watching, even as he kicks away from the edge and my face is exploded in a spiral of bubbles.

'What are you doing?' His voice hangs suspended in sub-tropical air.

'Just looking.'

There is going to be a briefly dramatic sunset. He tells another childhood story of his parents in Versailles, as the water becomes as vivid as expensive blue glass. It isn't the kindest of sunsets. Deep claws of lines come creeping from his eyes. He tells how unexpected desires could seize hold of his mother on market days. Often on market days. As though the anticipation of food and colour gave her unnaturally high spirits. She'd dress up and rouge her cheeks terribly red before swooping through the stalls: searching for spring freesias in winter and the best, freshest goose livers. She would declare it his job to carry the warm, squelching organs home. Almost dancing, she'd hold her flowers pointing down in the French way and imagined appreciative looks from every handsome man who passed. She'd buy fish wrapped face to face and tell him they were kissing; show him the pale wet puckers of fish lips with blood from the hooks still leaking.

Always, she was excessive. Always, the small rooms would be overwhelmed by the scents of early spring and rich pâtés. Eating her pâté, she'd forget her husband was meant to be a German imposter, and tempt him with smooth foie gras on the merest slivers of toast. There were noisier seductions with the bedroom door ajar. They forgot they had a son and once he saw her climbing on top of his father's shockingly bloated stomach and licking his pig-pink hairless breasts. For the first time he saw his father as a stranger in the middle stages of a self-inflicted decay: an excess of mottled flab. Her little pale breasts threatened in his hands. The pinkness of pâté on the edges of wine glasses. The erotic smearing of pâté, so that for days afterwards, when his father demanded a hug, he thought he could smell it still. And the hard father fat under the favoured, hairy wool suits, made his own tight little stomach flutter with fear or something else.

The mosquitoes, the fretful noises of the baby in the gauzed cage and the sound of his wife's car approaching from the road, take us from the water. His wife is pretty and French. Together, they are full of wisdom and laughter. They find ways to touch each other even as they serve up a simple meal. There is no talk now of his strange past. It is all baby talk, baby name talk, chatter. They want another child as soon as possible. I remember suddenly my old paranoia—of becoming pregnant, of breeding a Mongol child with my cousin. And until my periods came, erratic and dribbly, I would dream terrible dreams of blunt, yellowed baby faces. I was only fifteen but the pain of the imagined birthings was ferocious.

The wine is light and refreshing and I'm unable to feel drunk. Grains of rice are caught like confetti in hairs on his chest. He says they're thinking of calling the next baby after me, if it's a girl. 'Is that wise?' I ask. 'Alexandra,' he says, 'has always been the prettiest name.' When his wife kisses me goodnight, she whispers it is her favourite name too. She says my name so that it sounds enchanted. She is enchanting. She is so small, with small, light, fidgety fingers. Her belly is tight and warm and I can imagine how she must be when pregnant. Motherly, yet still intoxicating. He is attending again to the baby. When I kiss his hair, the smell of chlorine like the past, is acrid and ailing and hard to leave behind.

I have a strange night, half-waking with weird fantasies. In their spare bedroom, the wallpaper has thin flower patterns like veins. I peer in the low mirror to see that a hair has begun to grow on my cheek. I go to sleep knowing the wallpaper patterns are twisting in the dark next to me. At four, currawongs begin to sing in an approaching storm. I push the bedclothes off to watch what the wind does to my nipples. They turn skinny and hard. I tread lightly outside to watch the storm's progress. It comes fast and threatens the tinge of an early dawn. There is a strong, cleansing smell of rain. The wind knocks flowers from the stand of jacarandas. Soon a floating, mauve mass will hide the pool water.

The last time I saw his mother, it was the early seventies. A visit on my own. My holiday cousin, my holiday lover, was going to Paris to see his father who was dying, he said, of obesity and old age in the American hospital. The Fineflour tributary at the bottom of his mother's garden was sick; fish grey and reedy. I remember it gasping and sighing like some starved thing in front of us, as he asked to curl his tongue for one last time over my knob-breasts. We were cousins creamy with desire. Wild and ancient rhododendrons hid us. *Practise your French,* I hissed and flung my legs apart. *Will you write?* He sucked in strong, friendly rhythms and didn't answer. All the time, the river was there, dying. All the time, his mother was fretful in the house with her nail scissors and photo albums. Ants drowned in our mingling fluids. The river stank and drove us back to the house. His mother was hard at work, snipping and giggling as the small circular heads of her husband fell around her feet. She'd left no album untouched. We could see her face ached with the effort. Too much powder cracked it into a million terrible lines. Between her thumb and forefinger, the scissors pressed a deep welt. *Soon, soon*, her voice was high and as classy as ever. Then the scissors hung poised over an enlarged black and white print of the three of them, taken against some derelict cathedral. *Oh. Not Laon. No!* My cousin cried out even as she hacked. Something despoiled. They both cried. *He always obscured the view*, she sobbed and left the album open at the holiday in Laon, where my cousin was still a boy. Probably the last holiday before they left France and his father? I asked, but my cousin wouldn't say. He only mentioned that it was autumn again. Autumn leaves like jagged glass; the crackle of Catholic candles; a seven-towered cathedral alive with long-necked gargoyles; Laon; a hill town; barely recovered farming land; a shabby charcuterie; dripping grey alleys; the sound of his mother's bottom in the bath; the sound of her screaming; her bruised, braless, heavy breasts in the mornings—the same colour as salad de mer or dark mildewing strawberry tarts; vivid fragments. But he shook my questions away and began to blow balloons for that evening's poorly attended farewell fancy dress.

His mother dressed as Tilly Devine and painted her eyelids a shocking shade of mauve. I slunk about, thinking of Europe and the beautiful French women he would surely screw: the taste of French, not Australian, tobacco on his tongue. I picked up the small pipe he was ludicrously trying to cultivate and left teeth marks in it. I put his pipe between my legs and inside and in my mouth and sucked and sucked my waning desire. He was the Pacific Highway in a wetsuit painted with double yellow lines. His body was slight in rubber, inaccessible and amusing. I remember the night smell of the river: it was clotted: it was like thick bad cream at the bottom of a jug. Guests wandered uneasily about. I didn't know them or whose friends they were. They tapped the piano keys idly and were startled to hear the rich, perfectly in tune notes, hanging breathless in the balloons. Someone broke a pale jade horse and didn't confess. His mother was gay and bewildered by turns. The supermarket pâté, so coarse, so unfresh, caused her anguish. But she shrilled to people about her son's costume, *He's inspired, inspired* and called out all sorts of predictions and wonderful futures and pretended not to see his leave-taking as any sort of betrayal.

I saw visitors trailing out gaps in the back fence without so much as a goodbye, good luck or a piece of orange bon voyage cake with the special Grand Marnier filling. It was an exquisite cake. His mother had taken half the afternoon piping the right words of farewell into the icing. I ate untidy slabs of it—all the letters of his name, R H Y S—before collapsing into his bed. For the first time we slept together, as in sleep: unhidden, naked, his skin taking all night to unwrinkle from the wetsuit and I've never been sure if his mother saw us curled together or not: plump and cream-coloured cousins soon to part.

Only a little while later, she tried to drown herself. She found the most picturesque spot overlooking the upper Fineflour and stepped off an old timber bridge. The river was so low, her body didn't even float away and the cause of death was officially recorded as a broken neck. Someone wrote to my cousin but it was some years before he came back. And he found it difficult to settle. He flitted between France and Australia, Paris and Sydney, France and Fineflour and only now seems content to stay, far away from any river or relatives. Certain items arrived for me on the Northern Mail. I was not expecting them. I was not expecting everything to be so meticulously labelled for me, in his mother's elegant copperplate. I realised she'd taken more notice of me than I'd ever known. The crate had been carefully packed. There was some of her porcelain. Her French recipe books. An enlargement of herself as a young, rich mother, laughing at her baby boy, lipstick like a smear of berry sauce. A smaller enlargement, beautifully framed, of me and my cousin, soon after they'd arrived in New South Wales because we looked as skinny and boy-like as each other, but already full of cheek I think. We were grinning and naked under a willow tree. Only her writing beneath identifies who was who. Alexandra on the right. Rhys on the left—both holding hats over our most naked bits. My breasts were late growers.

Perhaps his mother knew all the time and loved me all the more. Another photograph shows her holding Rhys' hand carelessly, as if he was her young lover. In the crate that came for me, there were many recipes. A recipe for weaning yoghurt, using breast-milk. A mother's recipe. She might have thought that one day . . .

I kept everything. To show him. Only now has the moment been right. Tomorrow I will take out the leather cosmetics case full of forgotten smells and expensive scents in thick blue glass. There are butterfly hat pins with lethal points and other signs of flight and savagery: the way the powder puff is thrust just as she must have left it, deep in the awful beige powder. There's perfume. Jean Patou *Joy* in funny old-fashioned bottles that I've unscrewed before, when to sniff the strangeness of his and her past can be a temptation and a titillation. Always, I have worn the small heart-shaped locket. Someone's black hair is plaited and coiled inside.

I wear this locket on a long chain so that the misshapen goldness of it hangs just above my own uncertain heart. I've brought the recipe books to show him too, to give him. They're all in French so I've never been able to use them or to re-create her favourite recipes. Her favourites, or Rhys' as a boy, are easy to locate—the pages floury and butter stained. Easy to smell the sweetness of fine, long-gone pastries.

The rain arrives and suddenly it's cold on the veranda. Light is drenching and dislocating through the storm. Like memory, there are bands of colour and shade. I pad past the baby's bedroom. The door is half shut but someone is in there making murmuring noises. Impossible to say whether the voice is his, hers or both. With other lovers' children in the past Rhys has always been terrible and neglectful. With his own, he seems saintly.

I slide back into my own cold sheets and put knuckles into my eyes, like a child, to stop any tears. I comfort myself with a little blue tablet and with thoughts of strawberry tarts I might make tomorrow—with my cousin or his wife translating the stained pages, unravelling the mysteries. And I grow happier, thinking of the placing of yolks into a double saucepan; the beating of them into thick yellow ribbons; the rituals and the certainties of the kitchen; the sensual plucking of strawberries from the big beds out the back; the safe feelings.

The Beautiful Hour

It runs in the family, you don't have to go back a long way to see a pattern. Two generations past, and the signals are clear.

Prabhu, my grandfather, who all his life echoed the swaying coconut palms of Kerala in the gentle sway of his head, neither left nor right for certain—either *yes* or *no* depending on which way the winds of circumstance were blowing—was only a notch partway up the spine of this family's tree of ill-starred adventurers and their unscrupulous increase. Only continuing in the established tradition of the market magician, the smalltown shyster, the grave-robber, the odd pickpocket or two, when he gingerly reached his long fingers over the snores of his brothers, tangled in sleep like puppies in pyjamas, along the edge of the wooden bedframe, past his stepfather's oil-slicked head and under her thin cotton shawl to pluck the carefully folded pound note, creased and recreased through constant examination, from his sleeping mother's breast.

Her breath tickled the hairs of his forearm. The sunken half-moons of her breasts, once as coveted on the foreshores of Cochin as the grove of hybrid coco-apples cloned by his father in happier, long-gone days, collapsed with her outbreath against him like the oddly soft jaws of a clamp. Prabhu's hand was trapped, frozen like the rest of him in a cardboard cutout pose of comic strip terror. The pause between his mother's breaths seemed to last forever. He began to be afraid that she would never again breathe. Sweat ran down his cheeks like tears, remorseful or otherwise, and gathered in the ticklish corners of his mouth. He cautiously stuck out his lower lip to prevent incautious splashing. A drop swung from his chin.

Then his mother breathed once more and the pound note, snug in its homemade pouch of meagre treasures, slid into his palm.

I can see him now, slipping over the window-sill like a cat with tomorrow's dinner trailing precarious yet determined from its jaws. Scrambling through the rustly undergrowth on hands and knees and sometimes his belly, a shivery snake-shadow, he's that afraid of his older brothers and especially of his stepfather. Who knows which rustly sound, his or a lizard's, or a mongoose snapping its jaws on a rat, or a night-owl suddenly hooting, which might inadvertently wake them? Sit them up on their sleeping mats, snorting their nostrils and rubbing the sleep from their eyes. Those same eyes widening as his mother tears through the shell of her own sleep, hands flailing at the unfamiliar emptiness between her breasts. Eyes widening, then narrowing.

At the edge of the ruined grove of coco-apples, Prabhu rises to a loping run. The muddy track swallows his footsteps, sucks greedily at his feet and ankles as if it too, not just mother, brothers, stepfather, father (grave-bound and possibly only a little less disapproving)—not just them but the very earth itself is also against him. He struggles to lift his shivery feet. Curses softly, his stepfather's curses sliding like a torrent of sharp stones from his throat. In spite of a lifetime of hot oils, miracle herbs and curses of varying potency these feet will be his weakness.

So Prabhu said, sixty years later, lifting the edge of his sarong as daintily as a debutante. Slapping one flat hand, heavy with disappointment, against them while the Duchess winked beside him. Wig askew. A half-eaten sugar sandwich in hers. 'Amongst other things,' she intoned in a voice eager with secrets. 'Dear Boy, amongst other things.'

So down past the neighbouring huts he stumble-runs, best he can, sixty years earlier, past the first flickerings of oil-lamps, the first wingflaps of cockerels clearing their throats. A straggly group of milkmaids hoots as he rushes by them, clanking their buckets; a cow raises its stately profile; mynahs startle the treetops, dart wildly. Not for any of these does Prabhu stop. Not for the outer streets of Cochin slowly awakening. Down past the marketplace he runs, dragging his tattered breath and the yawning stares of the marketwomen behind him, past the spice godowns leaking their stream of coolies staggered under sacksful of turmeric, cloves and cardamom, down to the harbour-front where the ocean-going ships creak wearily and pull on their ropes.

Did I mention that Prabhu was fifteen? That he carried slung over his shoulder a small bundle? That he was barefoot, as I am now, and wore his *mundu* doubled up over his knees? His thick curly hair unravelling in the wind of his own making? These touches I add for myself, for Prabhu never mentioned them, interested only in the Grand Narratives, the Great Metaphors, the Momentous Sweep and Sidesweeps of History (admittedly, only insofar as they affected Prabhu himself—pausing to clear his throat emphatically, one long finger twiddling at an earlobe as one might twiddle the dial of a radio). Only the bundle featured regularly in the labyrinth of his dubious mythmaking, appearing and disappearing like a cork on troubled waters, its bundle-sized bulge growing and shrinking to suit any occasion.

Its folds were sometimes cavernous, its contents an inconstant list of treasures. Today's: the aforementioned pouch complete with pound note; two shirts, best quality Indian cotton; the last of the coco-apple seeds; one Certificate of Appointment from the Tiong Hwa Federated Malayan Gambier Estate Pty Ltd, 1924; a small bottle of Mother's milk, once held to possess miraculous properties; three gold coins, origin unknown; a silver crucifix, *Ditto*, claimed Prabhu, eyes flickering for a moment to the ceiling; a few common marbles hard won from the village champion; a lace handkerchief, love-token from a red-eyed girl; and so on, and on, and all of it such trinketry as to beguile even a Sultan's fusspot harem (the Duchess conceded, clapping her hands).

With the wide-eyed Duchess all-ears beside him, or some other female of opulent girth, grace and social standing (for that's how he liked his women, preferably also with fortune attached), Prabhu's bundle became a metaphor of Mythic Significance, our Family Inheritance, our Future Greatness now Lost through the Untimely Intervention of Fate or Nature, or Plain Bad Luck. The disclosure of which never failed to turn all attention towards me, Boy, lurking unobtrusively in some corner of the room. My awkward ankles and protruding elbow-bones were duly noted, vestiges surely of childhood privation. My sunken uninterested gaze. 'Poor Boy,' people murmured; some, like the Duchess, dabbing at the corners of their eyes. I was a shadow compared to Prabhu, young man as I was and he, walnut-wrinkled.

'You see, the very zest has gone out of him!' came his favourite observation.

The hungry hollow of my cheeks only elicited further sympathy, as did my mother Selene's religious vow, made when I was a squalling infant, which has kept my head as bare as a missing nest egg for twenty-two of my twenty-five years.

'Poor, poor Boy.'

Especially at the moment Prabhu lost it. Saw his soon-to-be-legendary bundle slide off the deck into the frothy expanse of a Straits of Melaka roused to unseasonal fury, never to be seen again (at least in its Entirety). The instant he gained first glimpse of his first new country, Malaya, looming shadowy and rain-streaked up from the edges of seasickness.

Prabhu saw his past dissolving like strings of vomit in the churning waters behind him while the future reared its head, curled up and potent. His shipmates, fellow immigrants, bonded coolies, a paying passenger or two, scattered in a flurry of shrieks and eye-whites as the future stretched its green skin to full capacity, filling the sky. Prabhu alone steadied his feet on the heaving deck. Stood his ground as never before, or since. He opened his arms wide. Released his precious bundle, clutched to his chest day and night for the past five weeks, to its own fate. For one moment, he says, he stared the future squarely in its face. Unafraid.

Then the future broke its glistening skin with a roar louder than any thunder and swept everything from its path. In that moment, Prabhu says, then and then only, he understood *everything*. All the manifold whys and wherefores of his existence evaporated to a perfect and singular clarity. For the first time in his life no familiar terrors collapsed upon him, no doubts fissured his resolution. No shivers assailed his feet. Have I, Boy, in my own short but crowded lifespan experienced any such . . .? I am not backward to admit it: I have not.

Prabhu waited calmly. He was ready for anything that the future held. Its veiled or blatant tyrannies, its periods of mundane forever-ness, its sweet fruit of surprise. Its *best shot*.

The moment he lost everything.

The Backyard Duchess, as Prabhu called her, was known for her Saturday 'At Home' afternoons, held outdoors all summer in Sydney. Languorous sparkle-wined affairs, they stretched on into the purple evenings, blazoned with green and golden sunsets from the smoke-stacks down Parramatta way, with jacaranda blossoms anointing the drowsy heads of her longest-staying guests. All afternoon the Duchess moved among them in her Saturday finery, gauzy and startlingly coloured, as busy as a worker bee tending its efflorescent crop.

'Will you take another glass, dear William?'

'Surely there's room for a morsel of sugee cake, Susan my love, Prabhu made it specially . . .'

'And you, Yakob, where have you hidden all afternoon? I do declare, Sir, that you have been avoiding me.' Whereupon the Duchess leaned forward and, as a houseproud housewife might return a straying curtain fold to its assigned position, tweaked the hapless Mr Yakob's hairy ear.

The sound of Saturday lawn-mowers cut the conversation into neat sections, no topic need extend beyond the time it took each part of that overlapping chorus (now louder, now softer, depending on proximity and competing engine power) to wend its way round each in the patchwork of quarter-acre blocks lining the street where the Duchess lived. In any case there was little conversation to be cut at this advanced hour, for by now her guests were sated on sunshine, wine (most of it homemade by the Yugoslav landlord) and an abundance of sugar: ants trailed around the remains of jam tarts and mango mousses; quarter trifles toppled sideways, jellies melted riverine. Her coveted lamingtons etched chocolate whirls on Sister Maria-Celina's collar, coconut candy added pink and green whiskers to the wealth on Mr Yakob's chin. A plane high overhead painstakingly spelt out *Happy 85th Mum, Y-o-* to the accompaniment of sizzled meat smells drifting over the back fence *-u-'-r-e- -a-* children's voices and pool splashes *-L-e-g-* the maddened dance of a small dog chasing *-e-n-d-!* its tail. 'How-waard,' the Duchess cooed, holding out a sweet biscuit. 'Howard!' to no avail.

'Why does everyone around here want to be a Legend?' Prabhu mused. He was in pontificating mood, staring dreamily at the steeple-point made by his fingers. 'I see it everywhere. I have noticed. On ice cream wrappers, for the influence of children. Signs around the Westfield Shoppingtown. Television of course. On the backs of multi-purpose vehicles. Smalltown criminals, overnight sporting heroes, millionaire yachtsmen, even eighty-five-year-old mums. Does eighty-five years a legend make? Or daylight robbery wearing a tin dustbin on your head? Regarding this most interesting phenomenon I will venture a proposition.'

'Yes, tell us,' the Duchess encouraged, returned from farewelling a last cluster of leavetakers, for no one remaining seemed capable of rousing themselves to answer. 'I have often remarked upon it myself. Haven't you, Mrs Phan?' and she turned her watery gaze upon the Professor of Linguistics's wife (herself a well-known poet in her own language), who smiled sweetly and covered her mouth with one hand.

'Yes . . . pardon . . . no,' her words barely audible. 'No— perhaps yes . . .'

The Yugoslav landlord, whose name no one could pronounce ('Call me Mike, mate, make it easy for ya, and the little lady's called Rosie'), started suddenly in his deckchair, eyes wide and blue as the photographs of his village on the Adriatic coast which adorned the dimly lit halls and passageways of the old house. He sat a moment, stiff-backed and staring, then sighed and snuffled a little, and promptly went back to sleep. Tilting his wineglass only slightly, a small red stain speckling one knee.

'Just look around you,' Prabhu began, for this was his pre-ferred foray into the arena of rumours and scandals, half-baked truisms, half-digested arguments, overdone outrage, underdone investigation, sundry experts' opinions and layman's philosophising. Every day he foraged for these in the ubiquitous babble of talk-back radio, newsprint broadsheets and sheets of somewhat narrower margins, overheard conversation (preferably in pubs, public toilets, the TAB) and afternoon TV: the facts, fictions and frictions bubbled to who-knows-what temperature and recipe in the high dome of his forehead and spouted like cure-alls at every opportunity.

'Just look around you, yawning cultural poverty, what else? Only such can make society grab at any story. Any character one hairsbreadth away from the ordinary and—*Hey presto!* Provide MGM staircase and trumpeting music for said new legend to ascend to the cultural pedestal of national consciousness. In my opinion, most useful for selling Landcruisers and breakfast bars, bonus number one. Soon after to be prized, analysed and agonised over radio airwaves, subjected to conference papers, debunked, later reinstated. Thereby contributing also to parallel buy-and-sell ideas industry, bonus number two.' Barely a pause before he added, 'Just look around you: teenage mothers, murdered pensioners, dogs fed better than people, paedophile priests. That Bondi woman marrying a shark—"better than any man she ever knew"—that's what happens when there is too much freedom. Children throwing stones at old men in the street. What kind of place is this? I ask you . . .' And so on, and forth, warming up nicely, until:

'You are a wicked man, Mr Prabhu,' Sister Maria-Celina chided. 'This great country, so kind to us, you and me both. Wicked.'

'Don't you think this place is needful of it, Sister?' Prabhu asked, wickedly flashing what remained of his betelnut-stained teeth. 'I assure you I am merely doing my duty. Making my contribution. Every denizen in society has his place and function, you follow me? Society needs him, priest, publican, get-rich-quick middleman, ditto politico, aristocrat, thief. All these goodly vocations taken when I arrived—luck of the late-comer—what is left to one such as me? Each to his Godgiven talent, you understand.

'And then I see it—Situation vacant. Start immediately. What is it, my job and duty? To provide society with service: the necessary flea, the fly, the derangedly buzzing gnat worrying the great white underpants of Australia, i.e. the status quo-to-speak. Though nowadays, I admit, patched here-and-there with multicolours. Yet still so doggedly endeavouring to cover up its black and ancient arse. Just look around you, I say . . .' And did so with theatrical flourish, for such speechifying took him back to the old whole-story-in-one-breath days (so necessary to discourage roadside audiences from sneaking away without trying or buying).

No one answered or interrupted, not even the Duchess or Sister Maria-Celina. If someone wanted to be a flea, a fly, a gnat (for God's sake) on the bottom of society—though not the very bottom—this was, after all, the Lucky Country, and he could. So let him, the frowning look on Professor Phan's face conveyed clearly. (Although the Professor's grasp on the English Language was fish-slippery and hampered by accents—Australian-English, Italian-English, Malaysian-English and so forth—it allowed him to discern the whale-shapes of meaning lurking below the surface, if not, as yet, to tell which really were submerged whales, or sharks or sardines.)

Since no freak meteorology greeted Prabhu's arrival here, no great wave of the future loomed up before him like a lightning flash-in-the-pan of existential understanding, he felt no obligation to express any gratitude for being allowed to *be* here. As seemed to be generally expected. Especially when third parties were listening. Prabhu felt he had earned his entry. In his usual fashion, with his usual finesse. In the established pattern of our family tradition, like water seeking its natural level, he had neatly sidestepped a mountain of paperwork all those years ago, a battalion of immigration officials, none too friendly, a phalanx of tests and countertests, because in his heart of hearts, and outside also, he knew that it all came down to a question of skin. Mind's skin as well as the body's. Red, black or yellow shades were prohibited and, though European i.e. Portuguese and possibly French via Pondicherry blood coursed its way through his arteries (alongside Chinese and

Madurai Tamil), Prabhu was dark—as dark as any ordinary Indian from Cochin. Miraculous Mother's breast-milk and Father's famous grove of hybrid coco-apples notwithstanding.

It was 1958. One year after Malaya's Independence, with many of her Eurasians still unsettled enough by the idea of 'native rule' to desperately scurry to whichever 'home country' would take them. (That ratbag band, half-and-half of this-and-that, sucked into history's blender, whirled around for several centuries and spat out still adamantly half-and-half.) If Mother England wouldn't have them, never mind, any one of her 'white' colonies would do, former or otherwise: Ireland, Canada, America, Australia. A list of wishes. Oh, the evenings spent agonising over atlases, the tea chests packed, scented with camphor balls or dried lemon-peel, the helter-skelter of tearful goodbyes (which my father Ashkar loathed and my mother Selene coveted).

We'll miss you! Come and see us, do! Hearts all the while a flutter, beating-beating-beating in anticipation of going *Home*.

The White Australia policy was still wholly functional at that time, though not functioning quite so hopelessly, as Prabhu could attest to: one fine day abandoning Selene, Ashkar, Molly, Angel and me in our rented accommodation in North Sydney. Our parents and we siblings three, soon after to be frogmarched 180 degrees (though, admittedly, at that stage I was still an industriously multiplying zygote deep in Selene's clenched and increasingly incensed belly). We were ostensibly on holiday in Sydney; in reality investigating permanence. And in spite of the many forms filled, interviews held, letters of recommendation produced, palms greased, silver linings sought and brazenly sucked-up to, all chance of our staying disappeared with Prabhu. (Slender pipedreams so long and lovingly nourished!) Our holiday visas expired and our savings account emptied. Return to Sender, Inquiries to Follow and our head-of-family gone—*Poof!* like the roadside magician he claimed to be. His finest trick.

Never forgotten.

From such a (new) beginning how could Prabhu be anything but irreverent? Fleaing, flying and gnatting to boot? To the shopkeeper refusing to see, let alone serve him, he cried: 'Ha ha ha, I am *in* already, me, my children and grandchildren. Completely fertile, thank you. Many in the family way also. What are you going to do about it, you slug-ugly prick?'

Which occasionally landed him on his ear on the pavement and me, Boy, celebrated neither for my brawn nor foolhardy courage, strolling nonchalantly down the other side of the street. Oblivious to Prabhu's bellows: 'Boy! Come back here, Boy!'

He sidled slyly up to the po-faced woman with political pretensions, handing out leaflets on street corners. Nodded and smiled as she edged away from him, her lips prim and gaze daggerish, keeping those leaflets firmly to herself. They were not for the likes of *him*. Until he swooped forward, leaning his curry-salt-fish-greenbanana breath into her face, hissing suddenly: '*Be afraid*!' And they were papery birds, those leaflets with their caw-caw message of division and hatred, released into the air and traffic.

Finally Mr Yakob cleared his throat. 'Mr Prabhu,' he said in his evenly measured voice. 'It's true this place isn't perfect. None of us is under the impression we have left the Earth and landed in Heaven. But the evening is lovely, is it not? And the wine is good'—raising his glass to the sleeping landlord— 'and the company most congenial. You may have noticed that the flies, bumble-bees and other stinging creatures seem to have retired for the time being. Let us enjoy this beautiful hour. Will you not tell us one of your stories instead?'

So my grandfather Prabhu, sixty years later, thanks to the Saturday inertia as innocuous as a giant, feather-light comforter descending upon the vast and lopsided suburbs of this, his latest (and lastest) adopted city, held court in the fading light under the jacaranda's whispery skirts. Out came his bundle, now voluminous as a dance of many veils, and out from it came—*Peekaboo!*—the spice markets of Cochin, the hill resorts of Penang, the Singaporean embrace of a grown-up, red-eyed girl, thrice-married and smelling not of soap-and-lavender-water but gin. One vision after another until the garden's edges were puddled in shadow and the neighbouring ones sliced here and there with windows of light.

Soon the Duchess would arise, somewhat distractedly, hurry into the house and emerge not long after with a trayful of tealights. She was a Duchess one would sigh over and breathe sweet nothings to if one could only shake off that terribly agreeable inertia, for so softly lit and golden-glowed is she that you can easily see the ruined face was once incomparable. Then she deposits a light here, by Professor and Mrs Phan's two silent daughters, another by Rosie Dobrosavljevic's ample elbow, and here and there throughout the devastation of the Saturday garden party until the last of the soft lights leaves her, cloaked in a little sadness, a little shadow, and she sinks back into her chair, sighing, 'Oh, doesn't it remind one of Fairyland?' As one might ask of Venice, or Suzhou, or even the moon-washed cliffs of Katoomba.

The sky was lit like stained glass in a cathedral window; below it, around an altar of picnic blankets, they gathered, subdued as a congregation. It was true, what Mr Yakob said: not-Heaven-exactly, but they were lucky to be here. Rather than elsewhere. Life was good, was it not? Each adequately eked out his or her living. Little comforts were aplenty and large ones not inconceivable. Everyone had a place. The beautiful hour seemed to stretch on forever.

There was an air of Sunday roasts in preparation, of the certainty of Sunday roasts being eaten tomorrow and in all the foreseeable Sundays of the future (or kebabs as the weather might have it), and of that future progressing as steadily as an ocean liner upon an ocean of earned and inherited merit. An unsinkable ship. The seven o'clock news (which they could faintly hear on Sister Maria-Celina's never-turned-off television set) might intrude with its exposition of disasters: famines, uprisings, genocides, lost Test Matches and such, but that was in the television. Out here all was well. Music tempered the traffic from Parramatta Road with easy listening. Families pottered about in their lighted windows. There was an enticing smell of coffee. And Prabhu's voice in certainty's cracks and interstices. (Bzz bzzz.)

'Don't get sucked into it, Boy,' he warned when I first arrived. Dragging behind me an enormous flamingo pink suitcase, a radio cassette player and a winter jacket, reversible and still smelling of the crush and swelter of Kuala Lumpur's famous Globe Silk Stores. Parting gifts: my sister Molly's once-used suitcase, the radio cassette player begged, borrowed or stolen by my father Ashkar, who all my life strove to provide me with ill-afforded extravagances; the jacket, practical as always but also 'classy', from my mother Selene. Who had beckoned me into the dim recesses of her bedroom on that last terrible night before my leaving, where she bent scrabbling amongst the boxes, plastic bags and cloth bundles under the bed, her hair tangled, her face streaked with mascara, until she produced—*hey presto* indeed—my Indian great-grandmother's gold stud earrings. Once encased in a carefully folded pound note, creased and recreased through constant exam-ination. Selene pierced those gold studs into my ears herself when it was certain that I was going. Really and truly, this time. Plane ticket in my pocket. A pinch to blacken my arm so I wouldn't forget her.

In a family given to stealing away in the dead of night, not to mention an ingenious array of other stealings, it was more usual to be showered with curses than going-away good wishes. Let alone such a wealth of gifts. But as the hours passed, we predictably dribbled back to form (water settling to its true level). By evening Selene was passed out on the kitchen table, the windows still care-lessly flung open, neglectful of neighbourly whispers. Molly's room lay empty as usual, only a faint trace of her perfume, and as for Angel—well, no one expected anything much from Angel. I loitered on the front steps, watching the shadows slant their way towards me, minute by slow minute, while our 'housing estate' awoke to its evening rituals—pots and pans clanging, motorbikes revving, a bath crooningly taken, voices raised and rising, a child shrieking—and our mongrel dogs skulked around my ankles. Surreptitiously tonguing their approval.

Only Ashkar accompanied me to the airport, lugging my suit-case over his shoulder like a coolie. He carefully perused my boarding pass and luggage tags for all the world as if he could read. Stood at the security barrier, ignoring the guard's tentative signals to let other people pass. Pressing his bulk against the glass. There was a look on his face, hovering somewhere between regret, anxiety and expectation, a ridiculous look on one so large and outwardly menacing. His clothes were stained and crumpled. A spot of saliva glistened on his chin. And on his face: that look, hungry to the point of hand-wringing, of lip-licking, of lifting hems to bowed foreheads—*Thank you, Baba! Your eternal health, Auntie!*—in humble appreciation of *anything*. Blessings, curses, averted gazes. Small change. I turned my shoulder. Fumbled with passport and papers. Have I, Boy, in my short but varied lifespan experienced any such . . .? I am not averse to admitting it: I have. Many times over, in the daily mirror of my father's face. And elsewhere.

Beyond the immigration check-point, I looked back once. Waved once, then mouthed our family motto: *Good Riddance to Bad Rubbish*. Thumbs up, Ashkar. Goodbye.

In the arrivals hall in Sydney, at the ungodly hour of six a.m. and surrounded by a scuttle of turtle-shaped travellers, back-packed and bleary-eyed, Prabhu examined me from head to toe and back again. Only a mild flicker of interest at those shiny, once-briny earrings (and my reddened ears, itching terribly).

'You don't look like anyone,' he remarked, turning abruptly on his heel.

We took the airport bus. Then a train, underground and over-ground. Then another bus. And walked through the echoing fluor-escent aisles of a shopping centre (my suitcase bumping into irate shopping trolleys), around three blocks of brick, fibro and aluminium-clad houses in various stages of grandeur, dilapidation and renovation until we came to his home and castle. The Yugoslav landlord's mortgaged-to-the-hilt old boarding house peered hunchbacked and gloomy from behind a raggedy stand of trees. Complete with its Duchess, leaning out from one of the upstairs windows, a yappetty dog in the crook of her elbow. Yoohooing us with a lace handkerchief.

'Just look around you, Boy,' Prabhu told me. 'Take in these wide spaces. See how big the sky is. How far stretches the land. All that is manmade here can be erased in the sweep of a bulldozer, that's how fragile its hold is on this ancient earth. In my opinion, two hundred years, bah! Such a thin historical skin, and mostly stolen also. Tacked down with colonial toothpicks. Here you can start again, Boy. Here a man can remake himself from the ground up, from a puff of smoke. So many examples around. Latecomers all. Even you can make your way here, if you're clever enough and quick enough about it.'

Prabhu wiped his feet meticulously on the worn doormat and motioned me to do likewise.

'I will help you resist,' he offered, fumbling in his pocket for the key. 'That will be my duty,' referring, I later discovered, to the soporific seductions of the 'Great Southern Lassitudes'—as he fondly nicknamed his latest (and doubly stressed lastest) adopted country.

Now also mine.

'Resist, Boy,' swinging the door open as Howard the dog, aquiver with outraged excitement, scrambled growling and pissing down the stairs.

'Welcome to Australia!' the Duchess cried, blowing kisses from the landing.

CONTRIBUTORS

Ethel Anderson (1883–1958) was born in England of Australian parents. She returned to Australia in 1924 after spending some years in India and England with her army husband. Throughout the 1940s and 1950s she published poetry and fiction. 'Peronel McCree and the Sin Called Pride: The Arch-sin' is one of a series of linked stories making up the collection *At Parramatta*, published in 1956.

Jessica Anderson (1916–) was born in Brisbane but has lived most of her life in Sydney, making a living writing drama scripts for radio. She became very well known after the publication of her prizewinning novel *Tirra Lirra by the River* (1978), but had written several novels and many stories beforehand, including the brilliant historical novel *The Commandant*, and has published more fiction since. 'Under the House' is from *Stories From the Warm Zone* (1987).

Thea Astley (1925–) was born in Brisbane. She has lived in Australia all her life and worked as a teacher in schools and at Macquarie University. One of Australia's most distinguished writers, she has been publishing fiction for more than forty years. She has won the Miles Franklin Award three times and has received most other major Australian literary prizes. She was made an Officer of the Order of Australia (AO) in 1992. 'It's Raining in Mango' is not strictly speaking a short story but rather a self-contained chapter of the novel *It's Raining in Mango* (1987).

Marjorie Barnard (1897–1987) lived in Sydney all her life and graduated with first-class honours in history from the University of Sydney in 1920. Best known for her collaboration with Flora Eldershaw, with whom she published fiction, criticism, and history under the androgynous pseudonym 'M. Barnard Eldershaw', Barnard has only recently become better known for her various and broad-ranging independent contributions to Australian intellectual life in the middle decades of the twentieth century. In 1980 she was made an Officer of the Order of Australia (AO) for her services to literature. 'The Persimmon Tree' is from *The Persimmon Tree and Other Stories* (1943).

Barbara Baynton (1857–1929) was born in Scone in rural New South Wales. Her biography makes lively reading, with mysteries about her date of birth and the identities of her parents, and three marriages, the last of which elevated her to the aristocracy, as Lady Headley. One of a relatively small number of women to achieve publication in the *Bulletin* of the 1890s, she is best known for the powerful and disturbing collection *Bush Studies* (1902) in which the prevailing Australian fashion for realism and her own plain style deflect the reader's attention away from the psychological complexity of her stories. 'The Chosen Vessel' is from *Bush Studies*.

Carmel Bird (1940–) was born in Tasmania, a place that figures prominently in her writing. She now lives in Melbourne. She has published numerous books of fiction and edited several anthologies; her most recent work is *The Stolen Children: Their Stories* (editor, 1998). 'The Hair and the Teeth' is from *The Woodpecker Toy Fact* (1988).

Jessie Couvreur ('Tasma'; 1848–97) was born Jessie Huybers to an Anglo-French mother and a Dutch father in London. She migrated with her family to Tasmania in the early 1850s. From 1873 onwards she travelled between Australia and Europe, writing fiction and journalism in and about both places, until her second marriage in 1885, after which she was based in Brussels. With Rosa Praed and Ada Cambridge she is one of the three best-known nineteenth-century Australian female writers. 'Monsieur Caloche' is from *A Sydney Sovereign* (1890).

Marian Eldridge (1936–97) was born in Victoria and became known in the 1980s as a 'Canberra writer'; she contributed to *Canberra Tales* (1988). She published a novel and two collections of short stories. 'The Woman at the Window' is from *The Woman at the Window* (1989).

Beverley Farmer (1941–) is a Victorian fiction writer best known for her 'Greek' stories. Several of her books have won awards. She has written novels, short stories, and the formally experimental *A Body of Water*, a collage of poems, stories, 'life writing', and meditations on reading and writing. Her most recent book is *Collected Stories* (1996). 'The Harem' is from *Home Time* (1985).

Mary Fortune ('Waif Wander' or 'WW'; ?1833–1910), born Mary Wilson in Ireland, travelled with her father first to Canada and thence to the Australian goldfields in 1855. She lived a colourful and sometimes precarious life in colonial Australia, a life reflected in her choice of pseudonym, although readers of her fiction will know that it is quite the opposite of waif-like. She made a living as a writer of poems, articles, and stories and has become known, through the scholarship of Lucy Sussex, as the earliest Australian crime fiction writer.

Helen Garner (1942–) is one of Australia's most highly regarded writers. She was born in Geelong, Victoria, and has lived most of her life in

Melbourne; she currently lives in Sydney. Her first book, *Monkey Grip* (1977), won a National Book Council Award, and she has won several other major awards with subsequent books of fiction. She has also written non-fiction and screenplays for film and television, and won a Walkley Award for journalism in 1993. She created a furore in Australian literary circles with *The First Stone* (1995). 'What We Say' was first published in *The Faber Book of Contemporary Australian Short Stories* (1988), edited by Murray Bail.

Kate Grenville (1950–) was born in Sydney and became well known as a writer when her novel *Lilian's Story* (1985) won the Vogel Award for 1984. Her most recent book is the powerful and disturbing novel *Dark Places* (1994), a form of sequel to *Lilian's Story*. 'The Test is, if They Drown' is from *Bearded Ladies* (1984).

Susan Hampton (1949–) was born in country New South Wales. She has won prizes for her poetry and is known for her skills as an editor. She won the Steele Rudd Award for her book *Surly Girls* (1989), which is a collection of prose poems, performance pieces, and stories. 'Conrad's Bear' was first published in *Transgressions* (1986), edited by Don Anderson.

Barbara Hanrahan (1939–91) was born in Adelaide and returned there to live after some years in London. She was initially a painter and printmaker and came to writing comparatively late. However, after *The Scent of Eucalyptus* was published in 1973 she published a number of novels and short stories, mostly with Adelaide as their setting, as well as continuing to work as a visual artist. 'Butterfly' was first published in the anthology *Moments of Desire* (1989), edited by Susan Hawthorne and Jenny Pausacker.

Elizabeth Jolley (1923–) is the daughter of a Viennese mother and an English Quaker father; she emigrated from England to Western Australia with her husband in 1959 and has lived there ever since. Her first book was published in 1976; since then she has acquired a national and international reputation. She has published novels, short stories, a book of autobiographical pieces, numerous radio plays, and her *Diary of a Weekend Farmer*; her most recent book is *Lovesong* (1997). She has won a number of national and international awards, and is an Officer of the Order of Australia (AO). 'My Father's Moon' eventually became part of the novel of the same name (1989) but originally appeared in the magazine *Australian Short Stories*, issue no. 17.

Gail Jones (1955–) was born in Perth and teaches at Murdoch University. She has published two critically acclaimed collections of short stories, *The House of Breathing* (1992) and *Fetish Lives* (1997). 'Other Places' is from *The House of Breathing*.

Joan London (1948–) was born in Perth and lives in Fremantle, WA. Her first book, the short story collection *Sister Ships* (1986), won the Age Book of the Year Award. Her second collection of stories, *Letters to Constantine*, was published in 1993. 'The Girls Love Each Other' is from *Sister Ships*.

Olga Masters (1919–86) was a journalist for most of her adult life and began writing fiction in 1975. Her first book was published in 1982 and won a National Book Council Award. She published a novel and two collections of stories before her death in 1986; another novel, another story collection, a stage play, and a collection of her journalism were published posthumously. 'The Christmas Parcel' is from *A Long Time Dying* (1985).

Gillian Mears (1964–) grew up in Grafton in New South Wales, and her writing is still strongly grounded in the northern rivers district. She won the 1990 Vogel Award for her novel *The Mint Lawn* (1991), after having published two collections of short stories; her most recent book is *Paradise is a Place* (1997). 'Cousins' is from *Fineflour* (1990).

Oodgeroo (1920–93) of the Noonuccal tribe of Stradbroke Island published her first six books—poetry, stories, essays, and books for children—under the name by which she was known for most of her life, Kath Walker; she formally reassumed her tribal name in opposition to the Australian Bicentenary celebrations in 1988. 'Mai (Black Bean)' is from *Stradbroke Dreamtime* (1972).

Katharine Susannah Prichard (1883–1969) led a dramatic and tempestuous life, which began in Fiji. It included such events as her foundation membership of the Communist Party of Australia, the suicide of her war-hero husband, and her nomination for the Nobel Prize for Literature. She worked as a journalist, travelled extensively, and was a prolific writer of fiction, poetry, drama, and the revealingly titled autobiography *Child of the Hurricane* (1963). 'Flight' is from *Potch and Colour* (1944).

'Henry Handel' Richardson (1870–1946) was born Ethel Florence Lindesay Richardson. Her trilogy *The Fortunes of Richard Mahony* (1930) is one of the classic texts of Australian literature. Like Christina Stead after her, she left Australia as a young woman and spent most of her life overseas. She wrote several novels and a number of short stories. 'And Women Must Weep' is from *The End of a Childhood* (1934).

Robin Sheiner (1940–) was born in Perth. She has published stories and two novels, *Smile, the War is Over* (1983) and *Beyond the Pale* (1989). 'My Sister's Funeral' was first published in *Meanjin* in 1985.

Christina Stead (1902–83) was born in Sydney, left Australia in 1928, and lived most of her life in Europe and the USA. She was a prolific novelist with a unique style; she also wrote short stories, translations, and screenplays. When her husband died in 1968 she returned to Australia, where she lived for the rest of her life. She won the Patrick White Award in 1974. 'The Old School' was first published in *Southerly* in 1984 and afterwards appeared in the posthumous collection *Ocean of Story* (1985).

Lucy Sussex (1957–) is a Melbourne writer, editor, and scholar. She has written books for children and young adults, has edited several anthologies, and co-edited the first collection of speculative fiction by Australian women, *She's Fantastical* (1995). Her first novel for adults, *The Scarlet Rider*, was published in 1996. 'A Tour Guide in Utopia' is from *She's Fantastical*.

Margaret Trist (1914–86) wrote three novels and two collections of short stories. Like many Australian writers she was involved in a number of the organisations and institutions that make up the country's cultural infrastructure; she worked for the ABC and wrote for the literary magazine *Southerly*. 'Twenty Strong' is from *What Else is There?* (1946).

Ethel Turner (1870–1958) is best known for her children's classic *Seven Little Australians* and for the other 'Misrule' books. She was born in Yorkshire in 1870 and emigrated to Australia as a child with her mother and sisters, subsequently spending most of her life in Sydney. 'The Carrying of the Baby' was first published in *The Coo-ee Reciter*, edited by W.T. Pyke, in 1904.

Alexis Wright (1950–) was born in Cloncurry in Queensland; her family are from the Waanyi people. She is the author of *Grog War* and editor of the anthology *Take Power*. Her first novel was *Plains of Promise* (1997); she is working on her second, and lives with her family in Alice Springs. 'The Serpent's Covenant' first appeared in *A Sea Change* (1998), edited by Adam Shoemaker.

Beth Yahp (1964–) was born in Malaysia and came to Australia in 1984 to study. Her first novel, *The Crocodile Fury*, was published in 1992, and she is working on her second, *The Water Trinket*. She has contributed to the writing or the editing or both of several anthologies, including *My Look's Caress* (1990) and *Family Pictures* (1994). 'The Beautiful Hour' was first published in *A Sea Change* (1998), edited by Adam Shoemaker.

Sources and Acknowledgments

The editor and publisher thank copyright holders for granting permission to reproduce copyright material.

Anderson, Ethel, 'Peronel McCree, and the Sin Called Pride: The Arch-sin', from *At Parramatta*, Penguin, Melbourne, 1985; by permission of the estate of Ethel Anderson. Anderson, Jessica, 'Under the House', from *Stories from the Warm Zone and Sydney Stories* by Jessica Anderson, Penguin, Melbourne, 1987. Astley, Thea, 'It's Raining in Mango', from *It's Raining in Mango* by Thea Astley, Penguin, Melbourne, 1988. Barnard, Marjorie, and Curtis Brown Australia for 'The Persimmon Tree', from *The Faber Book of Contemporary Australian Short Stories* (ed. Murray Bail), Faber & Faber, London, 1988. Baynton, Barbara, 'The Chosen Vessel', from *Australian Short Stories* (ed. Kerryn Goldsworthy), J.M. Dent, Melbourne, 1983. Bird, Carmel, 'The Hair and the Teeth', from *Personal Best* (ed. Garry Disher), Angus & Robertson, Sydney, 1989; by permission of the author. Couvreur, Jessie, 'Monsieur Caloche', from *Penguin Best Australian Short Stories* (ed. Mary Lord), Penguin, Melbourne, 1991. Eldridge, Marian, 'The Woman at the Window', from *The Woman at the Window*, University of Queensland Press, St Lucia, Qld, 1989; by permission of the estate of Marian Eldridge. Farmer, Beverley, 'The Harem', from *Fabulous at Fifty: Fifty of the Best from Australian Short Stories* (eds Bruce Pascoe and Lyn Harwood), Pascoe Publishing, Melbourne, 1995; by permission of the author. Fortune, Mary, 'The Illumined Grave', from *The Oxford Book of Australian Ghost Stories* (ed. Ken Gelder), Oxford University Press, Melbourne, 1994. Garner, Helen, and Barbara Mobbs for 'What We Say', from *The Faber Book of Contemporary Australian Short Stories* (ed. Murray Bail), Faber & Faber, London, 1988. Grenville, Kate, and Australian Literary Management for 'The Test is, if They Drown', from *The Babe is Wise* (eds Lyn Harwood, Bruce Pascoe, and Paula White), Pascoe Publishing, Fairfield, Vic, 1987. Hampton, Susan, 'Conrad's Bear', from *Transgressions: Australian Writing Now* (ed. Don Anderson), Penguin, Melbourne, 1986; by permission of the author. Hanrahan, Barbara, 'Butterfly', from *Moments of Desire: Sex and Sensuality by Australian Feminist Writers* (eds Susan Hawthorne and Jenny Pausacker), Penguin, Melbourne, 1989. Jolley, Elizabeth, 'My Father's Moon', reprinted by permission from *My Father's Moon*, Penguin, Melbourne, 1985. Jones, Gail, 'Other

Places', from *The House of Breathing* by Gail Jones, Fremantle Arts Centre Press, Fremantle, WA, 1992. London, Joan, 'The Girls Love Each Other', from *Sister Ships* by Joan London, Fremantle Arts Centre Press, Fremantle, WA, 1986. Masters, Olga, 'The Christmas Parcel', from *A Long Time Dying* by Olga Masters, University of Queensland Press, St Lucia, Qld, 1985. Mears, Gillian, 'Cousins', from *Fineflour* by Gillian Mears, University of Queensland Press, St Lucia, Qld, 1990. Oodgeroo Noonuccal, 'Mai (Black Bean)', from *Stradbroke Dreamtime* by Oodgeroo Noonuccal, Angus & Robertson, Sydney, 1992. Prichard, Katharine Susannah, 'Flight', from *Australian Short Stories* (ed. Kerryn Goldsworthy), J.M. Dent, Melbourne, 1983. Richardson, Henry Handel, 'And Women must Weep', from *Favourite Australian Stories* (ed. Colin Thiele), Rigby, Adelaide, 1963. Sheiner, Robyn, 'My Sister's Funeral', from *Meanjin*, vol. 44, no. 2, June 1985; by permission of the author. Stead, Christina, 'The Old School', from *Ocean of Story* by Christina Stead, Penguin, Melbourne, 1986. Sussex, Lucy, 'A Tour Guide in Utopia', from *She's Fantastical* (eds Lucy Sussex and Judith Raphael Buckrich), Sybylla Feminist Press, Melbourne, 1995; by permission of the author. Trist, Margaret, 'Twenty Strong', from *Favourite Australian Stories* (ed. Colin Thiele), Rigby, Adelaide, 1963; by permission of the estate of Margaret Trist. Turner, Ethel, 'The Carrying of the Baby', from *From the Verandah: Stories of Love and Landscape by Nineteenth-Century Australian Women* (ed. Fiona Giles), McPhee Gribble/Penguin, Melbourne, 1987; by permission of the estate of Ethel Turner. Wright, Alexis, and ACM (Aust.) Pty Ltd for 'The Serpent's Covenant', from *A Sea Change: Australian Writing and Photography* (ed. Adam Shoemaker), Sydney Organising Committee for the Olympic Games, Ultimo, NSW, 1998. Yahp, Beth, and Barbara Mobbs for 'The Beautiful Hour', from *A Sea Change: Australian Writing and Photography* (ed. Adam Shoemaker), Sydney Organising Committee for the Olympic Games, Ultimo, NSW, 1998.